I0134181

Critique of Pure Passion

An Excavation into Gaia's Inhabitants and Their Delusions Concerning the Truth

Jorge Majfud

Humanus

San Diego-Acapulco

Critique of Pure Passion. An Excavation into Gaia's Inhabitants and Their Delusions Concerning the Truth
© 2025 Jorge Majfud
ISBN: 978-1-956760-42-2
Crítica de la pasión pura
© Graffiti Editorial, Uruguay, 1998,
© Baile del Sol, Spain, 2002, 2007, 2019
© 1998 by Jorge Majfud
majfud.org | jmajfud@ju.edu
© Humanus 2025 humanus.info
editor@humanus.com
All rights reserved for any commercialization of the full text. Any part of this book may be reproduced or used by any graphic, electronic, or mechanical means, including photocopying or information and retrieval systems, provided the original text is not altered.

Critique of Pure Passion was mostly written in Mozambique in 1997 and first published the following year in Uruguay. It consists of 358 compact essays, each of which is a self-contained unit. However, this collection of essays revolves around a few basic themes: the formation of ethics and morality from the persistent fears and anxieties in history—renunciation; the ways of understanding and representing the world, life and death, history and the present, humanistic evolution, and the reactions of traditional powers.

Tacuarembó, 1998

We know there is a planet covered with life, and among it, there are restless and strange beings that we cannot define. We only know that they are distinguished from the rest because they have created themselves or Someone has created them with something different from cosmic dust. That is why we have called them Metaphysical Creature.

Years later

In this new edition of *Critique*..., I have adhered to the same criterion as always: to keep the text as it appeared to the public for the first time, even though today I think I should have omitted some paragraphs or clarified an innumerable number of other points. For example, the obvious and necessary clarification that these reflections belong to a child of the West, occasionally inspired by other lands. However, that kind of correction seems to me a form of falsification. A lie to the readers and a possible betrayal of that young man who took notes on an island in the Indian Ocean or in the impenetrable regions of Mozambique, by the side of the road under a suffocating sun or in a hut hallucinated by a moon outside of history. What right do I have to correct the one I no longer am?

I hope to have the life and clarity to formulate better questions and attempt more satisfactory answers.

J.M.
Athens, April 2006.

Index

Preliminary Note

What follows is an ordered set of free reflections; they do not aim to teach any Truth but rather a vision of the world (I believe the difference between the two lies in the fact that the former is always a pretentious version of the latter). I apologize to all those who, in error, have the misfortune of agreeing with me.

Valle Edén, Uruguay, August 1998.

GNOSTIC-EVOLUTIONARY PATH

	HEAVEN	EARTH
4	FOURTH MIRACLE?	
Achievement	**D.** Afterlife Eternal life (West) Cessation of existence (East)	**4.** Survival of the individual and society. Material progress.
Effect	**C.** Benefit of the gods	**3.** Benefit of creatures
Ethical-theological *Rational level*	THEOLOGY **B.** Reflection on the unquestioned truth.	ETHICS **2.** Reflection on unquestioned duties
3	THIRD MIRACLE (Neolithic) Problematic conscience of the individual	
Moral *Irrational level*	**A.** 3, Worship of the gods 2, Renunciation-sacrifice 1, Sin of pleasure **First Tablet**	**1.** Rules of coexistence, modesty, taboos, and tolerance. **Second Tablet**
	Repression of sex	
	Fear of the distant future Rejection of death	Fear of the immediate future Survival instinct
2	Second Miracle: Human species consciousness (Paleolithic)	
	Individual and social experience of sex	
	Emergence of sex: 2 billion years ago	
1	First miracle: life 3.4 billion years ago	
	EXISTENTIAL EXPERIENCES	

I: History and Nature

1. CURRENTS. Different verifications (such as the possibility that all human races can interbreed) have demonstrated the biological monogenesis of the creatures of Gaia. Absolutely all human creatures share a common origin, and it is likely that, due to some mysterious or significant event, all descend from a man and a woman who lived in Africa 200,000 years ago. Because of this and other discoveries, linguists have concluded that all languages spoken on the planet also share a single origin. Myths are similarly useful for anthropology and the idea of a common or restricted birth of humanity. — For its part, the modern theory of paradigms assumes independent units of thought, but at the same time, it is possible to see how some derive from others. The process that leads from one thought to another is similar to that of languages: each one derives from earlier ones and, often, several arise from a common root. Bantu and Latin are the roots of at least ten African and European languages; Sanskrit and Mandarin, say the Asians, are the roots of at least all languages. Thought behaves similarly, and this is one of the hypotheses underlying this report.

2. INTERIOR. All living beings are the result of an outer history, which refers to biological evolution. Plants and animals evolve by influencing and adapting to their environment. Their history is dictated by external agents. In contrast, the history of the Metaphysical Creature is, above all, a consequence of its own spirit; that is, of its inner universe. Only this creature is the result of both histories. —Each creature thinks and feels conditioned by the collective inner history, just as it is by its personal history. A Uruguayan of our time carries within him the dialectic of Socrates, Christianity, and the rule of Adolf Hitler. Even if he is unaware of it, he must see the world through all that historical dust. His dog, if he has one, will have only received from Hitler's dog some genetic mutation (which will have nothing to do with the war or its owner). —What differentiates one society from another, one individual from another, lies in the inner history of the species: in the collective history of its spirit. Because of it, a 20th-century Westerner thinks and sees the world differently than a contemporary Hindu; he thinks and sees it differently than an 11th-century Westerner. It is the *inner history* that differentiates the Metaphysical Creature from the rest of the animals and from itself.

3. LEAPS. The inner history of the West consists of a *flow* of permanent and irreversible changes, which shapes the model of a "true" history. In opposition to this image is the inner history of the East and the so-called primitive peoples who, by denying change and affirming repetition, we say have no history. But denying an inner history to mythological peoples is an inaccuracy. It would be like equating a Maya or a Hindu with a tiger. —Mythological peoples also possess an inner history, not formed by flows but by *leaps.* The entire social structure of India and Nepal (I refer to the caste system) and many of their founding myths were produced by the invasions of the Aryan horsemen. The mythological world of Homer was also based on concrete and specific events, such as the Trojan War. —Both modern Hindus and those Greeks of the 7th century B.C. saw the world through traditions born of concrete events and protagonized by the same creatures —historical events.

4. CONDITION. A person is not born with a language or with the Pythagorean theorem. But they are born with the capacity to learn and develop these cultural products. Similarly, they are not born with a specific morality, but they do have the biological capacity to learn it from their environment, a capacity that began to develop at a certain point in evolution. Noticing proto-moral, cultural, and even political faculties in certain groups of

monkeys, some biologists have deduced that morality is more of a neuronal formation than a cultural one. To this virtual or analytical dichotomy, another scientist, Frans de Waal, responded in his recent book, *Good Natured*: "Is morality a biological or cultural phenomenon? There is no simple answer to this kind of question, which is like asking whether percussion sounds are produced by the drums or by the drummers." And then he gives a metaphorical example: A plant may grow tall and strong if exposed to the sun, while another will not do the same if condemned to the shade. The size of each plant depends not only on its genes or the environment in which it develops but on both. —But even after clarifying this point, other questions remain. To what extent do the taboos and psychological characteristics of the creature belong to its outer history, and to what extent are they perpetuated in its inner history? Is there a transfer of data from the inner history (culture) to the outer history (biological)? An institution like the prohibition of incest, could it have been perpetuated for millennia without the intervention of genetic inheritance? —Some believers find it repugnant and even immoral for a Catholic priest to have sexual relations with an adolescent. Priestly celibacy is an institution established by the Church less than two thousand years ago, and there is no biological reason to feel repugnance for such an act, just as there is no biological reason to condemn incest. But if the prohibition of incest is an institution many times older than celibacy, how could it not be more universal and profound? The cultural mechanism that provokes the rejection of the priest's sexuality, is it not similar to the one that universalized the rejection of incest? —The theory of the collective unconscious considers a kind of inner history inheritable through an inner and inevitable path. This mnemonic material, which supposedly we all, or almost all, possess, is the basic sketch of the unconscious. This would mean that we are not only born with a *moral ability*, as Frans de Waal defined it, but even with some megabytes included; something as if we were born with *language ability* including some words in Russian, French, and the occasional Chinese ideogram, depending on the travels of one of our ancestors. —In any case, what shapes and conditions almost all the freedom of the creature is the inner history that is inherited through an outer path and not entirely inevitable. The paradox arises, then, that the outer history is internal to the organism, because it resides in genetic inheritance; while the inner history (the history of the spirit) is external to the organism to a great extent, because it resides in cultural inheritance. If the Atlanteans had existed, today we would have some "mnemonic sediment" from them, according to a Jungian. But our lives and our vision of the world would not be conditioned by that lost culture as they are by the history of the Hebrew people.

5. HISTORICISM. Already in the 18th century, Giambattista Vico had considered that creatures are nothing outside the history they themselves produce. G. E. Lessing also understood that the pretension of knowing absolute truth was absurd. What is admirable is not so much this first observation but another that seeks to confirm it: because achieving absolute truth would mean stepping out of history. That is, ending the effort to seek it. In *Human, All Too Human*, Nietzsche reproached the philosophers of his time for their historical negligence. There is no eternal creature, just as there are no eternal truths, but rather a creature that is in process. Later, in *The Decline of the West*, Oswald Spengler repeated a similar warning: Immanuel Kant had considered in his reflections only nature, when the metaphysical creature was a being marked by time, a historical being. (This reproach is somewhat paradoxical and unfair, since it is easy to conceive ideas like "paradigm," "mentalities," and "historicism" after the analysis of Kant's synthetic *a priori* judgments.) In 1951, Jaspers had understood that "the unfinished character of the creature and its historicity are the same thing." In 1962, T.S. Kuhn introduced history and controversy into the sciences or, more precisely, into scientific epistemology: objective realities depended on a mental perspective called "paradigm" (I believe that a century earlier Dilthey had coined "*weltanschauung*" to

name a similar idea). After the controversy, that is, after the success of the Kuhnian paradigm, the concept and its name spread to the rest of thought and represented the most radical alternative to the prestigious closed systems of the 20th century. Now, let us observe that the historicist paradigm assumes not only the learning of a new way of seeing the world; it also implies the forgetting of the previous form. We assume that we cannot see "reality" in the same way as the ancient Babylonians did. We can only suspect that they saw it differently, just as we can understand the actions of a psychopathic murderer but cannot experience their inner nature, their own worldview. This means that although the creature is an "unfinished" being, it surely always will be. Or, at least, it will be as long as forgetfulness, stupidity, or perfection do not bring history to an end.

6. CONTINGENCY. Ours is no longer the frozen universe of Laplace. Not only has absolute space been destroyed by the relativity of space-time; the laws of physics have also lost their former condition of eternity. Because the historical paradigm extended its understanding to the natural sciences as well, and now Darwinism is taught in physics courses: its laws *evolve.* But, like species, the evolution of the laws of the Universe is historical. This means that event B1 may be the consequence of A, but it is not a *necessary* consequence: A could also have been followed

by B2, B3, or Bn. Once effect B1 has occurred, the process is irreversible: C1, C2, or Cn will then follow. The history of the Universe is built on contingencies: we live in a cosmic moment where the speed of light is *c* and the energy of electrons is *e*. But these constants could well have been different, and one day they will be. Contingency destroys one order and creates another, unpredictable one that cannot be calculated or conceived by the laws of the previous order. This paradigm resembles, in some way, Kierkegaardian thought: reality is not a single rational process; it is an indefinite set of possibilities, including nothingness. —Once, the Universe was concentrated in a point of zero extension and infinite density (to many, this idea may seem fantastic, but let us consider that an astronomical theory can be refuted in many ways except for being exaggerated; exaggeration does not exist for modern astronomy, just as it did not exist for the ancient Hindus). For that point to have been disturbed in an explosion, we must assume an external action. This leads us to the idea of a Megaverse or the recognition of a Creator. But if even the laws of physics are not significant at those thresholds of time, why should the rest of our rational understanding be?

7. ABANDONMENT. Our time no longer uses history to predict the future and condition the present. Not only because it understood that the future is unpredicta-

ble but also because it has renounced the Grand Projects. The future of humanity no longer matters more than the present of the individual. —The new history is a symphony of histories, coherent or contradictory but no longer structured; it does not explain the whole but each of the parts, from infinite points of view. Each moment is the simultaneous result of unpredictable contingencies. The physical law of *indeterminacy* reigns. —The contemporary landscape almost no longer includes nature. Almost everything surrounding the creature possesses memory and awareness of change. Everything is now the result of some evolution. Not only the creature and living beings; even inanimate nature: I refer to *The Evolution of Species,* to *A Brief History of Time.* After Charles Darwin and Alexander Friedman, nature ceased to be the world of *being*, of the static and the eternal, to have its own history. A history with a superhuman or Hindu scale. Forms and physical laws are no longer *fixed* but are instead in perpetual transition. Like the apparent human nature. Every time the creature reconsiders the anachronistic question "*what are we?* ", it turns to history to see "*how we were.*" Now, every human experience finds its meaning in its own history. The histories of madness, love, sensitivity, privacy, sex, hatred, beauty, and image have been written and scrutinized. There is a history of Good and a history of Evil, a history of happiness and a history of history itself. That is, every human experience has a relative meaning. For the postmodern creature, everything is relative to history; the world of *what-should-be* and the rest as well. There are no novel events subject to any law. Now, it is the events (both physical and spiritual) that dictate their own laws. And in their dictation and abolition lies History and its provisional death. There are no longer Greek philosophers reflecting on being, and those ontologies are now innocent chapters in the history of paradigms. —Truth was revealed to the Hebrews; each Greek found it one day in the agora; the moderns *arrived* at it after centuries of accumulating knowledge. Those who came after relativized it in history, or simply lost it. Karl Jaspers said that in almost all times doubt existed, but in our century it was not just a problem of solitary individuals but the great problem of the "mass." Of course, it is also possible that those famous Certainties of the past were never as popular as they seem; and that the new thing is, for some mysterious reason, our obsessive awareness of abandonment.

8. IMPROBABLES. Why does the "arrow of time" always point to the future? According to scientific thought, this is due to the second law of thermodynamics; because we always move to a state of increasing disorder; because in every cosmic process, information is irreversibly lost (the *Big Crunch* will not be identical to the *big bang;* or it will not happen, because the Universe is open and will

never stop expanding). And why? Because we start from an *ordered* state of the Universe, and any change will always point toward disorder, toward chaos. Because a puzzle has only one order and countless disorders; and if we start from the first, any change will lead us further into the second (the future). That is, we are in a particular cosmic moment, or we start from it to live and understand something of the Universe. —The physicist Ludwig Boltzmann related entropy (S) and the probability (P) of an event in the formula: $S = k \,.\, (\ln P)$. This means that the more improbable something is, the lower its entropy. Schrödinger proposed the term *negentropy* to designate the inverse of Boltzmann: $N = 1/S$. Thus, scientists agreed that the phenomenon with the highest negentropy was life; though they could well have started by saying that life was the most improbable or absurd thing they knew of in the Universe. Moreover, it would be pertinent to recall another extravagance of that same phenomenon: living beings *excrete* entropy, such as carbon dioxide in respiration, etc. —Life on Gaia began 3.6×10^9 years ago. Considering the radioactive nature of the planet, scientists believe this phenomenon was triggered by another explosion: a supernova. But let us observe that not only is life on Gaia a strange and perhaps unique phenomenon; the metaphysical creature is also a strange phenomenon on Gaia. The emergence of consciousness in an animal is only comparable to the emergence of life in the Universe.

As the biologist Julian Huxley described, the emergence of conceptual thought required the confluence of countless conditions in one of the innumerable species inhabiting the planet. Conditions that the metaphysical creature met or was gradually meeting. —If we had been forced to deduce a logical judgment about the creatures of Gaia, we would have said that they do not exist or cannot exist. All these phenomena are a miracle or the convergence of infinite improbabilities. What makes the metaphysical creature a mystery of the second or third degree.

II: Writing

9, MEMORY. It is true, with writing, history was born; but let us not say this merely for its historiographical significance. The invention of writing (3500 B.C.) not only made the recording of data possible; it also provoked a metaphysical revolution, difficult to match by any other invention: mythological time was replaced by a "historical" one, and with it, an entire world crumbled to make way for another. —It is not true that with writing began the recording of human actions. Long before, creatures preserved their past in a kind of collective memory, transmitted orally. For its preservation, this type of memory required perpetual repetition, and in this process, the records underwent modifications. We know that these changes were not arbitrary and that they occurred for the benefit of a certain archetype: the myth. As the Romanian Mircea Eliade showed, archaic cultures could not bear history; they annulled it by translating real events into archetypes through repetition. Even in our time, a specific event does not persist for two centuries in collective memory without losing its historical particularity, a time we should reduce to a few years if we consider the great popular idols of the 20th century. The archaic mentality only preserves the general and casts particular details into oblivion. This habit of the human mind is still with us. In his History of Eternity, *J. L. Borges, free from the superstitions of modernity, forgetting or contradicting the existentialism of the time, observed: "The generic can be more intense than the concrete."* I had just analyzed Platonism and remembered: "As a child, spending summers in the north of the province, the round plain and the men who drank mate in the kitchen intrigued me, but my happiness was immense when I learned that that circle was *pampa* and those men *gauchos*." —Just as we find the same pyramids in different cultures, we also find the story of Creation as different versions of the same tale. Oral memory, imprecise and fleeting, relied on archetypes, on the "natural" structure of early cultures. The invention of writing was a long process, and its consequences were not as immediate as those brought about by Edison with any of his toys. The ancient myths and, above all, the mythological behavior of the archaic mind were preserved in the novel clay tablets of Sumeria and the papyri of Egypt. But from then on, time ceased to be circular and imprecise. Individual events began to be ordered according to their sequence. The demigods and intellectuals of the Nile expanded and elevated the ancient obsession with preserving the bodies of their dead: better yet, they began to preserve their memories; feats, misfortunes, family histories, and stories of the empire. Further east, Sargon and Hammurabi delved into the depths of time, but they never ceased to be concrete men, the authors of laws and victories on the battlefield. Forgetting was no longer possible, and they, who did not want to be forgotten like their Hindu neighbors, busied themselves with recording events, dates, and names.

10, IMPRECISIONS. When Hegel described the Indian spirit (hedonistic, sensual, and dreamlike), what he did was describe the European fantasies about that exotic country from which the most intense aromas came, not the Hindu spirit. But he noted a significant characteristic: the Hindus lacked the historiographical concerns of other nations. He often describes them as disproportionate liars. "The Indians," he wrote, "cannot comprehend anything similar to what the Old Testament recounts about the patriarchs. Implausibility, impossibility do not exist for them." He then recalls that, according to Hindu memory, there were kings who ruled for thousands of years. He recounts, for example, that the reign of Vikramaditya was a glorious moment in the history of India. But it was also known that there were eight or nine kings with the same name over a period of 1500 years. Implausible, he attributes it to a defect in the decimal system that takes fractions for whole numbers. Sir, any people could be accused of this mathematical slip, except the inventors of zero. Well, but Hegel made other important observations: the Hindus, who achieved great fame in literature, algebra, geometry, astronomy, and grammar, completely neglected history. Most of what was known about Indian history in Hegel's time had been written by foreigners. —This disinterest in history by the Hindus is explained by their own conception of time: deeply mythological, circular like *samsara.* Because in India, even today, the most concrete reality is seen through the doctrine of cosmic cycles that leads souls to transmigrate and the Universe to regenerate eternally, including in the same wheel creatures, gods, and stones. "The Indian man," observed Spengler, "forgets everything. In contrast, the Egyptian could forget nothing. There has never been an Indian art of portraiture, of biography *in nuce.* Egyptian sculpture, on the other hand, knew no other subject." Other examples must be added: the idealistic sculpture of classical Greece and the portrait sculpture of Rome. The former, a mythological people; the latter, obsessively historical. —Sanskrit is one of the oldest languages of Gaia. In its use and perfection, a powerful culture, the Indian one, matured long before the appearance of written Sanskrit. The Hebrew people, on the other hand, are marked by writing, and this is because they formed and matured (not before 1250 BC) on a powerful written tradition; whether we consider the Egyptian tradition in Moses or the Sumerian civilization in Abraham.

11, REVOLUTION. In Homer's time, Greece was still immersed in a mythological culture. That is to say, those Greeks did not recognize the concrete past or the different future. Therefore, until the ninth century before Christ, they left no inscriptions or great works as in Egypt and Sumeria. Only shortly after Homer completed his famous mytho-poetic compilation did alphabetic writing appear in Greece, brought by Phoenician sailors. The *Iliad* and the *Odyssey* were not indifferent to this arrival. Not a few have seen in these epic poems the spontaneity of oral verse and the complexity of writing. Shortly after (if we consider that then four hundred years were not that immense stretch of historical time as it is in our time), a revolution occurred in Greece that was not only cultural: a new spirit was born that Europeans later called *Western.* Perhaps Plato is the most charismatic representative of this change from an oral culture to a written one. Almost everyone knows his attacks on poets and his proselytism in favor of philosophers as educators of Greece. But between Plato and Homer are the "first philosophers "; Zeno is a precursor to Socrates, and if he were not earlier, one might say he is his caricature; Socrates himself was not a writer philosopher, but he participated in the new culture to a greater extent than Parmenides, who did leave written thought. Socrates eliminated all archetypal simplification; because dialectic seeks the new, the truth still unknown to the one who uses it. In contrast, myth is not a path *toward* a truth still incomplete; it is the expression of that hidden truth. To argue that an arrow shot through the air does not move, as Parmenides and Zeno did, one must be willing to contradict all our intuition of reality. Different, myth can only sustain what is intuitive. Intuition may show us, without intermediaries, a horse with wings pulling a chariot of fire through the skies. But it can never shoot an arrow that does not move.

12, IRREVERSIBLE. With writing, the germ of a historical and dialectical spirituality begins to incubate. The biblical God is a historical God, beyond sharing mythological elements. Yahweh differs from the archaic gods by what is historical in Him, not by sharing ancient myths with the infidels. From *Genesis* or from the creation of the world, He made it clear that time is linear, with a beginning and an end; not round like a Hindu wheel. In contrast, the Eastern gods are victims of the wheel that contains them and makes them spin, eternally. The hierarchy of the Hindu gods is flawed or attenuated by a kind of triumvirate or parliamentary collegiality. But, above all, they are subjected to a kind of Supernature that diminishes them. Creatures and gods dissolve in the whirlpool of cycles, because not even *Brahman* is definitive. The incorruptible memory of the sign on paper makes it almost impossible to confuse the past with the present. If every event is unique and each has a before and an after, then lost time is irretrievable. It is not a wheel but the terrible stroke of a god—and it leads somewhere.

14, EVENT. For the mythological mind, everything was circular, and the duty of creatures was to preserve that Order. There could be nothing new in the world, and if there were, there could be no world. The only new thing in the Cycles is the end of the Cycles. But since time *is* the Cycles (it does not contain them), the new and the End are everywhere and nowhere. In contrast, historical peoples are formed in the habit of writing. Writing fixes a concrete past, and from this perception the awareness of novelty is born. The new is what is not written. Linear time is made of novelties and obsessions with novelties. The Roman people were a historical people par excellence, according to Eliade, and they lived obsessed with the "end of Rome." For the historical mind, the End is not the only novelty that can exist in the world, but it is the only inevitable one. In the Christian West, the End can only be remedied by an eternal present; not by the Eastern repetition. Because nothing ever repeats, and *what is written* will be read only once.

III: Mind and Spirit

15, MIND. For Homer, the creature was a battlefield where external forces of divine and contradictory origin converged. Later, Plato invented the mind and its modern divisions. He decreed that reason must dominate passions; because one was above the other in the hierarchy of virtue, and this order meant health and balance. Centuries later, when Peter Abelard reflected on ethics, he did not rely exclusively on demons to explain and justify the creature; a captive heir of the Greeks, like almost everyone, the scholastic preferred to involve *nature* as well. This time referring to the human mind. Not long ago, Freud revisited the Platonic model of the *psyche* to develop his positivist philosophy. Only now the order of factors had been reversed, and the famous balance was different: health consists in freeing the unconscious from the old rationalist condemnation. That said, with a certain measure—a Platonic measure.

16, MENTALITIES. In archaic times, every mental phenomenon belonged to the external nature: rivers, men, ghosts. Anaxagoras and Heraclitus imagined a kind of universal mind they called *Nous* and *Logos.* (The word "logos" could also mean "discourse" or "thought.") When Plato invented the human mind, he made it the repository of some of these phenomena. Until Berkeley came along and placed *everything* within it. By then, for the bishop and his followers, not only demons and ghosts were mental phenomena; trees and stones were as well. That is, physics was a branch of human metapsychology.

17, STRUCTURE. For our contemporaries, all societies in all times have created myths, seemingly different but similar at their core. The obsession of modern researchers has been to find the common elements that compose this Platonic structure. And they have done so with success or at least with elegance. But since this structure could not be of divine origin (a scientific premise), it had no choice but to be the *expression* of the human mind. According to this prestigious worldview, Hercules and Samson are to the brain what bile is to the liver. Thus, by distilling myths, noticing the similar in the diverse, the psychological skeleton was drawn. —The myth of Creation and the myth of the Flood repeat in Black Africa, ancient Mesopotamia, and Polynesia. Pepe Rodríguez, a Spanish academic and successful book seller, wrote in 1997: "God, to give a couple more examples, was not very accurate when he attributed to Moses the same mythical story that had already been written hundreds of years earlier about the great Sumerian ruler Sargon of Akkad (c. 2334-2279 BC), who, among other things, was placed in a reed basket and abandoned to his fate in the waters of the Euphrates River shortly after birth, only to be rescued and adopted by a water carrier. This type of legend, known as the 'saved from the waters' model, is universal and, apart from Sargon and Moses, appears in the résumés of Krishna, Romulus and Remus, Perseus, Cyrus, etc. Did God know He was plagiarizing a pagan story?" This type of observation is classic in 20th-century anthropological literature, though it is not always so arrogant. In another time, the same verifications would have testified in favor of God; now they serve to refute Him, who knows why.

18, SIMILARITIES. The modern creature is so conditioned by its memory that anthropologists, always in pursuit of the immanent structure, must go to more primitive societies to simplify or purify the problem. Throughout the 20th century, whenever an anthropologist sought to understand European madness, they invariably moved to New Guinea or some similar place. There, among the Papuans, the task was imposed of studying our supposed ancestors in the flesh. (Not long ago, I ran into two or three anthropologists in Africa. Excellent Europeans, by the way.) Anthropology is a science that aims to study the human creature, both physically and morally. But none of these scholars would think of staying in Paris to study the Parisians, who are still human; no, in such a tangle, how would they distinguish the fundamental elements? What repeats among the Papuans is easier to observe, easier to imagine as true, authentic. And it costs nothing to import it into the unconscious of the most rationalist Frenchman. —In the de facto sciences, the recurring methodology consists of "seeking similarities." The study of the mind and body especially relies on the common elements present in different individuals. And from this activity arise medicine, psychology, and charlatanism.

19, MEANINGS. Anthropologists study dozens of cultures in order to discover common elements. That is to say, anthropology is the science that studies cultures in order to nullify the meaning of culture. The more common an element is, the truer and deeper it must be; as much for a Papuan as for a Japanese. Once isolated, this element is attributed to prehistory. Since prehistory seems quite uniform (thanks to our erudite ignorance), it is assumed that creatures repeated the same customs for hundreds of thousands of years. It is deduced, then, that what was formed in the human mind there must weigh equally on every creature now. Thus begin the tempting comparisons: —a. The nomadic societies of prehistory went out hunting and gathering; so too, after the industrial revolution, one goes out hunting for money and food outside the home. —b. Male chimpanzees exchange food for sex, as cavemen did; so too, an executive who invites a woman to dinner is courting her, and it is likely they will end up in bed. —c.

Soccer is a repetition of hunting practice. —d. While women talk (and talk) face to face, men do so sideways, almost always paying attention to a game or another activity; just as they did when they went out hunting together. Anyone can add other examples. For instance, modern states represented the concentrated authority of the king or pharaoh, while current societies represent a return to tribal times, as power is distributed among the owners of large private companies; and, as among the chiefs of those clans, their interests are opposed. —All these observations may be valid. But is it fair to extract social, moral, and psychological predictions from them? Fair or not, that is what is done. Well, let us consider that all these tendencies or impulses form a large part of our psychological skeleton; but let us see that the act they drive has changed in meaning (which is what should really matter). That structure no more determines our social behavior than our culture does; it is merely the old structure of a rebuilt building. Let us think that the old Punta Carretas prison in Montevideo is now a shopping center, and none of its visitors would notice if they lacked that prior anthropological information. Taking off one's hat and bowing before a person once meant absolute submission to a sovereign; when does it mean the same in our time? The practice of the act, the custom or reflex, remains, but the meaning has completely changed. —The same could be said of religious rites. Many, or almost all, once meant sacrifice or fearful submission; none of which prevents them from later coming to mean Enlightenment or mystical love. And that spiritual process must be significant; that is, it should not be a random or arbitrary change, but a necessary or, at least, historical one.

20, COMPLEXITY. In the first instance, concrete knowledge consists of the recognition of differences. In a later stage, abstract knowledge meant the opposite. The recognition of the common in diversity was an intellectual progress. Sábato observed that "Commercial exchange always carries a germ of abstraction, as it is a kind of metaphorical exercise that tends to identify distinct entities by stripping them of their concrete attributes. The man who exchanges a sheep for a sack of flour is performing a highly abstract exercise." Years later, he has one of his characters say: "A genius is someone who discovers identities between contradictory facts. [...] Someone who discovers that the falling stone and the Moon that does not fall are the same phenomenon." —But there are complexities and complexities. The prestigious hypothetico-deductive method requires as few variables as possible. For a reason, it first shone in astronomy and then in physics. Until it encountered a real problem in human behavior. Psychoanalysis, for example, needs (and indeed possesses) more than two thousand starting hypotheses, a particularity that does not refute it but excludes it from the simplicity of rigor. And let us not speak of sociology, which must navigate the diverse and millennia-old field of cultures.

21, SPIRIT. The mere mention of the word "spirit" makes reductionists nervous, those who have everything translated into amino acids and Oedipus complexes. Who, at this stage of Civilization, can believe in the soul? Of course, the soul cannot be weighed or measured. Nor is it deducible. The refutation by the impotence of ignorance is not new. Before, everything unknown was attributed to the existence of some god or demon. Now, since gods and demons have taken to fleeing the scene, it is deduced that where the light of the Method does not reach, there is emptiness. How, then, does the soul or something called spirit exist? Well, let us think (as in the 19th century) that dreams are physiological phenomena, and that this verification does not rule out that *they are also* a psychological phenomenon. Then, if we verify that they are a psychological phenomenon, would that rule out that *they are also* a manifestation of the soul? Similarly, the fact that the Kaaba is a meteorite does not exclude that it was sent by Allah. It is perfectly valid to study myths and metaphysics from a psychological perspective, just as it is to study dreams with electronic instruments. But that should not mean reductionism. The intellect does not function without neurons, but Christianity, Sartre, or Lagrange's theorem are something more than a simple neuronal order.

IV: Facing Death

22, EXPERIENCE. I must admit that I do not know what death is; I have only been allowed to discover its mask and not without the emotions that hinder understanding. But if I were immortal, I would have no authority to speak of it; and although I have no experience in dying, I do have experience in living with the awareness of that inexorable future.

23, COMPANIONS. One lives surrounded by people and animals and deposits feelings in them; one associates emotionally with them to ward off the irremediable cosmic loneliness to which we were condemned. But then those beings disappear, one by one. Because it is always the others who die. Then society dissolves, the ancient pillars that held up the world crumble, and we fall into the void where memories are useless mirages of water for the one who is dying in the desert. Then we bring children into the world with the hope that the new pillars will outlive us. Because the destiny of the metaphysical creature is not entirely terrible.

24, FAILURE. It is in childhood the only time when the creature is capable of fully living the *present*. Later, in maturity, it will no longer be able to do so, because the *future* will always intrude without a defined form. Until it is made, and then, in old age, it will be the *past* that claims its right: to complete the work of time; that the creature never dies satisfied. —It could be said that many creatures only cared about the present, like Omar Khayyam. But it was not this kind of creatures that were responsible for almost all our metaphysical and material history. For better or worse, all the creature's action has its motivation in the future. In that time is deposited every "why," every meaning, material or metaphysical. Death not only means, in principle, the denial of all future; it is also the denial of all past, because with it every previous achievement fades and crumbles. A 12th-century poem expresses it thus:

Where is your glory, Babylon? where is the terrible

Nebuchadnezzar, and the mighty Darius, and the famous Cyrus?

Where is Regulus, where is Romulus, where is Remus?

The ancient rose is but a name, only names remain to us.

How, then, can one not understand the religious response? Metaphysical exploration is the only thing that can lift the creature defeated by its own consciousness, by the powerful interrogative force of its memory. Definitely, its greatness is not on earth but in heaven. But does all this mean that the creature invented God to fill its voids or that, simply, it discovered Him while traversing the experience of its metaphysical destiny? Similarly, did it invent mathematics to understand the world or did it discover it after a millennial experience?

25, ATHEISTS. I suppose that in the face of death neither Democritus nor Lucretius should have experienced any anguish. Logically, brains like theirs (I almost said "spirits") should register this *event* as just another one: with the death of a brother a new molecular order has been established in the Cosmos, similar to a stone that breaks or a tree that burns. And yet...

26, NEOMYTHOLOGY. The death of a famous or simply well-known person, known like a family member but not actually one, rekindles in the creature the mystery of disappearance, of departure, of abandonment. But without the unthinking pain that accompanies the death of a friend or a family member. Therefore, it is experienced by the people as a Greek tragedy.

27, ANSWERS. But are there answers to the incomprehensible death? That is, are there answers to the mystery of life? Well, if there are any answers, let us be sure that the creatures have already explored them after facing the same experience for millennia. Because, what a coincidence, these beings have been dying for a long time, and for almost as long they have been anguished by it. — Those contesting institutions are, undoubtedly, religions. Imprecise answers, it is true. But what more can be expected from precarious and imperfect beings who are swallowed every day by the unfathomable abyss? The body can never deny death; the spirit, on the other hand, though mistaken, is the only one capable of such audacity. And it is there that its greatness lies. The creature, in the face of life and death, is a doubtful being. At least compared to a tiger or a rhinoceros. What to do, what to feel? When one of those poor beings decides to be guided by a certain religious creed, it delegates the responsibility of being wrong to a leader; or, better yet, to an entire people and an entire millennial tradition. Even knowing that millions of other creatures are guided by different and even opposing creeds, the individual is no longer anguished by the idea of being wrong alone. If Buddha, Christ, or Muhammad said it, what Judge would condemn them?

28, TRAUMAS. The modern spirit did not forget traditions and taboos but quite the opposite. It violated them. Because its epic was to "unveil" and subvert the ancient order, forgetting that those traditions and taboos were not there by chance. The ancients did not invent their founding myths because there was no television then. Myths, like taboos and the rest of spiritual traditions, responded to strict needs: they meant psychological protection as well as metaphysical answers. For thousands of years, creatures have been facing the same experiences of sex, life, and death. None of that has changed, but then they did it with some *protection* and now they find themselves completely naked. —The pretense of unrestricted truth (which is always an illusion) usually leads to an excess of psychological exposure. And the most exposed are, as always, children. In the face of sex, life, and death, today's children ask the same questions they did in the times of Hammurabi or King Arthur. Only now they are explained reality "as it is," because it is not good to deceive them with fantastical stories (after all, myth and taboo mean deception and repressive censorship). One does not need to be Jean Piaget to realize that a child's mind is not like that of an adult. Hardly will a terrible experience permanently alter the psychology of an adult, but we know that any experience can mark the future personality of a child. In some cases, "mark" can mean "trauma." Hardly will a fiction, a fantastical story, provoke any trauma in an individual; until now, all traumas have been provoked by reality. So, if the main problem lies in "reality," what is so perverse about facing it with some defense? Are not, perhaps, dreams themselves the first to understand this need by using symbols to allude to reality? To say that a fantastical story, like

Alice in Wonderland, can affect a child's mental health is almost like saying that their dreams can affect their future personality. Telling a child that a person who dies goes to heaven cannot be worse than explaining to them how the soul disappears and the body remains in a coffin. Not only because heaven is more beautiful than the coffin, but, above all, because even we adults do not know where the soul goes when the body is left alone.

29, LIBERATION. All religions signify a rejection of death. All presuppose the dualism of body and soul. The former is destined for old age and decay; that much we know. Therefore, nothing good can be expected from it in the long term. The soul, always perfectible, can *become* virtuous, whether in the body of a dwarf or in the body of a giant. —Since the times when men scrutinized the silence and darkness of caves, the soul has been *that* which is present in a living body but does not alter its weight when it leaves it. Therefore, it is a weightless quality; or it weighed as much as air, according to the Greeks. And like air or anything that has no weight, its destiny is the high heavens. But of course, there was something that was not right: the fact that creatures continued to be born meant that, for some reason, souls would *fall again*. Because that is their nature, according to the Indians, or because that is their divine punishment, according to others. In any case, the soul is "a stranger on Earth," and it can only be liberated or return to its original state through the *knowledge* of its current condition, not through mere death. According to all religions.

V: Sex and Punishment

30, MODESTY. Power is diversely related to sex. To dominate is to monopolize the object of desire. But since domination is a universal aspiration, conflict is inevitable. Therefore, the object of desire must be hidden, or else the dreaded disorder will ensue. Children are allowed to walk naked in the street, but the rest of humanity is condemned for the same. In almost all countries, exhibitionists are imprisoned, and the act of copulation in public places is penalized. The concealment of sex is an ancient practice translated into *modesty.* Not content with hiding sex, some excited Islamic extremists also suppress the bodily existence of their women and punish them for showing their lips, arms, or any other tiny area of the body capable of arousing desire in the male. Because Chaos is evil, and Order is of God.

31, CONDEMNATION. In the earliest religions, in the cults of the Mother Goddess and fertile earth, in agricultural societies and the first cities, in Babylon, chastity was considered a sin. And sterility a curse. Later, these considerations changed; obviously, they were inverted. When and why did the religious spirit begin to condemn sex with such fury? Why was Mary a virgin if she was married? All spiritual leaders were in their time considered sons of virgin mothers, from Krishna to Confucius, from Buddha to Jesus. (Some blasphemers attempt to explain this fact by suggesting that only a holy spirit can impregnate a woman without penetration; and that this was the go-to argument of adulteresses. But let us note that there are other stories, as vulgar as this one, that never entered mythological celebrity.) Saints are supposed to be virgins, holy men must be chaste, *and so on*. Concrete examples abound, and some of them are caricaturesque. Some have attributed the sexual austerity of Christianity to its original reaction against the pagan culture of Rome. Others have pointed to economic motives for the imposition of castrating measures like celibacy. For example, unmarried priests are more economical, as a family would imply a larger budget for the Church or, otherwise, the distraction of the priest in civil production. On the other hand, at least in more religious times, priests could inherit property from their families, but upon death, they had to donate it to the Pope's coffers, as they had no descendants. —However, we can say that Christian austerity is common to *almost* all religions, if we were to commit the imprecision of calling tantra a religion. The religious spirit is, above all, *renunciant,* and few renunciations are more valuable and significant than the renunciation of sex. The renunciation of sex carries a dual meaning, one religious and the other social: the renunciation of the present in favor of the future, and the renunciation of promiscuity in favor of order. Both imply a victory over the most basic instincts. An already irreversible divorce of the creature from the rest of the animal kingdom. If primitive man renounced *a* woman in ritual sacrifice because she was the prized symbol of life, religious man renounced woman, the despised symbol of precarious life, as a tribute to something greater than what was renounced: eternal life. But since it is a renunciation too costly for a creature that was once an animal, the renunciant must protect themselves from temptation. Some defend themselves from demons, others self-flagellate. Others, like the monk Peter Abelard, resort to a kind of alter ego: reason. With it, the scholastic justifies the condemnable desire for women. "Let us consider the case of a religious man," he wrote, "bound in chains and forced to lie among women. The softness of the bed and the contact with the women around him lead him to delight, not to consent. Would anyone dare to call this delight, born of nature, a sin?" —The history of religions lists not only ascetics and voluntary martyrs; it also includes creatures with the habit of tearing things from themselves: eyes, tongues, testicles. Origen of Alexandria, for example, not content with the asceticism he practiced, castrated himself as a way of correctly interpreting the Gospels.

32, CHALLENGE. Is it necessary to be an atheist or a blasphemer to recognize the neurotic character of religious renunciation? Might it not be that by doing so we are taking a step toward a more authentic spirituality? Is not that *step* the most important step in human evolution? Is not *spiritual evolution* the only one with any meaning? Is not that, perhaps, the greatest goal of a God who still cares for His creatures?

33, OFFERING. Why were sacrifices preferably performed with virgin women? It is clear that they were not killed because they were despised, but *quite the opposite.* Virgins are those women who have not yet stolen life's share of pleasure. The progress that leads from the sacrifice of the best ox to the sacrifice of a pure young woman is the progress of a collective neurosis. The economy of the gods begins to suffer inflation, and, as always, the solution is to oppress the people with higher tributes. And the most that men could offer without offering everything was one of those parts that symbolized the most desired: the pleasure of sex. As Bronislaw Malinowski observed, in human memory the testimony of a positive case always overshadows the negative case. (At least in the superstitious mind, because modern anxiety refuted this law with Murphy's.) However, the frequent negative cases of magical inefficiency must have led to a veiled skepticism, which is reflected in the inflation of offerings. Once the sacrifice was consummated, the grateful gods were expected to respond with earthly benefits: good harvests, abundant game, rains—security, the survival of the group.

34, AUDACITY. In excessive pleasure there is no renunciation, and thus only the aesthetic spirit can celebrate it without remorse. Sex is the consummation of the greatest desire of primitive man—and, in some cases, of modern man as well. But once obtained and consummated, one falls back into ordinary life, which is *always* less pleasurable and, often, painful. Even the most prosperous farmer was threatened by a fearsome and unpredictable future: poor harvests, old age, illness, and unavoidable death. Excessive pleasure was an audacity against reality, always threatening and unpredictable, before which one had to pay tributes in "pains." The sacrifice of virgins has an unequivocal magical-religious meaning: a request for well-being on earth through a symbolic act (magical), but to the gods of heaven (religious). And why women and not virgin men? —Well, almost all cultures are expressions of the fears and desires of the male, the tender and brutal tyrant for thousands of years. Just as defeated enemies served for the fatal ritual, within the same community the most vulnerable were women. Moreover, the generic woman represents for man the mystery of life, of fertility for agricultural societies. Because it was symbolically the most powerful element in the ritual. If sacrifice meant renunciation, woman was the most valuable renunciation. For this reason, the veneration of the female body in the Paleolithic era and its subsequent sacrifice share the same direction and meaning. —In summary:

human sexuality, or its repression, carries a dual meaning, both moral and metaphysical, social and religious. Modesty and family taboos seek to control its excessive energy for the benefit of social order. The abolition of pleasure seeks the abolition of pain in Gaia and the attainment of true happiness, eternal pleasure, beyond.

35, EXPERIMENTATION. The fetishization of women on television is the commercial translation of that asymmetrical, one-sided relationship: male dominance. Although now she is no longer condemned; she is forced to dance, once again. It is the aesthetic spirit that expresses itself in the exercise of sensuality. Its only "renunciation" consists of not moving much faster than the ethical changes that are always unfolding, whether in its favor or in favor of its opposite, the religious spirit. Thus, it avoids chaos to prolong its practice. Meanwhile, the religious spirit, renunciant by nature, condemns it. And the market exploits it and its women.

36, SENSITIVITY. In our Western culture, sexual relationships are pseudo-liberated. Intercourse is surrounded by traumas, complexes, judgments and prejudices, modesty and strict rights, rules that regulate, protect, and castrate it. In less repressed cultures, such as African ones, it is simply practiced.

VI: The Last Commandments

37, THREAT. Darwin had already observed that the struggle for survival is more intense among individuals of the same species. The creature could not be an exception and experienced this problem as an individual, family, clan, tribe, race, and, finally, as a nation. Throughout civilized history, and long before, the creature has faced, with obsession, a single external threat: other creatures.

38, INCEST. There is an undeniable relationship between the prohibition of incest and the formation of human societies. It is generally accepted that such a prohibition triggered the spark of culture and civilization on Gaia. But the inverse relationship must be no less true: the need for societies larger than the family required exogamy, as a pact or sign of familiarity. —For hundreds of thousands of years, creatures were hunter-gatherer animals. They took from nature what nature offered them, and for this reason, they had to move from one place to another in groups not much larger than the family unit. In this way, competition was avoided as much as possible. At that time, raids by neighboring males in search of new females or more power must not have been uncommon. Incest must have been the common practice, and exogamy the crime, since, contrary to what is believed, incest is the norm in nature, and its prohibition a fundamental abnormality of metaphysical creatures. (Something similar occurs with homosexuality. It cannot be said that this human condition is "against nature," because, for nature, homosexuality is no more a deviation than wearing clothes or prohibiting incest.) A clan more or less closed off by the necessity of survival and conflicted by the sexual development of its younger members must have imposed sexual rules, that is, taboos. Later, creatures experimented with convenient but unstable societies; they associated on a larger scale for defense or hunting. Until, not long ago, the greatest of revolutions occurred, which would change a million years of prehistory: agriculture. Then the creatures had to accept the neighbor, the former enemy. The old endogamous zeal was no longer just a factor of family conflicts; it became the first antisocial element, a threat to the unity of the community. Exogamy, on the other hand, became an institution of vital importance for society; and incest, a dark memory. —From then on, cooperation among creatures became more important than competition; the family or clan expanded into tribe, village, and city. Not without paradox, it can be said that the first step toward civilization, toward the *zōon politikón* (political animal), was agriculture. Because it not only gathered creatures but also forced them to organize, morally and legislatively; and it also enabled the division of labor and commerce thanks to overproduction.

39, MOSES. According to the Old Testament, Moses wrote the Decalogue on Mount Sinai; probably 1450 years before Christ. With the Law, the Hebrews achieved the failed effort of Akhenaten: monotheism. However, the last five commandments (do not kill, do not commit adultery, do not steal, do not lie, do not covet) predate the first ones and the heretic pharaoh. These were already known among the Hindus as "General Duties." Buddhism also has five precepts, four of which coincide with the last ones of Moses. Not long ago, the German theologian Hans Küng wrote that long before what the Bible announces as God's Commandment, it was already written in the Code of Hammurabi (18th century BC). —No matter how you look at them, it is evident that the First and Second Tablets have different origins and meanings. Surely, if we were to abandon a pair of children on a distant planet similar to Gaia, over time the new generations of creatures would repeat all our myths, found religions similar to ours, ideologies, and the deaths of ideologies. But before anything else, they would start again with the dictation of the last five Commandments. Today, it is not uncommon for religious authorities to recognize that a creature without religion can live according to a "human

ethic," and in them lie the hopes for an end to "holy wars.
"

40, PROHIBITION. The insistent preposition *do not* indicates the preexistence of its opposite. Because, as Freud said regarding taboos, "we do not see why there would be a need to prohibit something that no one desires to do; what is prohibited must be the object of a desire." Lévi-Strauss says exactly the same in *The Elementary Structures of Kinship*: "There would be no reason to prohibit what, without prohibition, would not run the risk of being carried out." The origin of the prohibition (he says) must be sought in the existence of a danger that threatens the group. "...We still need to discover the reasons why incest implies a detriment to the social order." Precisely, psychoanalysis tells us that this type of prohibition is internalized in the form of horror towards the act that is prohibited. We think that in the depths of prehistory, creatures lived in permanent conflict with nature and with themselves —even in times of peace, security and conflict must have been present as concerns. As still happens with the rest of the animals and some creatures, males fought among themselves responding to the most basic instincts and out of respect for Darwin's laws. The victorious male killed (6) the defeated, fornicated (7) with his females, and took (8) what his adversary or neighbor left behind. Later, the more evolved and intelligent creatures used subtler instruments for the same purpose: they coveted (10) and lied (9) for their own benefit. —Another question remains: why does the most universal prohibition of all (according to ethnologists), incest, not appear explicitly in the Decalogue? Neither in the Decalogue nor in any other foreign Law. *Perhaps because it is implicit?*

39, GREEKS. In *The Republic* of Plato, the thesis, known at the time, is presented that nature is unjust *by nature* and justice is the product of a social contract, something like a non-aggression pact. Glaucon argues before Socrates: "...when men began to commit and suffer injustices, and to witness the consequences of these acts, those who had no power to avoid the harms or to achieve the benefits decided that the best thing was to establish mutual agreements in order to neither commit nor suffer injustices. And from then on, they began to dictate laws, and called legal and just what the law prescribes." (These words of the Greek are not far from Freud's assertion that justice arises from the feeling of impotence, characteristic of childhood). Later, when Socrates responds to Glaucon, what he does is argue in favor of justice as a power superior to injustice. However, the Greek intuition had made an anthropological observation that Socrates overlooks and does not refute. For his part, Glaucon sees this contract more as a written document than as an internalized demand, and thus underestimates (like Thrasymachus) the perseverance of the just creature in the face of the hypothetical abolition of "laws." This abolition is no longer a legal or political problem but a psychological one, and to make it effective, an anarchist dictator is not necessary but rather a brainwashing. Which is not impossible, and history records many of them.

40, PRICE. The Confucian maxim "do not do to others what you do not want done to you" formulates the basic principle of tolerance. Jesus later confirmed it in his own way or in the way of the Father. The Pythagoreans prescribed the same; Sextus formulated it thus: "Whatever you wish your neighbor to be for you, be you for your neighbor." If there were not, in the deepest part of creatures, the propensity to overlook it and the fear that others might overlook it, these recommendations would never have been perpetuated in the way they were. (The three men said the same thing: the individual and the group are one. If the individual is sick, so is society. And above all, the inverse: no individual is entirely healthy in a sick society.) These formulas, which we might call *ethical,* have legislative translations; among the most famous and ancient are the Code of Hammurabi and the *Torah*: "An eye for an eye and a tooth for a tooth." Both obligations, some internal to the creatures and others internal to the written law, are decisive in the functioning of a society.

41, PUNISHMENT. In a society with a high ethical consciousness, criminals are scarce. They are also fewer in societies where the law punishes more severely. When, after the war, Mozambique fell into a wave of crime, it was countered with public executions of extreme cruelty. A simple thief or an innocent person could be burned alive in the midst of popular excitement, and the memory of this spectacle ended up discouraging a large number of future criminals. An inverse example is found in a neighboring and more *civilized country.* The end of an unjust and rigorous regime and the greater permissiveness of the new government turned Johannesburg into the most violent and dangerous city in the world. And to realize this, one need not walk down *George Street.*

42, RENUNCIATION. The renunciation of personal benefit is always well-regarded by the creatures of Gaia, and it has no limits other than the renouncer's own endurance. Societies applaud and venerate martyrs who sacrifice themselves for the benefit of a group, or simply for another person. Creatures call this *altruism* or Che Guevara. Conversely, the selfish individual represents a threat to the group, either by effect or by bad example. —In all societies, one of the most valued elements is the order that keeps them alive. When one travels in an unknown country, the first word one seeks to learn is the one that means gratitude, despite having no immediate utility; the second, to say good morning or to greet. Both represent the will of non-aggression. So-called "good manners" also reflect this secret pact. Not speaking in secret at a gathering, not using a language foreign to the group is not just a matter of form or "bad manners "; it also signifies a renunciation in favor of the other.

43, SPIRIT. Nevertheless, the creatures of Gaia are not reduced to the simple laws that helped them emerge from their most primitive state. Their spirit is also an achievement, and it is formed not only in their relationship with others but also *with themselves.* The creatures of Gaia are not only the consequence of a higher ethical complexity but also of a variable and sometimes contradictory metaphysics. Karl Jaspers summarized it thus: "The first step toward the repression of mere instincts is external violence, which produces terror and anguish. Then comes the already indirect violence of the *taboo*; afterward, the appropriate overcoming of the belief that man dominates himself through the sense of his actions emanating from belief." —The last five Commandments refer to survival through coexistence; the first five belong to a metaphysical level; they come after the last five and are the primary foundation of the three great monotheistic religions —the true contribution of Moses to history and to the creatures of Gaia.

44, TIMES. The thesis of a common or restricted origin of humanity is affirmed or confirmed by the weight of religious dogmas and scientific evidence: Adam and Eve, the monogenetic nature of human beings, the retrospective convergence of languages and myths, the intellectual habits in their search for truth. Let us see that something similar occurs with what we understand as ethics and morals. There are moral principles, few and common to all or almost all creatures, and they are summarized, with some omissions, in the second Tablet: incest, homicide, adultery, theft. Ethics, on the other hand, are far more diverse and complex, as are cultures and languages: the culinary ethics of India, Protestant ethics, socialist ethics, military ethics, if such a thing exists. One could say that moral principles are prehistoric, unconscious, and more stable; while ethics were formed within the cultural complexity of inner history, they are influenced by a certain rationality, are more recent, and more vulnerable. Anthropology has concerned itself with the former, with taboos and prohibitions; while science or sociological philosophy has dealt with the latter.

VII: The Consciousness of the Species

45, CONSERVATION. According to the oldest fossils, life on Gaia emerged at least 3.5 billion years ago. For much of this time, the inhabitants of Gaia were unicellular organisms, similar to bacteria. Like modern bacteria, these organisms were very simple (compared to higher animals), so we could not say that something akin to the "instinct for self-preservation" existed in them. However, these mysterious cellular units fought against death just as a tiger or Amnesty International does now. Modern bacteria possess an almost insignificant appendage that, through a rotational movement, allows them to approach a favorable environment or flee from a dangerous one. This means that the impulse for self-preservation is not exclusive to higher animals, endowed with a complex network of neurons. The struggle for survival is a piece of information that was born with life itself. Life is a struggle in favor of itself; otherwise, it would never have existed, or it would have immediately returned to its mineral or inorganic origin. —The impulses of conservation and destruction are part of animal nature; but the predominance of the impulse for the preservation of life is always greater than its opposite, and this is demonstrated by our very existence. Almost all creatures on Gaia die unwillingly. —Morality and religions, in different ways, deny death. One resists physical death; the other resists true death. Religions, which are initially independent of morality, respond to the same *vital impulse,* almost always by denying it. An extreme and paradoxical example is preached by Buddhism: in its attempt to deny death, it also denies life. But not just this life; the other life as well. For their part, moralities are the cultural expressions of that common impulse for survival and have existed, in various forms, before and after religious precepts. The last Mosaic Commandments are both prior to and subsequent to Moses and form the basis of almost all the ethics that abound on Gaia. —Well, among creatures, there are many and varied definitions of *ethics,*which makes it almost impossible for me to pinpoint a consensual definition. But precision and consensus need not be the primary virtues of this report nor a characteristic of the creatures of Gaia. I, at least, understand ethics as a code of duties and behaviors that, unlike morality, consists of a rational discourse. Or, at least, it aims to be. Ethics and morality should thus form a single body, hierarchical and coherent in its internal discourse. The last five Commandments are the a priori elements of all ethical discourse, which will seek to confirm them from the lowest to the most complex levels. And it is perhaps due to this very complexity of discourse that creatures often arrive at different and even contradictory ethics. And they kill each other over it.

46, ANIMALS. Moral prescriptions consist of rendering Darwin's laws ineffective among metaphysical creatures. What is good in the natural kingdom is bad among animals that produce culture. Wars, the dominance of the strongest, and the suppression of the weak are condemned when practiced among humans and admired when the protagonists are two reindeer. In ecological reserves around the world, creatures have reimposed the *Law of the Jungle.* To this end, they have prescribed that animals kill one another, according to the measure imposed by the victors. And for this ancient and innocent mechanism of conservation to function, human creatures declared themselves out of the competition, given their high professionalism in matters of power and extermination. Of course, genocide continues to be practiced among creatures even as it is condemned. But this happens because, although they are cultural animals, they do not cease to be simply animals.

47, ANSWERS. It is clear that the greatest strength of the metaphysical creature lies in its own weakness. Through it, the creature developed not only its entire material culture, which allowed it to overcome the challenges of its environment, but also its entire ethical and metaphysical culture, which enabled it to rise above social conflicts and existential conflicts with itself. When a creature moves across Gaia into an inhospitable environment, or when such an environment encroaches upon it, it does not perish or adapt according to Darwin's laws: it protects itself with clothing and modifies its surroundings according to the laws of intelligence and culture. With religions, it responded to existential enigmas; and with moral precepts, it organized societies that were vaster and more complex than primitive hordes.

48, AUTHORITY. As ethical discourse ascends from the basic Commandments, its complexity increases, and unanimity begins to dissolve. Obviously, debates arise over the corollaries and are often intellectual, religious, or political discourses aimed at *justifying* a particular code of conduct. We all agree that stealing and killing are wrong, but discussions arise over the exploitation of workers and the death penalty. Often, the correct course of action is not clear to the individual, so they turn to an authority or leader, not always unconsciously. The intellectual authority or religious leader will then dictate the "correct" behavior, not always at the request of the individual. While the axiom that prohibits murder is universal, it is no less universal to overlook it in the name of a particular ethic. According to a certain type of modern revolutionary, killing is wrong, but when done as a means to achieve a more just end (the death of the exploitative bourgeois), it becomes good. For this kind of rationality, there are ethical crimes and immoral crimes.

49, BALANCE. Moral consciousness repudiates the imbalance of forces. For this reason, it repudiates power concentrated in groups or individuals. Of course, the debate arises when it comes to identifying those groups or individuals. Even dictatorships and tyrants end up being justified by this same rationality, in these cases paradoxically. Except for "immoralists" like Nietzsche, moralists will always side with the weaker. Group sensitivity is no different. Discriminations, for example, are fiercely repudiated when they come from groups in power. The very frequent racist expressions of a poor Black person in Africa never have the same effect as those of an Englishman or a white American. The former are often met with a smile; the latter, with deep or superficial contempt. On the other hand, let us recall how feminism is accepted or tolerated while any expression of machismo is repudiated.

50, ANTI-RACISM. Ethics and morality are also based on prejudices. What we should hope for is that they are always healthy prejudices. "Thou shalt not kill," "Thou shalt not steal," are basic prejudices because they do not depend on any discourse to justify them. Anti-racism is the same. Once, I mentioned to some friends the research by Charles Murray and Herrnstein on *"ethnic differences in cognitive ability,"* and other statistical studies conducted in Canada that showed graphs of IQ scores clearly favoring the white race. Automatically, my friends reacted with outrage, insulting Murray, Herrnstein, American racism, and Coca-Cola. I admit that the conclusions of those Harvard professors elicited the same rejection in me. But was it a scientific rejection? What arguments did my friends and I have to refute research we knew nothing about? —Arthur Schopenhauer once wrote: "That the Blacks have fallen, by preference and in large numbers, into slavery, is evidently a consequence of their having less intelligence than the other human races, which, however, does not justify the fact." Well, no one can deny intelligence to the German philosopher; but neither can they deny his imprecision. For the fact that there are races or peoples who were more often subjugated does not mean they are more or less intelligent. In any case, it would mean they have less *enslavement intelligence.* That would be like saying that bank robbers are the brightest intellects in a society. All of which is possible, but the reasoning remains an *imprecision.* And a professional philosopher can be forgiven for being completely wrong; less so for being imprecise. In other cases, it is not precision that is lacking: for example, in the *Dictionary of Psychiatry* by Antoine Porot (third Spanish edition, 1977).

There, a disease is defined as "psychopathology of the Blacks," and it refers to the intellectual incapacities of the indigenous peoples of Africa. After listing various syndromes, which I imagined to be cultural traits (such as dreaminess), "soma-psychosomatic" conditions (like depression, alcoholism), and economic factors (such as intestinal parasites and syphilis), the specialist recommends the repatriation of sick Black individuals, not without a significant number of escorts, given their dangerousness. —Now, let us suppose that one day it is proven that there are less intelligent races (and that it is precisely defined what is meant by "intelligence," without falling back on a schoolbook or zoological explanation). In that case, the creatures must be better prepared for the truth. This means that we must expect races to treat each other as if none were above the others but rather on the same round surface of Gaia. That is, they should not treat each other as they do now, assuming a uniform racial intelligence.

51, INTELLIGENCE. During the most savage times, physical strength was decisive in the selection of parents, but after the establishment of societies and civilization, the determining factor for success became intelligence. From the Neolithic period until not long ago, having numerous offspring was an aspiration of every creature on Gaia because, among other reasons, that was the only form of Social Security. If we consider evolutionary theory, we will agree that first the strongest reproduced, and then the most intelligent. This also suggests something more: the peoples with the oldest cultures should be the most "intelligent "; that is, they would be the peoples who have invested the most time in selecting their members for intelligence rather than strength. (We know that intelligence is a heritable trait. A creature with a high IQ is generally a member of a family with an average intelligence higher than the rest.) Well, but let us not forget that human intelligence was not born at the same time as its cities and cultures. The creature's brain has been developing for hundreds of thousands of years, while civilization and the oldest cultures are no more than ten thousand years old. That is, in any case, we spent more time developing wild intelligence than cultured or civilized intelligence. Therefore, we must think that, although the antiquity of a people may be reflected in the average intelligence of its members, this difference should not be very significant between different peoples or races.

52, PENISES. There are not a few specialists who have repeated the same observation: in a man's self-esteem, the penis and his intelligence are the two most important elements. I agree, and I also suspect that in white racism, these two elements play an especially important role: since the sexual inferiority of Blacks is not suspected, the focus is instead on their intellectual deficiencies. Sometimes, when I see on the news that in one of those rich countries a white man dragged a stranger with his truck until he bled to death, just because he was Black, I cannot help but think that the impulse behind that act of rage is the same that drives a husband who discovers his wife in bed with a lover.

53, CONSCIOUSNESS. A dog discovers a bone on the other side of a metal fence. Immediately, it begins to dig under the fence, but soon it hits an impenetrable stone floor. Its goal is close, but the stone prevents it from passing there. Tired, the dog decides to go around the fence, initially moving away from its goal, until it finds an entrance and finally manages to retrieve the bone. —This is a simple definition of intelligence. Now, what matters to us is its analysis. We immediately notice the existence of a renunciation; and the process that contains it is ordered as follows: Intelligence—Renunciation—Consciousness. The dog we were observing does not yet demonstrate consciousness. But let us see that, subjected to a similar situation several days later, our dog renounces the first attempt to dig (self-denial) and begins to look for an entrance. It is at this moment that we can begin to think of some principle of consciousness. —The mere development of intelligence in the metaphysical creature would not explain the emergence of consciousness without the intermediary of renunciation. It is in self-denial that the processes of the external world begin to be realized and mature *within* the individual. And this is what I call *consciousness.*

54, RENUNCIATION. Morality means a renunciation of the individual in favor of the group. Religion, a renunciation of the world in favor of the individual. The act that links morality to religious metaphysics is *renunciation.*

55, CONSCIOUSNESS. The British scientist James Lovelock believes that living things have a particular capacity to associate. An organ of an animal body, for example, artificially nourished, can live in isolation; but together with others, they form a unity. "The energy-transforming entities that act in animal cells (mitochondria) and plant cells (mitochondria and chloroplasts) were once bacteria living independently." And then, Lovelock summarizes: *"Life is something social."* —But let us not confuse a society of organs with a society of consciousnesses, even though both signify the same process. In the animal world, there are societies of organs that are confused with societies of individuals. For example, let us think that ant colonies and beehives are not "societies" of individuals; they are *individuals,* because both function as a single organism. Why, at times, do ants transform into a criminal army, attacking, robbing, murdering, and enslaving another ant colony, without apparent reason? Do they truly act as an army of wills or as a single warrior? (Human armies, do they not possess the artificial will to act as a single individual, where it is expected that one head thinks and the rest act without thinking?) Among bees, the workers have no sexual activity, but the hive and the ant colony do: the head and the sex in both is the queen. Killing the queen is cutting off the head of the individual, and it is from the lack of individual sexes in the hive that its good organization derives. Otherwise, there would be terrible and permanent internal conflicts that would threaten them as a unit. Conflicts like those the metaphysical creature has had to overcome, even if only partially, that exuberant little animal that is in heat all year round and for almost its entire life. —A bird flying south and a beehive are two animals. Neither in an ant colony nor in a beehive do their members exercise any kind of renunciation. A gorilla protecting her own offspring or another's is moved by a positive feeling: love. In this, there is no renunciation. Different, human societies do not function as an organism; they are not a body but a *consciousness.* Each member could well not renounce many of their desires, but commonly they do so for the benefit of the group. Because morality lies in negative actions of the creature for the benefit of a group or the species; it is not an original feeling but a *consciousness.*

And consciousness, I conjecture, was born from the psychological conflict provoked by self-denial, by the creature's renunciation of certain instinctive impulses (let us think of the most transcendent of taboos: incest). To that *collective consciousness* I call ethics and morality.

56, SOCIOBIOLOGY. The theory of the savage struggle for the survival of the fittest was challenged by other theories that had formed from the observation of certain cooperation among animals. The Russian Kropotkin, perhaps, was one of the first to observe the importance of cooperation among individuals of the same species for the defense against a common enemy (*Mutual Aid*, 1906). But what kind of association are we talking about? When a group of hyenas associate for hunting, each one gives to the group what the group gives to each one, and the act of giving-and-receiving is resolved immediately. A case still unresolved is that of those animals that emit alarm sounds upon detecting a predator, saving their comrades and losing themselves. ("a chicken is an egg's way of making other eggs"). I believe that to explain this human character of the victim, it is not necessary to resort to the humanism of animals; it is enough to consider only instinct. The emergence of the instinct of cooperation among animals can still be explained by Darwin's theory: the "cooperators" survived more often than the "selfish" in a regime of immediate give-and-receive, and thus their characteristics were transmitted preferentially over those who remained alone. In this way, the animal that gives its life by alerting its companions to a nearby danger does not do so out of altruism (renunciation) but because *it cannot help it*, just as some fish cannot help but commit suicide on the shore to spawn and thus ensure the conservation of the species. In some other higher mammals, such as chimpanzees, it has been observed that they are capable of giving some of their food for the benefit of another member of the group; but this "renunciation" always signifies a short-term investment when the giver is not emotionally connected to the recipient; or it is an instinctive act of love when it involves a close family member or a female being courted. Even in special captive situations (and when food is not scarce), it has been observed that some monkeys give some of their food only to those companions who are accustomed to returning the favor in equal measure. However, while the observation is highly interesting, the enthusiasm often overlooks another more common observation: this trade is almost nonexistent in the wild, where the law of the strongest still prevails, and "selfishness" is overwhelmingly superior to socialist altruism. In humans, selfishness and altruism exist, but morality represses the former and prescribes the latter until it becomes the rule rather than the exception, as in chimpanzees. This makes us think that the maxim of Confucius and so many others, "do not do to others what you do not want others to do to you," is hundreds of times millennia old and forms part of that "Gnostic-evolutionary Path." In metaphysical creatures, morality has extended this time of give-and-take indefinitely, to the point of imposing and demanding the obligation of not expecting a reward for renunciation. "The best reward for a good deed," says a popular saying, "is the deed itself." This idea is an ethical formula, that is, a teaching that aims to confirm an attitude favorable to the group from the conscious level (maturity) to the unconscious level (childhood). It is a renunciation and not an instinct because the individual can break the law if they so choose. (Here we derive the theological value of freedom: from the unnatural choice, from the renunciation of instincts, depends salvation or chaos). And, above all, because for it to work, it must be preached. It is not an observation; it is advice. That is, culture (ethics) took from nature an exception (democratic solidarity) and contradicted it by turning it into a rule. Thus, it would be absurd to say that morality is a product of nature and not of the renunciation of that nature: even metaphysical creatures are inclined to do what the unconscious prescribes and consciousness (moral and individual) prohibits. And usually, we do not do it. —But there remains a dimension of terrible importance. The most recent ethology has shown that relationships between animals are not based exclusively on strength and deadly competition, as in capitalism, but include a repertoire of feelings very similar to those of humans: clemency, solidarity, friendship. But even so, these behaviors respond to a reason of "sympathy" and not *yet* to renunciation, as we define it in the metaphysical creature. One responds to a positive impulse and the other to a negative one. The metaphysical creature also responds out of sympathy (rescuing a child in danger, etc.), but we do not see the signs to think that another higher animal is capable of renouncing any of its impulses without some more or less immediate and external coercion (ritual sacrifice of that same child). Sociobiology studies morality from ethology with excellent observations on some species of higher animals and from there draws its conclusions about human ethics since, inevitably, it subscribes to evolutionism. But, even while traversing the path of human evolution, it forgets an important dimension for ethics and morality: the metaphysical; its relationship with sex, life, and death. And that is not studied by observing monkeys.

57, PROGRESS. The material progress of the creature does not lie solely in its intelligence. Many other animals possess some of the same and none of the material or spiritual progress. The power of the creature was possible because it could *channel* that intelligence by constructing an external history: its culture. But all that construction, driven by instincts of power, love, and destruction, would never have been possible without a collective consciousness, without a society of consciousnesses, without some kind of morality; that is, without the *renunciation* of the low for the benefit of the high. Because the metaphysical creature is the only animal that renounces; and humanity the only consciousness of Gaia.

58, PUNISHMENTS. Social control, which was initially exercised by the leader of the horde, king, or pharaoh, eventually accepted an intangible and less precarious nature, personified in the gods or in God. Initially, all gods rewarded or punished human actions right here on Gaia. But, faced with the apparent failures of divine justice, the gods themselves ended up postponing their judgments for the *hereafter.* In this way, the judgments became unappealable. And, therefore, more effective. Thus, the preservation of life (morality) and the denial of death (religion) were unified into a single body; God and the Consciousness of the species became One.

59, INDEPENDENT. If the well-being and happiness of the people depended on the conduct of each individual (morality), then their fate in the afterlife must also depend on it. From ancient Egypt to Sumeria, life in the Underworld depended on life on Gaia. But morality and religion come together because they were joined. Not because they are one and the same. To realize this, it is enough to observe that metaphysical creatures often possess the first component and lack the second. And the inverse is also true. *There are not a few "immoralist" doctrines that occasionally arise on Gaia, and yet they do not cease to be religious. Carpocrates, for example, in the 2nd century, taught a wisdom or superstition very similar to Buddhism. The difference lay in the means and not in the ends. According to this Christian sect, the soul could attain knowledge and liberation not through asceticism but through the commission of all immoral acts that a creature could commit. For Carpocrates, as for the more distant Heraclitus, good and evil were mere matters of opinion. —On the other hand, let us remember that for Buddhism, it is preferable to perform a good action rather than a bad one, because in the worst case, a kind creature is rewarded with a better rebirth. But even better than a good or bad action is none at all. And in this choice lies the greatest Buddhist achievement: the definitive abandonment of kamma* and the nightmarish series of rebirths—liberation. Well, all religions have moral implications, but the Meaning of each one neither originates nor is exhausted in these provisional measures. Morality and religion are intertwined in the thought of Peter Abelard, yet without losing their hierarchical order. When the medieval monk reflects on sin, he does not condemn desire (internal) but rather the consent to act on it (external effect on others). But first, he emphasizes the value of pleasing God as the greatest virtue. Because at that point in the Middle Ages, the First Tablet was still placed above the Second.

60, RATIONALITY. Ethics is to the last Commandments as theology is to the first. Both ethics and theology are reflections that seek to confirm, with a certain rationality, a priori unquestionable precepts.

61, PARTNERS. Before Plato, the most sensible considered it a virtue to harm the enemy. It cannot be said that this idea has been eradicated on Gaia, but since then it has been famously refuted. Confucius and later Jesus moved from an ethics of isolated tribes to one of *coexisting tribes*. The Confucian maxim of not abusing others expanded from the village to become universal. Or at least that was the intention. The enigma of life and death leads to the acceptance of God; the impulse to live and coexist leads to the acceptance of the other. The meaningless sacrifice of the other not only affects the stability of the group; it also represents our own destiny: death. A double reason, then, ethical and metaphysical, to stand in solidarity with them. Because the other is our partner, in life and in death.

62, BARBARISM. In the face of the threat of disorder, religious prescriptions have differed: punishment for the guilty (the Law of Retribution, Luther's doctrine) or passivity in the face of injustice (the Buddha's detachment, Christ's other cheek). Both attitudes or recommendations seek to prevent the return of barbarism, the reign of the senses; the Darwinian order or the chaos of the fearsome creatures.

63, BALANCE. There are two basic goals in every society: security and freedom. Morality limits, controls, and enhances freedom, because in its origins freedom opposes security. It is in unconditional freedom that sexual and power instincts are culturally expressed. If the creature were to renounce *everything* it would die, like a good Jainist; and if it did not renounce a part, it would also die. That is, the health of a society depends on the balance between renunciation and freedom.

64, TRANSLATIONS. In the early biblical and Quranic times, the fundamental relationship that bound the creatures of Gaia to God was fear. A faithful creature, first and foremost, was a creature who feared the Father. And that was its greatest possible virtue. It was Christ who placed the emphasis on *love.* And here we must distinguish between love for God and love for one's neighbor. Both loves are positive translations of the First and Second Tablets. In the New Testament, it is written that once, when Jesus was asked which commandment was the most important, He replied (Matthew 22:37): "Love the Lord your God with all your heart and with all your soul and with all your mind. This is the first and greatest commandment. And the second is like it: Love your neighbor as yourself. All the Law and the Prophets hang on these two commandments." The ancient Fear of God is translated into Love, and the prescriptions against mistreating one's neighbor are summarized in the obligation to love them. If I am not mistaken, it was Saint Augustine who wrote: "All other precepts are summed up in this one rule: love your neighbor as yourself," an ethical piece of advice that indirectly acknowledges that selfishness is more universal and more powerful than altruism.. —Untranslatable is the act of the *bodhisattva* who, having attained nirvana, is capable of renouncing it to share it with others. But it doubly represents the consciousness of the species. But it doubly represents the consciousness of the species.

VIII: THE TRANSLATION OF EMOTIONS

65, EVOLUTION. If we are optimistic, perhaps we can indeed say how or from where a particular characteristic of the metaphysical creature arose. But that characteristic will, in any case, be the result of countless and unsuspected progressions that end up making it unrecognizable from its supposed origin. As unrecognizable as civilization is from the taboo of incest. —To accept the idea that metaphysical creatures are the result of evolution, it is not necessary to deny the existence of something called spirit or to succumb to materialist doctrine. It is true that in an Australopithecus there was no conception of God or any idea of justice. But neither was there infinitesimal calculus or Chaos theory. Noticing that the butterfly emerges from the caterpillar does not invalidate its beauty or its ability to fly. Because one thing is to seek the origin of things, and another is to reduce them to their origin.

66, REDUCTIONISM. We can consider the emergence of some human feelings from others that precede them. I conjecture that Malinowski had a similar idea when he pointed out that "the moral value of harmony and goodwill is shown on a higher plane than the merely negative taboos that constrain the main human instincts." Erich Fromm also derived the feeling of justice from the infantile feeling of helplessness. Now, are these "reductionisms" valid? Only a materialist worldview can be reduced to reductionism as a principal method. However, reducing one phenomenon to another can be fruitful in several respects. With great clarity, Claude Lévi-Strauss observed, in *The Savage Mind,* that a reduction can only be legitimate when it does not impoverish the phenomena subjected to reduction. "We cannot classify the levels of reduction as superior and inferior. On the contrary, we must expect that the level considered superior will retroactively communicate something of its richness to the lower level to which we have reduced it. [...] Scientific explanation does not consist in the passage from complexity to simplicity, but in the substitution of a less intelligible complexity for a more intelligible one. "

67, INCEST. No anthropologist explains the rejection of incest as irreducible. Psychoanalysis also tends to start from a prohibition implying a prior desire. And that is fine. However, the emotional experience itself of the individual excludes everything prior. The horror of incest may well have a social origin in the infancy of the human species (the first *no* of man to nature and the origin of all institutions, according to Octavio Paz; the most universal institution, according to Lévi-Strauss and almost all ethnologists). But, for the individual, the emotional value refers to themselves, and everything prior is of no importance. "I have seen and perceived," wrote Malinowski, "how savages abstained from an illicit action with the same horror and disgust with which the fervent Christian recoils from what he considers sin. Well, this mental attitude is partly due to the influence of society insofar as the particular prohibition is stigmatized by tradition as repugnant and horrible. However, it functions in the individual and through the forces of the individual's mind. From this, it follows that it is neither exclusively social nor exclusively individual, but a mixture of both." Sartre, the lucid Sartre, observed that psychoanalysis had been the first to warn that every state of consciousness is worth something other than itself, and that for consciousness, a forbidden desire is never implied in its symbolic realization. And, being an existentialist, he used an existentialist example: Human presences are not contained in the ashes of a bonfire; they are linked to them by a causal relationship, but those remnants are what they are—ashes, that is all.

68, FEELINGS. Psychoanalysts say that the opposite of love is not hate but indifference. But I suppose they derived such a valuation from those inspiring muses that are their patients. Because it is the ontology of the insane. —For me, there are at least four basic feelings. Love and Hate, Security and Fear. Two pairs of opposites that can be considered as the starting and ending points of communal norms (morality) and religions (metaphysics). Morality may prescribe love for one's neighbor or the obligation not to hate them, but it is not the origin of either. Both were already included in the creatures of Gaia. Let us remember, for example, that the handshake once meant non-aggression. The man who offers his hand, like the one who raises it open, intended to show that he was unarmed. Now, the same gestures signify friendship. And the same happened with so-called "good manners," such as removing one's hat or bowing before a person who centuries earlier was a king, tyrant, or Lord.

69, FACULTIES. Our contemporaries, when they do not belong to some mystical or Hindu sect, tend to place the inventions and discoveries that characterize them in times more recent than the exact ones. Many are still surprised that the ancient Babylonians could solve quadratic equations and other mathematical problems attributed to the Greeks or the Renaissance. However, if we consider a larger time scale, for example one that measures in millennia, we will agree that there are quite a few differences between Cro-Magnon men and Gandhi. The biologist Julian Huxley wrote that "it is perfectly possible that the so-called supra-normal faculties of modern man are in the same case as his mathematical faculties were during the Ice Age [...] Even operations as simple as multiplying two three-digit numbers would have seemed completely magical to those Stone Age men." Well, he wrote these words shortly before the Second World War.

70, EMOTIONS. Just as we consider abstract thought to follow concrete thought, we can also consider some feelings to follow others. Charity, for example, may have a historical root (offering and petitioning the gods or the trade of goodwill among creatures). But its current meaning may well refer to a character that has *evolved*. Enough so to deserve its own name. It cannot be said that feelings of justice, envy, or solidarity are common to all animals. Ethics and aesthetics are two human faculties, the product of perhaps millennial learning. Why should we assume that body and intelligence are the result of evolution, but not their emotions? A hundred thousand years ago, sapiens and pre-sapiens occupied Africa, Asia, and Europe, and it is estimated that they numbered no more than one and a half million. Thirty thousand years ago, they were six million and occupied almost the entire world, a thousandth of what the creatures number today. If today there are six billion and they still survive, it is thanks to a new behavior that regulates a far more complex coexistence. And if so many barbarities still occur that offend them as metaphysical creatures, it is not because of these new feelings but in spite of them. Therefore, the urgency of a more humane and rigorous ethics is justified because now the creatures are more numerous and possess greater destructive power. Those Cro-Magnon creatures who exterminated the Neanderthals are their ancestors. That is to say, for both religions and anthropology, metaphysical creatures are the daughters of homicidal sin. If any or a few of those prehistoric genocidal beings had taken power in any of the world powers of the 20th century, they surely would have acted like Adolf Hitler.

71, INVOLUTION. Let us remember that Hitler was not a primitive Cro-Magnon man, but his Darwinian ethics possessed much of the attributes that despise tolerance and compassion for the other. Between Hitler and Genghis Khan, the difference is negligible or merely formal. In the German case or in the Argentine case, the result is more complex and apocalyptic. Because a couple of aggressive cavemen are not enough; a culture of aggression and extermination is also necessary—along with the corresponding technical and logistical support.

IX: The Near Beyond

72, FORESIGHT. In the beginning, the creatures of Gaia took from nature what was closest at hand. When the population grew and the grasslands began the process that turned them into the deserts of Africa and the Middle East, they became sedentary; then, little by little, they began to think about the future. They cultivated and stored food; they built dams, canals, and patient walls. Later, through more developed intelligence or their culture, the creature lifted its gaze a little further. And then it built temples, organized and imposed more complex duties, more subtle and rigorous prohibitions. The metaphysical creature had to perform a double renunciation of the world. Then they invented or discovered the existence of gods with their two meanings, one sociological and the other metaphysical: the gods represented the Law and channeled the questions without answers.

73, SACRIFICE. The ritual of sacrifice lies at the origin of agricultural societies and all religions. Both Yahweh and the humanized gods of Olympus demanded this tribute in the form of slaughtered oxen and rams; in Greece, it gave rise to the *tragoidía,* which refers to the sacrifice of a goat (the future "*bouc émissaire*" or scapegoat) in honor of Dionysus. The Maya and the Aztecs went a bit further by offering the lives of men and women; and some of the genital blood of their own kings. In ancient Sumer and in not-so-ancient Zimbabwe, it was common practice to periodically sacrifice the most valuable member of society: the king was returned to the celestial planets. Even in the Vedic origin of Hinduism, the source of the most famous doctrines of non-violence, there existed ritual sacrifice. None of this is strange on Gaia. The sacrifice of a valuable animal not only channeled the violence of the creatures in a controlled manner; above all, it held a metaphysical meaning. —It was common among myths, the idea that the creation of the world and life had been the product of a divine sacrifice; pain and the end of immortality, the consequence of an original sin. Existence was nothing but a descent into imperfection, a state far below the aspirations of the creature. There are exceptions, of course: the archaic Greeks and some Sumerians imagined a gray and swampy afterlife; something in any case worse than this life. But the general rule is different, at least for the historical creature. The Arabs and the Alexandrians believed that eternal life could only be achieved through pain; and in the 16th century, the famous Saint Teresa agreed:

On the cross lies glory
And honor,
And in suffering pain

Life and comfort,
And the surest path
To heaven.

Neither East nor West could stop blaming this existence for having displaced a happier one. Because, it was evident, Peace and Paradise had slipped away like a dream.

74, TRIBUTE. The sacrifice of the best bull in the herd never meant gratuitous self-punishment. Lévi-Strauss already demonstrated that the system of sacrifice was independent of the system of clan affinities, which accompanies these reflections. In totemism, no other species or phenomenon can replace the eponymous one: one beast is never taken for another. But in the case of sacrifice, *the opposite occurs.* Clearly, the French anthropologist observed: "The fundamental principle is substitution. One thing can replace another *as long as the intention persists*, which is the only thing that matters." Sacrifice is an irreversible process of giving the goodwill of the mortal creature and receiving divine grace. Through the magical or religious rite, the god is shown the path it must take when administering the fate of the creatures, which must take the form of supplication and submission. "Sacrifice would be the connection between two separate domains ", and the scheme would be as follows: Creature —Victim —Sacrifice {lack and response} Divinity. Also in this way, recognizing the persistence of magical thinking in the religious rite, we understand why the renunciation was not carried out with a simple abandonment of the good (as in the cases of the Hebrew scapegoat and the Greek *pharmakòs*): the only door to the beyond is pain and death. And if, in addition, that beyond is identified with the heights, there is no better messenger than the holocaust, to send the soul with the smoke. Now, the custom of sacrificing an animal has changed over time. What was once the absolute detachment of a lamb offered to God has become more relative to the believer's inner state. In the 7th century, the Muslims warned: "God does not pay attention to its flesh and blood, but to your fear of Him." And to avoid the waste of these animal sacrifices, it was prescribed that the victims be distributed among the most needy. Once again, we see that religion is not pure metaphysics, but a dialectical relationship between the first five Commandments and the last.

75, ALMS. The prescription of almsgiving (one of the five pillars of Islam and a virtue according to all religions) has a religious meaning before a social one: through alms, creatures detach themselves from a part to preserve the rest and, if possible, win the favor of the Almighty without Him or the donor even realizing it.

76, INSURANCE. Like their creatures, the Greek gods formed an almost democratic society. In ancient Greece, each city preferentially worshipped a goddess or a god. A creature could also show their individual preference for one of these Olympian beings, and generally, the choice depended on their occupation. The relationship between the Greeks and their gods was very close, almost material. In Homer's time, the sick would go to sanctuaries to be healed; they could even consult their gods through the oracle. In the rituals of sacrifice, each Greek offered their gods a portion of what they wished to keep—the future was always uncertain. In this way, the Greek earned the gratitude of the god who was to provide them with *the very same thing* in times of scarcity. A kind of metaphysical insurance policy, so to speak. This same material relationship between creatures and their gods is found in Sumeria. There, the temple was the place where surplus production was stored, awaiting worse times.

76, PROMISES. The institution of renunciation is vast and has ancient versions, such as the sacrifice of an animal or a woman; and more fashionable forms, like almsgiving or self-immolation. But it also has modest and even ridiculous variations: if the saint invoked from the dust of the basement grants the championship, the sudden believer will walk a hundred meters on their knees, throw themselves into a pond, or go out in drag if they are not a drag queen. Even the sacrifice can be performed without the supposed divine creditor. As in public events or official inaugurations where ribbons are cut and champagne is wasted, the ritual is emptied of transcendent meaning, and only the form inherited by creatures through custom matters.

77, CONSCIOUSNESS. Perhaps the passage of time would not worry metaphysical creatures so much if they had never awakened to consciousness. —Even in the Paleolithic, the presence of weapons and tools in graves is evident. An unmistakable symbol that the spirit of the dead continued to live and that their new life was not very different from the previous one. With no further questions about the beyond, this society of common spirits formed the sufficient metaphysical framework for the primitive mind. Now, if we repeat this image for the beyond of birth, we are just one step away from the doctrine of reincarnations, which is the only one that has somewhat addressed the rest of the animals and the prenatal metaphysics. But generally, religions emphasize what lies beyond death rather than beyond birth, which shows the importance that the *fear of becoming* has had over any other.

X: Magic and Religion

78, EVOLUTION. Modern thought saw the world as the evolution of different stages. Freud ordered them as follows: animistic, religious, and scientific. Earlier, in Darwin's century, Auguste Comte thought that the intellectual evolution of the metaphysical creature stemmed from its primitive theological ascendancy. "Man assimilated the physical world to his own actions —he wrote—, which are the only ones he is capable of understanding. Thus, he populated nature with wills compatible with his own." Similar but fruitful was the path followed by Max Weber.

79, HUMANIZATION. Since prehistory, creatures have seen nature with their own attributes. Even the amusement we feel at a chimpanzee, its gestures and movements, is explained by our tendency as creatures to humanize everything. What entertains us about a chimpanzee is not its monkey-like qualities but its human-like ones. After all, for over a million years, creatures have been scrutinizing human faces with patience and obsession. And even if collective or mnemonic memory were merely an illusion, we would still have our own individual experience, which is never insignificant: the figures that occupy us the most are shaped like human beings. That a family might adopt the fox as a totem did not mean—I imagine—that they took on the attributes of a fox, but rather that they identified certain group characteristics in that animal, which were then represented and confirmed by their descendants. (Something similar happened with certain surnames. Fumagalli, for example, means "chicken thief," which might have been true for a man who lived in Italy five hundred years ago, but it is certainly not true for those who work for the IMF.) By identifying with an animal due to some slight similarity, they distinguished themselves from their true peers. (Later, inter-totemic wars allowed for the universalization of a few victorious symbols, as in the case of the ancient Egyptians, which enabled the unification of a larger people and their differentiation from others.) For although creatures are as gregarious as any other animal, their personal and group relationships are ordered according to differences.

80, INGREDIENTS. Once, the cosmos was a community of spirits. Both the physical world (thunder, rivers) and the metaphysical world (gods, spirits) possessed human attributes. Distorted or not, exalted or diminished. Not only did the later gods of Olympus possess our psychology; so did a more abstract and ineffable god like Yahweh. So, what is the difference between the superstition of witchcraft and the belief of a Christian? Once, in a village in Africa, I was asked the same question, not without irony. The answer is: *many.* Because magic or witchcraft signify a *physical* relationship of the creature with nature, with the same pretensions as science and technology. Let us remember that the Renaissance was characterized by a renewed interest of the creature in nature, and that this interest translated into the proliferation of proto-scientists and erudite magicians. For both, the exploration and experimentation of the world mattered; not the circus or transcendence. —A religion, on the other hand, implies a *metaphysical* relationship of the creature (renunciant) with its own destiny. As Lévi-Strauss once put it: "Religion consists in the humanization of natural laws, magic is a naturalization of human actions. (Human actions as if they were part of physical determinism)." Religion would, then, be the result of the anthropomorphism of nature, while magic would be the inverse—the physiomorphism of man. Both types of thought often appear simultaneously, in different proportions. —We should also remember that no historical moment has been devoid of magic, science, or religion. On a superficial level we can observe the persistence of a kind of formal totemism in the mascots of clubs or sports tournaments, in the brands of standardized products (logos, cars, sportswear). All of them include some feline, some bird of prey. At another level, we see how cultures of witches and sorcerers practice a kind of science, and the most technologically advanced societies are animistic. The latter is exemplified by the fear of psychosomatic illnesses (many people believe that by thinking about an illness, they end up acquiring it; for now, what is certain is that the mere thought is a form of suffering it). Or also, if we revisit Freud's tripartite classification of history, we can see that the *healer* has gone through various stages: the witch (animist), the priest (religious), and the psychoanalyst (scientific). And anyone can see that these three types possess different quantities of the same thing. Nor does blind faith in psychoanalysis cease to be a kind of superstition on the same level as witchcraft: the patient surrenders to recounting their entire childhood in the belief that dialogue or mere confession will bring about a magical cure. Because that is what authority demands. If the patient has no faith in the analyst, the miracle will not occur, and the disbelief will be scientifically defined as a case of "resistance." An attitude erroneously attributed to Jesus, since, if one pays attention to the Gospels, the Messiah reproached his fellow healers for lacking faith, not their patients.

81, TRANSCENDENCE. In predynastic Egypt, the dead were buried alongside some of their belongings. It was even customary to sacrifice the master's dog to serve as a companion in the afterlife. Due to a magical condition of things, animals of greater value, such as cattle, women, and other family members, could be replaced by clay representations. In Xi'an, China, the emperor was accompanied by the most famous terracotta army. Only shortly afterward was the sacrifice of people preferred for the same purpose. Gordon Childe proposed that the idea of an afterlife in the Nile basin must have been induced by the good preservation of corpses in the desert sands. For my part, I believe that this peculiarity of desert corpses only led to another peculiarity of Egyptian civilization: the obsessive practice of mummification. —It cannot be a coincidence that the first great civilization of Gaia was born under the obsession with death. What differentiated those Egyptians from other peoples was not the idea of an afterlife, but the obsession with which that idea was experienced. What explains this coincidence? Was it the obsession with death that produced this great civilization, or was it the greater spiritual development of those new creatures that made them capable of lifting their gaze a little further? —The idea of the survival of the soul was not exclusive to the Egyptians. To realize this, one need only glance at the tombs of other peoples. Because the persistence of the memory of the dead is enough to prevent the idea of a definitive disappearance. Memories are our own existences without their bodies.

In contrast, the *void* is a much more recent metaphysics, or anti-metaphysics, the product of a dialectical brain, more developed but just as impotent as ever. The custom of providing the spirit with weapons, figurines, and other symbols is characteristic of magical thinking. But this is only an instrument that first served the physical world and later the metaphysical—the *other* reality. In the same way that art and magic first served hunting and healing, they later served to act upon the new world.

82, DIFFERENCES. Religion is to magic as alchemy is to modern chemistry. Only a very superficial glance could confuse one with the other. Even today in Africa, magic is a respectable instrument for acting upon physical nature, hunting, and enemies. In contrast, religion arises from the experience of death, from the awareness of existential questions; from the Enigma. Every religion seeks to be an Answer to the inexplicable. In Africa and America, magical rites for the dying are performed to save them from death. In contrast, Christian sacraments are offered to the dying to provide them with a better fate in the afterlife. In the first case, the sick person expects nothing but for magic to restore their health; in the second, when the sick person hears the chants and prayers, they can already abandon any hope of remaining on Gaia. Therefore, primitive magic cannot be considered more religion than medicine. It is more a physical science than a metaphysics.

83, INFALLIBILITY. Either magic is a pseudoscience or science is a pseudo-friend. Both act upon the physical world, upon the forces of nature, but they are epistemologically irreconcilable. For example: a single negative case is enough to dismantle a prestigious scientific theory; and a single positive case is enough to confirm the reputation of a sorcerer. The same principle applies to astrology. To attempt to prove the scientific validity of astrology through "verified" predictions is like proving the validity of a mathematical theorem through one or two correct results. No one would think of demonstrating that $a^2 = b^2 + c^2$ by measuring three or four right triangles. Well, it is true that Kepler's laws were confirmed by observable predictions. But this gentleman's laws were considered valid because they could be confirmed *for any possible case.* Not for nine or ten cases arbitrarily chosen by astronomers. Pierce said that sciences reason in three different ways: inductively, abductively, and deductively. None of these forms is present in divinatory science. Granted, astrology is also based on a scientific observation: the stars influence life on Gaia. I partly agree. Indeed, I believe the Moon influences the birth of a chicken, as my grandmother used to say. *But not its destiny*, because that is already the business of the creatures who dedicate themselves to poultry farming. And I suppose that for Mars or Saturn, a chicken and a man are the same thing. —I remember that once a fortune-teller predicted I would live many years, and another that my life would be very short. A gypsy assured me I would have two children, another said one, and the last told me I would have none. I am sure that not all of them were good, and that the best among them could divine my future, which will soon be demonstrated to the pride of divinatory science.

XI: Men and Women

84, FERTILITY. Even in the Paleolithic, the creature was a timid and physically weak animal. Some ancient bones found in caves show that it took what the beasts left behind. That is to say, they were not yet the main predators of Gaia. Fearful, in their free time they dedicated themselves to an art mixed with magic and religion. Luck in hunting concerned them, and since they could not accumulate prey, they sought to accumulate luck. Drawing a wounded bison accomplished the symbolic death of the beast, which had to precede the real death. —Another recurring theme of the time were those small sculptures known as *Paleolithic Venuses*, representations of women with exuberant breasts, prominent bellies, and buttocks. Well, one might think that women of the time looked like that. But let us note that these images are all female and lack faces or feet, two characteristics unthinkable for the ancient inhabitants of Gaia. The theme being exalted is clear: sex and fertility. Men and some women expressed in some way their greatest desires and their admiration for physical life. Long ago and far away, women were venerated and respected. For those primitive minds, lust was not yet a sin. Later, perhaps in the Neolithic, a more refined female figure predominated. Seven thousand years ago, in Mesopotamia and Greece, worship was given to a kind of great Mother Goddess. In Crete, she was the goddess of reproduction, life, and death. A characteristic symbol of antiquity was the *serpent*, a recurring feminine symbol linked to the cult of Mother Earth. Because all worship of the feminine is tied to ancient agricultural activity. And agricultural societies venerated everything in the universe that was fertile and vital.

85, ABSTRACTION. From the fields, they moved to horses and then to cities where movement, conquest, commerce, the first forms of accounting, and writing developed. They advanced toward abstraction, the quintessentially masculine element, according to Ernesto Sábato. In the Neolithic, and afterward, female deities were replaced by male ones, which culminated in monotheism and other more abstract answers. Matriarchy is followed by patriarchy, now also ideological. The masculine element will be overwhelming, and women will become the lifelong representatives of sin, the culprits of all the evils of this world (the condemnation of the body and the obstacle to enlightenment). —The fact that almost all myths have men as positive protagonists and women as negative agents reveals their masculine origin. If we consider myths as the first form of non-practical thought, we would have to attribute the greatest mental activity to men. Why was the female, closer to children, not the one tasked with creating these myths or, at least, modifying them in her favor? Possibly because there was an ideological factor, imposed by the force of the male. Myths could be modified and censored whenever they came from the female imagination. Or, more likely, the female imagination itself worked in favor of male authority. —The story of Creation is either true or male-centric. A simple economic analysis reveals this: if God had created woman first, a second intervention would not have been necessary to explain the existence of the other sex. Nor is it a coincidence that in the Apocalypse, Saint John identifies Babylon as the Great Prostitute, an immoral woman dressed in red and purple. The biblical condemnation of Babylon is the condemnation of the revolutionary male spirit, abstract and moralizing, to the ancient feminine reign, sensual, fertile, and vital. —From the horizontal repose of Mother Earth, we move to the restless verticality of the erect obelisk. The sacred rivers of Mesopotamia were born from the womb of the great goddess (in some Semitic languages, "mouth" meant "vagina of the great goddess"). The horizontal is feminine and the vertical masculine; Mother Earth, Father Sun. Mountains became the sacred places par excellence, but not for what they had of earth but for what they aspired to of heaven. The sacred mountains of Taoism in China, Mount Sinai,

Zion, Jerusalem, and Mecca are all high places. The *ziggurat* of Mesopotamia, the *stupa* of Hinduism, the *teocallis* of the Aztecs are artificial and more perfect mountains; while the minarets of mosques and Gothic cathedrals point to the sky. —In ancient Egypt, the *key of life* was the configuration of an oval over a cross; the first element represents Isis, goddess of life and reproduction, and the second Osiris, god of the dead and the eternal beyond. The vagina and the phallus represent coitus, but the isolated cross is only the masculine, the unsettling awareness of the beyond. It will not be Osiris, the god of the dead, who is forgotten by tradition, but Isis—the goddess of life. Because woman represents evil, the element of *life* that binds souls to the precarious earth.

86, WITCHES. There are not a few cosmogonic myths that blame woman for all the pain in Gaia. When a myth begins by blaming her, one can already guess that it will end by proposing a transcendental vision of death. A logotypical example is that of the swastika. Almost everyone knows that this cross belonged to the most ancient Eastern traditions. Now it does not only serve to adorn all the temples of Asia; it also scandalizes the proper tourist of the West. Because there are two versions whose most terrible difference lies in a detail too subtle for the eye: the clockwise rotation symbolizes masculine energy and the counterclockwise rotation symbolizes feminine energy. One of these turns was traditionally used as a symbol of black magic and negative energy. As is obvious, that turn is the one that represents feminine nature. —Being a jungle continent, vital and mysterious, woman was always associated with the forces of the night. They were the sirens who deceived sailors to sink ships among the rocks; the terrible Medusa, the Furies, or the Harpies. When Dionysus arrived in Greece from the populous skies of Asia, he was already famous for his irresponsibility, and before he dedicated himself to drinking in Rome, he used to abduct Greek women to dance in his honor. Even an adolescent and uninhibited people like the Greeks showed in their mythology the characteristic fear that woman, or the sex of woman, produced, which for mythology and for Freud is the same. For psychoanalysis, this is due to the child's fear of the phallic mother. But that is only for psychoanalysis. Let us remember that for both the mythological Greeks and a people as different as the Islamic Arabs, the female orgasm and, therefore, the desire of woman is more intense than that of man (see the myth of Tiresias and the story of Kamaru-s-Semán). Which does not mean it is true, but the idea derives from the same sexual act: woman expresses herself with less control. —Man, surely the main producer of myths, expressed in his culture his fear and admiration for woman. She represented desire, the competition to the death, fertility, and the obligation of his own role as a male. In this sense, I believe that the repression of woman and the condemnation of homosexuality have the same meaning: both are expressions of masculine fear of the orgasm of his protégée, of not being able to fulfill his role as the dominant and reproductive member. It cannot be a coincidence that all original religions have repressed the feminine and sodomy. Nor can it be a coincidence that for the most intolerant political groups (which resurface in times of fear and insecurity) being black, Jewish, and homosexual is the same thing, in addition to being repugnant. —For the men of Gaia, woman is the representation of the irrational, the most desired and the most feared, that which has no control, that which cannot be fully understood or dominated. In the skies of Europe, witches became famous, not warlocks. In the midst of the Renaissance, a historical period identified with reason and humanism, hundreds of thousands of these fearsome creatures were burned. Even witchcraft was considered a feminine profession par excellence, like that of a secretary or a telephone operator. As was customary, the confession of crimes such as causing bad weather was extracted through torture. The ecclesiastical methods of martyrdom were so infallible that for the interrogated, death was not only tolerable but also a blessing from heaven. Of course, this kind of theological cleansing that spread from the 15th to the 17th century was not the *copyright* of the Catholic inquisitors; the Protestants, from Germany to Scotland, including the Puritans of the Thames, were also staunch defenders of this display of macho fear.

87, REPRODUCTION. Agricultural societies celebrated fertility and the reproduction of life. Therefore, eroticism and sensuality were good. In contrast, later religions avoid it when they do not condemn it. Sex is lust, something like a necessary evil. And it is woman who is the ruling goddess of that world. Even when a religious creature speaks of life and love, both obligations of the second Table, they will never hesitate to consider them secondary matters compared to the true objective: the transcendent beyond. First, the *here and now* is relegated, then it is condemned for representing a distraction and an obstacle to the *beyond.* Joseph Campbell wrote that "Life, the acts of life, the organs of life, woman in particular as the great symbol of life, become intolerable to the extreme purity of the soul." From the deepest antiquity, religious leaders resisted the other half of humanity. Not only because all the great religions were founded or led by men, but because the transition to the religious state implies an abstraction and a renunciation of the world. Both conditions are difficult for a being like woman, who clings to life. Even Solomon, the wisest of kings according to Ecclesiasticus 47-19, had a moment of *stupidity* when he gave himself over to women and gave them "dominion over his body." It was then that the kingdom was divided in two and the Hebrew decline began. Further east, Buddha and Jina Mahavira long refused to accept Buddhist or Jainist women. Because Buddha aspired to attain Enlightenment, an achievement that implies concentration on an abstract goal—the ineffable *silence.* The preliminary step of the entire series that leads to nirvana is the annihilation of desires and the renunciation of the sensible world. Love spoils the sight, and for a Buddhist, it also spoils the rest. The spirit that falls in love will relapse (we know this) into what Hindus and Gnostics call the prison: the body. Eventually, Buddha accepted women among his disciples, but it was due to pressure and indifference, not out of approval. After all, he was a Buddhist. But even so, a tradition held that every woman had to be reincarnated as a man before attaining enlightenment. That is, she first had to ascend from her lamentable state. —The Old and New Testaments are also predominantly masculine. Or at least patriarchal. The Jews who wrote the Gospels gave women far less importance than they later gained in Europe. According to Richard Tarnas, the cult of the Virgin Mary stems from the pagan sensibility of the ancient Roman Empire, as in the Scriptures she was only a passive and secondary figure. We know that Christianity is not founded exclusively on the Gospels; it is also the result of a cultural mixture that considers Jewish, Hellenic, and Roman influences. The prominence of the Virgin Mary marks the great difference with the other two monotheisms. As Erich Fromm said, "Catholicism signified the disguised return to the religion of the Great Mother who had been defeated by Yahweh." But none of that prevented the religious spirit (or its pathology) from turning against women. Let us remember that Dorneus, in 1602, managed to demonstrate *theologically* that the *binary* represents evil (the loss of unity) and woman. Thus, he found it evident the symbolic and carnal relationship of woman with the Devil. —In these times, Catholics led by the Pope also resist the ordination of women priests, arguing that Jesus did not have disciples belonging to that sex. Well, Jesus didn't have many things... But if we are to use that kind of theological rationalization, we could start by asking: if Mary had a husband, why don't nuns marry? Without even considering other facts and sayings of the Master that are usually overlooked. (We know that in Gaia, orthodoxy is the most coherent doctrine within each religion. And the least practical as well.) —The rejection of women priests responds to a tradition, but its root lies in the threatening nature of the feminine. And while the Anglicans were able to ordain women instead of men, it is not due to a religious impulse but to the predominant ethics of the West: permissive, like the ancient Greek. Through the same Hellenizing digression of the Church, Luther and his Protestants founded a freer and more intolerant religion.

88, RENUNCIATION. The famous Danish theologian and philosopher Søren Kierkegaard was in love with a beautiful and vibrant young woman named Regina. After an initial engagement and other hesitations, the Dane decided to leave her against his own wishes, because Regina was too interested in *this* life. Regina "had not surpassed the aesthetic stage in her spiritual ascent." And she was incapable of following him. By renouncing Regina, he renounces this precarious world and does not allow himself to be deceived by happiness. In contrast to the renunciant, the aesthetic spirit chooses to challenge existence, opting for the experience of *being.* And for this reason, I also call it the *spring spirit.* It should not surprise us, then, that in all the arts, love and women are the most recurring themes. It could be said that in Gaia, many women have been important figures in the most popular religions; but compared to men, they have rather had secondary or supporting roles. On the contrary, in the arts, they have occupied a central place since the Paleolithic era.

XII: The Emergence of the Enigma

89, SUSPICION. Secretly, but relentlessly, the existential dynamic is characterized by posing questions. The secret questions about the enigma of existence constitute the entire foundation upon which any metaphysics in Gaia is built. But creatures cannot live on such a nature, just as they do not build buildings on water without first finding points of support. The creature would not be what it is if it had not recognized the Enigma of its existence. Nor would it be what it is if it had resigned itself to its own impotence in facing it. The creature needs to think and believe in a truth, in an answer. Or it needs to think, to feel that it can reach it. The Answer is unattainable (we already know this), but the creature lives and acts as if it already possessed it. The philosophical position of the materialist atheist, the aspiration of the religious, the action of the politician, the revolutionary, the public servant, the conviction of the scientist are the institutional forms that the answers to the Enigma take. From politics, no unquestionable truth ever emerges, only convenient truths, that is, contradictory positions. The same goes for religions and the rest of the "contestatory" institutions. Not even science can boast of being the instrument of any absolute truth. —The creature glimpses Something eternal to which it always aspires. But it never comes to know *what* it is; it only lives as if it knew.

90, CONSCIOUSNESS. Even more mysterious than the now-famous unconscious is consciousness. The unconscious can still be considered as a separate entity from our own. The unconscious can commit all kinds of crimes while the Self washes its hands; it can be formulated with psychological laws that seemingly do not directly involve us. But consciousness, *that* which we are without intermediaries, *that* which perceives the world and perceives itself like eyes in a mirror, *that* which formulates answers and enigmas cannot be explained without its own intervention. In fact, *it cannot be explained.*

90, PATHS. The Tradition of Greek thought eliminated the possibilities of new prophets. If almost a thousand years after Aristotle Muhammad could emerge as the last great prophet, it was due to the little influence the Greeks had on the intelligence of the nomads of Arabia. And if nowadays some minor prophet occasionally arises, it is simply due to a lack of intelligence. Because among celebrities, the role of prophet was taken over by reformers, and their main instrument was no longer revelation but commentary and speculation. Theology is a hybrid species, the product of the crossbreeding of Semitic faith and Greek rationality: Saint Augustine, Thomas Aquinas, Luther, Kierkegaard. Even Philo of Alexandria, perhaps the first theologian in history, practiced this fertile mixture. A century before Christ, he sought to integrate the *logos* of Plato and the Jewish God. For this reason, it is not surprising that he was a favorite of the Scholastics. Since then, theology has always started from a truth to arrive at it again after a long detour; a rational path but not necessarily a logical one. This thought will always respect a tradition, although in successive variations it may end up denying it with some *ism*. In contrast, philosophical thought will begin by postponing any intellectual tradition (or at least suspending it). Often, and since Thales, it will begin by opposing it, seeking new answers to ancient questions. But this search will also be doomed from the start to mere variations on old propositions; because it is unlikely that a metaphysical creature has anything radically new to say about the human condition.

91, INTERIORITY. For all philosophy and all religion, what matters is the *knowledge* of the truth. In this sense, and in opposition to secular or postmodern ethics, it matters less what a creature of Gaia does than what it thinks or feels. The first step toward salvation is the re–*cognition* of the proposed truth, in most cases summarized in the person of God. In verse 187 of the second sura, the Quran reminds us that "the temptation of idolatry is worse than the slaughter of war." And if science is good, it is only because sooner or later it will end in the one Truth. For any deeply religious creed, a criminal believer is worth more than an honest atheist. It goes without saying that contemporary ethics has inverted this preference after centuries of secular tradition. And if we consider it superior to the previous one, it is because it is currently in use. Only for that reason

92, EXAMPLE. The lack of faith of one metaphysical creature does not condemn another. But it threatens it. Creatures have always feared anything that subverts the established order, *even when it was unjust.* The fear of chaos is the fear of the end of the world in ancient cultures and the fear of madness among modern ones. Because of these fears, sick societies submit to despotic powers, which are always accompanied by some divine or pharaonic aura. The condemnation of the loss of control varies according to the conditions of the moment and extends to anything that threatens the balance through bad example. For this reason, suicide and homosexuality are condemned. When the Colombian poet José Asunción Silva committed suicide in 1896, society and even his own friends reacted with scandal. The poet was buried in "unsanctified" ground after having quicklime thrown over his face. But why? A suicide is not a murderer, and yet it is common for them to provoke a similar or even greater fear. Therefore, society will condemn anything that could spread as a bad example. And it will do so with more virulence in those moments when religious conceptions of the world predominate over aesthetic ones. The condemnation of the "bad example" is, in the second instance, related to the preservation of a social order; but, in a prior instance, it refers to a metaphysical level. Both reject chaos. The fear of suicide and the loss of saving Truth are intimately linked. Quicklime was not thrown over the poet's face simply (a symbolic act, moreover), but over one's own fears, though unrecognizable. They threw quicklime over the fearsome questions that always press from within, like desire in the puritan.

93, TRADITIONS. Myth and religion have been known for a long time, but they are not confused. Both signify a response to the enigma of existence. Myth does so spontaneously and without subsequent implications; religion offers a response but, moreover (and above all), an obligation: *it demands the obligation not to doubt*, not to question the revealed truth at any moment. —The fourth symbol attributed to Pythagoras says: "Doubt nothing concerning the gods or related to divine dogmas." These words are enough to make us realize that Pythagoras, more than a philosopher and much more than a mathematician, was a religious creature. Like Moses and so many others, Pythagoras of Samos began by demanding unconditional respect for the gods and then lingered on a long list of prohibitions.

94, STABILITY. The first condition of a religious creature is the acceptance of the proposed truth, revelation, or initiatory knowledge. A religious creature must maintain its faith at any cost and never doubt the resolution of the Enigma. Therefore, the exemplary figure will be the martyr, and his main adversary will be the one who does not accept or questions the Resolution. Whatever friendship exists between a believer and an atheist, it lacks a religious dimension. Members of sects and religions always strive to marry among themselves; and although they do not always succeed, this is due to a simple practical problem. This reminds us that orthodoxy exists because orthopraxy was sacrificed for its benefit. The theology that justifies a tolerant relationship between different creeds will prioritize the last five Commandments, which were never more important than the first five for the original religion. Let us remember that Servetus was burned at the stake for claiming that it was enough to be a good man to earn heaven. Nor was goodness sufficient for the

Indian religions, from which the world's most radical doctrines of non-violence emerged. And the biblical massacres leave no doubt either: in the name of the first Table, the prohibitions of the second can be overlooked.

95, PRIORITY. In the Hebrew Decalogue, dictated by Yahweh to Moses, seven prohibitions and three prescriptions are listed. Their order aligns with the priorities of the religion. The first two obligations refer to belief in the Supreme, and what a secular person today would consider a priority (thou shalt not kill, thou shalt not steal) is relegated to sixth and eighth place in the ranking. The Catholic version modifies it slightly by removing the prohibition against making idols, perhaps because after the fall of Rome, the Jews were the primary concern, and one could not prohibit what was being preached. The same is observed in the *Five Pillars* of Islam. —Moreover, let us remember that a Muslim does not enter Paradise solely by falling on a battlefield against the infidel. *Jihad* does not only mean "holy war." The idea of a holy war originates from the Christian world and was officially sanctioned by Pope Urban II to encourage the bloody Crusades of 1095. For his part, Bhaktivedanta Swami Prabhupada reminds us that there are two kinds of creatures capable of reaching heaven: as almost everyone knows, one is the renunciant; the other is the *kshatriya* who dies on the battlefield fighting under the orders of Krishna. Faced with the battlefield, the hero Arjuna laments to the Lord that he cannot be happy if he sees his enemies, who are also his relatives, die. And for this show of weakness, unbecoming of an Aryan, he is rebuked by God. The Bhagavad Gita, a sacred book for hundreds of millions of people in the world, says (II–31): "Considering your duty as a kshatriya, you should know that there is no greater occupation for you than fighting based on religious principles. Therefore, you have no reason to doubt. (II–32) Oh, Partha! Blessed are the kshatriyas to whom such opportunities for battle present themselves without seeking them, opening the doors to the celestial planets." Priority: to confirm, at any cost, the proposed Truth. In all its versions, this response denies death, doubt, and chaos. A second constitutive body will seek the organization of religion so that this truth can be perpetuated. And for this, some kind of social order is necessary, rules—thou shalt not kill, thou shalt not steal, thou shalt not fornicate, thou shalt not covet.

96, KNOWLEDGE. For no religion is there salvation in a state of ignorance. For none was goodness ever despicable, but it could do nothing for a man if he did not receive or attain knowledge. The Hindu god tells us (17–28): "Whatever is done as sacrifice, charity, or penance, oh son of Partha!, is not permanent. It is called 'asat,' and it is useless both in this life and the next." One can attain consciousness in Krishna in an instant, and everything else will be erased. It is said that Khatvanga Maharaya attained this knowledge minutes before his death; a confession that must have discouraged less celebrated aspirants. Even Buddha, who could only point the way to the ineffable, attained liberation at the same time as knowledge or Enlightenment, after which he allowed himself all kinds of liberties. (Tradition has it that the famous ascetic died of indigestion. But his disciples are not ashamed of this apparent lack of orthopraxy.) For its part, the ancient doctrine of reincarnation assumes that a soul is punished when it is reincarnated in an inferior being, such as a heron or a tiger. Although there is no apparent reason to assume that a heron or a tiger is more unfortunate than any metaphysical creature. For Hindus and Buddhists, life is suffering since it cannot be eternal happiness. The difference between a tiger and a man is that man *can come to know it*. And it is in that wisdom (in the *samsara*) where liberation begins. The tiger, on the other hand, can only be content with being somewhat happier than men.

97, MOTIVE. Emotions are the primary force that drives creatures to reflection. If the creature lacked feelings, not only would it not have produced a single verse; it also would not have sought to explain the Universe, which means that not even a significant portion of technology would have developed; starting with astrology and alchemy and ending with interplanetary travel.

98, SCREEN. Once, the Abyss was hell and paradise; once it was inhabited by gods and demons. Once, the Abyss was being and non-being. And yet it was *Something*. But one day, somewhere, everything collapsed, and where there had been Something, the creature's gaze was lost in a dark and ineffable depth. A true abyss, unfathomable. And perhaps it was precisely for this reason, out of terror, that they later erected enormous screens in front of it, stage curtains, virtual realities that prevented the gaze from reaching the abhorred beyond. The Great Screen occupied and preoccupied the amused eyes that were once metaphysical eyes. And although the creatures retained the obsession of judging their own actions, no one could ever prove whether that was good or bad.

99, IMPOTENCE. If the desert of our Ignorance is infinitely more vast than our small oasis of knowledge, why should we think that Reality is reduced to that exception surrounded by palm trees?

100, IGNORANCE. The most important question for the metaphysical creature will always be whether its existence has meaning or not, whether there is a transcendent reality or not, whether the history of the individual and the history of humanity have a purpose and a destiny or not. Any answer, affirmative or negative, will depend exclusively on the creature and, in both cases, will be a metaphysical and arbitrary response. And this is because the creature is endowed with an intelligence that is not yet equal to its powerful spirit. —Creatures of almost all times have been proud of their own generation, because one always hears more about the ignorance of the past than the future wisdom. Or because, while they are occupied with their own time, they never manage to recover all the little wisdom that is produced and lost along the way. The history of the human spirit is the expression of an endless conflict: the eternal search for truth and its inability to definitively attain it. Myths, religions, science, thought. Humanity is not so much the product of its wisdom as of its Ignorance, to which it will never resign itself. And that is why it must be admired.

XIII: Obsessions of Truth

101, STRUCTURES. Once, I had the opportunity to dine with N., the son of a famous African revolutionary.[1] N. had studied in Europe and at the time was leading military operations in the north of his country. Our conversation that night revolved around certain stories of animal spirits that had invaded a village. Considering his urban origins and European education, I asked him if he believed in the magic of sorcerers. N. furrowed his brow and pursed his lips like someone who hesitates to admit they believe in God in the midst of a gathering of atheists. But finally, he answered yes with a story. When he was younger, a witch had predicted that either he or his brother would die soon. Before the month was over, N. fell ill, and shortly after, his brother had a car accident. And he died. When he finished his story, N. looked at me like a professor who has just demonstrated a theorem and looks at his student to see if they have understood. With my most Western expression, I said, "Well, and where is

---

[1] It refers to Nteuane Samora Machel, son of the liberator and first Mozambican president Samora Machel, who died in an accident in 1986. Currently the stepson of Nelson Mandela. Ed. note.

the proof?" Someone next to me sighed in annoyance; it was impossible for someone to have so much trouble understanding an *irrefutable* proof. "I don't see the proof," I insisted; "all I see is an induced crime." I think my friends chose to change the subject when they noticed that the viewpoints had become too polarized. But let's look at it from a psychological perspective, which, if not the best, is no worse than the magical interpretation. Let's consider that, after the revelation, both N. and his brother must have been deeply disturbed; especially since they were both pure-blooded Africans and very susceptible to the words of a renowned diviner. N.'s illness must have directly affected his brother, as it indicated who the mortal in question would be. Isn't this the best psychological state for an accident to occur, whether real or involuntary? —I admit I'm being somewhat unfair by presenting a reasoning that is typical of our Western mentality to readers who will surely be Western. I'm not claiming that this is the truth, but rather that neither of the two realities can be absolutely proven. We creatures project onto all of reality a particular worldview that has been suggested or verified *by a minimal part of that reality.* Because Reality is infinite and our intellectual faculties are limited; because we cannot avoid generalizing understanding; because we cannot see the world through two different truths. —We can only say that a proposition is true when it integrates with those basic truths we are unwilling to modify. This commitment is simple when it relates to mathematical axioms and corollaries, but it becomes highly complex when it escapes that tautological science.

102, INSTRUMENTS. In 1748, Hume spoke of relations of ideas and *matters of fact.* Pythagoras' formula merely expresses a relationship between the sides of any right triangle and is independent of what occurs outside the intellect. "That the sun will rise tomorrow —said Hume— is no less intelligible nor implies a greater contradiction than the assertion it will not rise tomorrow. In vain would we attempt to prove its falsity." For Hume, there were two possible types of propositions: one based on the senses and the other on pure intellect. The first is knowledge of the concrete and refers to the contingencies of the world; the second is formal and tautological knowledge and possesses an existence independent of the world (synthetic and analytic judgment; physics and mathematics). Therefore, reason cannot extract any definitive truth from concrete reality, that is, from concrete reality it is not possible to extract any universal and necessary law. —The very history of science shows us that different realities were translated into numbers and mathematical laws, which later had to be replaced by others with the same pretensions. Using geometry ingeniously, Ptolemy was able to explain the irregular movements of the planets, a cosmic defect that had distressed the Platonists. And he did so without abandoning an anthropocentric prejudice of the time: Gaia as the center of the Universe. For a long time, the absurd idea (conceived or repeated by Aristarchus of Samos) that Gaia revolved around the Sun was set aside. Until an eccentric Pole named Copernicus proposed it again, and later Kepler confirmed it with simple and elegant mathematical formulas about ellipses. Of course, this was possible thanks to another prejudice. We know that the humanist Neoplatonists of the time venerated the Sun as a direct manifestation of God. This belief created a favorable environment for the birth of the Copernican (heliocentric) paradigm with its numerical relationships characteristic of Pythagorean mysticism. Very well, except that now the creatures of Gaia know, or believe they know, that in reality all movement is relative to a frame of reference. Thus, as Gregorio Klimovsky says, "from Earth we observe the Sun rotating, but from the Sun we observe the Earth rotating. If we were to position ourselves at the center of mass of the solar system, we would see both rotating around us. In fact, the semantics of scientific terms seem to have a strong influence on understanding what we are talking about when we state the hypotheses of a theory." —Let us recall the case of Newton; his laws remain very useful even though the universe they represent no longer exists. Those optimistic formulas that explained how the world worked are now a poor translation of reality.

103, MADNESS. If a Uruguayan or a Frenchman sees a ghost, they will surely attribute the phenomenon to a psychological disorder (though no one has yet proven the nonexistence of such beings). A Makua or a Makonde will say the opposite. Each relies on the most solid cognitive structure they possess. This structure is given by the culture to which one belongs, and no one lacks it, no matter how poor it may be. Perhaps it is the mad who have partially destroyed these foundations. It cannot be said that they are incapable of seeing reality *as it is,* but rather that they have lost contact with the previous reality, the one they shared with the rest of the group. A madman is, above all, one who has subverted the common rules a group has for conceiving and living the world. Mad was that Makonde who preached Marxism in his village, while outside the spirits of the dead roared in the bodies of lions. Mad would be Plato in a 7th-century monastery, Picasso in Brunelleschi's workshop, Homer in Aristotle's Lyceum, Moses in Egypt, Christ in Jerusalem, Galileo in Rome. Each epistemological structure always seeks *cohesion.* It flees from chaos, from the multiple and the diverse, and tends toward order and unity. When a new proposition contradicts the group's paradigm, the proposition is eliminated. It is the so-called "postmodern" who have grown accustomed to the opposite: questioning the paradigm first; sometimes, to the extreme of being left without any. —If I am not mistaken, Jean Piaget thought something similar. According to the Swiss thinker, to know is to construct a structure adapted to the world. Each new "object" must be assimilated by a preexisting structure. Or the structure must accommodate itself when the objects cannot be adapted (apprehended). And the Uruguayan theologian Juan Luis Segundo affirmed the same: "To explain is to unify" —Assimilation, adaptation, integration: different wills of the intellect that seek the survival of the body and the spirit in unity.

104. NON-CONTRADICTION. Bertrand Russell said that the investigation of causal laws constituted the essence of science, and that the scientist must always postulate determinism as a working hypothesis. More recently, the epistemologist G. Klimovsky pointed out: "It is very important to note that scientific knowledge can be hierarchized in the sense that much of our knowledge is obtained from other knowledge that is more fundamental or, at least, that has already been obtained and accepted. The hierarchical logical scheme that makes certain truths depend on others is what transforms the sciences or, at least, scientific theory, into a system." Over time, epistemologists have become softer. Now they are more cautious and modest. From Aristotelian discussions

on logic, we have moved to a kind of behaviorist psychology of the sciences. Like T.S. Kuhn's epistemology. The mere word "determinism" has lost much of its prestige since Einstein was no longer around to defend it. It is not well understood what creatures call *science*, but we could say that until now its fundamental principle has been the principle of *non-contradiction.* A principle that aims at nothing other than maintaining the cohesion and unity of knowledge. The truth that comes from reason or experience is ordered according to certain rules to form a single body. What biology says must not contradict chemistry, and what Lagrange's theorem says must not contradict the laws of psychology. In principle, because it is still not known what relationship could link a differential to a crime of passion.

105, MATHEMATICS. A paradox is an inverse tautology. While the paradox says A ≠ A, the tautology says A = A. As is easy to observe, the first proposition is far more interesting and mysterious than the second. However, no science is based on the principle of contradiction, but there is one that has the tautology as its main axiom: mathematics. Contradiction is not possible in mathematics because, by definition, it is the development of the proposition A = A.

106, UNITY. The word *cosmos* is of Greek origin (as usual) and means "order" (the ancient Egyptians pronounced *maat*, and besides order, it also meant law or justice). In numerous cosmogonic myths, the universe arises from chaos, even in those that presuppose the intervention of a Creator. Others replaced that chaos with a more abstract nothingness. The first case alludes to creation from the multiple, undifferentiated; in the second, it is the opposite: the multiple, though not chaotic, arose from *unity* (God). Both are alluded to by the scientific cosmogony of the 20th century: the Universe arose from a disordered point. That is, that entire point (the future space or the *res extensa* without extension) exploded without physical laws. The universe would be, for myth and for science, an intermediate state between chaos and unity. Both, respectively, are identified with Evil and Good, with ordinary life and liberation. According to each belief, sin has separated us from the first Being, has trapped us in *samsara*, in diverse and painful matter. On the contrary, virtue should return us to Unity, to Brahma, to Nirvana, or to the definitive liberation from the individual. For the ancient Chinese, the Universe arose from chaos (*hundun*). According to the Tao (in *Dao De Jing*, 25), the original chaos was a sphere where the entire Universe could fit in an undifferentiated form. Here, multiplicity and unity merge into a single cosmogonic image. Our diversity is an intermediate state because it shares both multiplicity and unity: diversity exists, but it is governed by a certain order or law. This order, which is largely physical, is above all psychological. Mircea Eliade observed that every New Year celebration signifies the re-creation of the cosmos from chaos (festival-orgy); in this way, the natural order is renewed. In the *akitu* ceremony of the Akkadian era, the battle of Marduk with the monster Tiamat is reenacted. Marduk's victory ended the original chaos by creating the cosmos from the dismembered body of Tiamat. (The Hittites also had a similar tale, but the protagonists were Teshup and Illuyankash.) In this cosmogonic myth, the cosmos—our intermediate order—emerges from the triumph over Chaos. But at the same time, it partakes of its diverse nature: its own body, the material. (The Akkadian tale becomes doubly significant when we discover that Tiamat was not only a sea monster; she was also the feminine personification of the original abyss.) The same ontological concern is found further east. According to the oldest *Upanishads* , beyond the multiple lies unity. For Hindus, the world is composed of pairs of opposites, which will one day be unified in a higher state, in Brahman. The same is true for Taoism. Among the Chinese, the symbol of *yin-yang*, a kind of tennis ball, describes the world as the *interaction* of a pair of opposites. But at the same time, united, they form a sphere, the original unity, the equilibrium to which one aspires. The same idea was the ideological basis of alchemy: reality composed of pairs of opposing forces, male and female. The goal of knowledge was the *re*-union of opposites, which is why androgynous or hermaphroditic figures were recurring among their traditional symbols. Among the ancient Greek philosophers, the idea that the world was formed by pairs of opposing forces was also common. Consistent with the symbolic equivalences already noted, we find Empedocles, for whom multiplicity arises from unity through hate, while love tends to re-unite. For his part, Heraclitus argued that this diversity of opposites was, at higher levels, a unity. But it could only be perceived with reason and not with the senses. The senses (he said) can only identify the multiple and the diverse. Unity, on the other hand, can only be known indirectly *"because the true nature likes to hide."* This idea of Heraclitus is a common precept in all theological and scientific thought on one hand, and mystical thought on the other. For the former, the path is reason; for the latter, enlightenment or initiatory knowledge. For neither are the senses, because they can only perceive the *diverse* aspects of the world.

107, INTEGRATION. Systematizing knowledge is an obsessive endeavor of *homo-ratio*, because systematization flees from the diverse and tends toward unity. "Scattered" knowledge is mythological, magical, and animistic, three attitudes condemned by science and theology. Already for Plotinus and the Neoplatonists, unity meant good and the multiplicity of matter meant evil. Since Anaxagoras, the Greeks sought to assimilate scattered matter into primary elements first, and into the ordering Intellect (*nous*) later. That intellect then became reason, if they were ever two distinct things. The same integrative obsession has persisted to this day. Recall that in Newton's time, different physical laws were known for different phenomena (Kepler's elliptical motion of the planets, Galileo's concept of inertia, Descartes' solar attraction that resolves the integration of the two, etc.). With his propositions (inspired by his alchemical studies), the same could be explained, but from a single theory. Consider, moreover, that Isaac Newton achieved the most significant intellectual unification in history: for the first time, he explained celestial phenomena with the same laws that explained terrestrial phenomena; the divine planets and the fall of an apple (the realization that "a falling stone and the Moon that does not fall are the same phenomenon"). Later, when it was discovered that light sometimes manifests as a wave and other times as a particle, scientists set themselves a clear and concrete task: to eliminate one of the two. Because reality cannot be dual or indefinite (The idea of the "indefinite" behavior of light is absolutely novel. According to Niels Bohr, it will never be possible to eliminate this duality.) In the 20th century, when the results of quantum and relativistic physics appeared as independent bodies, physicists eagerly sought a theory that would unify them into a single expression. Today, scientists live and suffer in an illusory or Newtonian space, trying to unite the microcosm with the rest of the Universe.

108, EINSTEIN. Throughout the *Theory of Relativity*, there is an obsessive will for *unification*. The *special* theory united space and time, and the subsequent *general* theory did the same with matter and the geometry of space. But reality is sometimes rebellious and produces paradoxes (logical paradoxes, as Hume would say): the same *general theory* divided reality into two. Above remained a geometrized macro-universe, and below, a non-geometric micro-universe. This dualist heresy was the greatest concern of the scientific community in the 20th century. And especially for Einstein, who always started from the metaphysical principle that reality was a rigorously coherent unity. For this reason, he imagined and proposed a *unified field theory*, which should be based on geometry and not on statistics. Behind or alongside it, countless mathematical theories emerged that aimed for the same. But none escaped their own abstractions and instead produced skepticism, like that of Max Born. As everyone knows, Einstein was a staunch supporter of the hypothetical-deductive method and opposed the statistics of the new quantum physics and any principle of "uncertainty."

I suppose this reaction is due to the fact that statistics represent the threshold that separates chaos from mathematics, ultimate reality from the first idea.

109, WATERS. Water in controllable quantities signifies Good, but gathered in marine quantities (unfathomable) it represents Evil. This observation, which is initially of psychological origin, has metaphysical implications. Baptism is performed with a small amount of water; in Africa, the first thing offered to the god is a bit of this vital element. In countless tales, sea monsters are the animations of chaos. If any of those advanced men of the ancient East had witnessed a documentary by J.I. Cousteau, they would surely have sworn they had seen a vision of hell. —There are not a few ancient myths that make the world emerge from the waters; that is, our order or semi-order emerging from chaos. Genesis tells us that in the beginning, "Gea had no form, everything was a deep sea covered in darkness, and the Spirit of God moved over the water." Later, it will be the waters of the Flood that will once again submerge the world in destruction, in chaos. Also, according to Sumerian cuneiform texts from the 4th and 5th centuries BC, first there was the original ocean, which gave rise to An, father sky, and Ki, mother earth. The marine world was, for those creatures, a blind world, multiple in its products and always unknown. Unlimited downward and sideways. According to the Torah,

Leviathan is a sea monster, like Tiamat. A Jew who respects the *halakha* (primitive rule) will refrain from eating sea products and any fish without fins or scales. Because, according to this same rule, the marine kingdom is impure. Maurice Ruben-Hayoun says: "the ritual of tashlich, from the Hebrew ('you shall cast') which comes from Micah (7:19): 'you shall cast all their sins into the depths of the sea,' consists of throwing pebbles (which symbolize sins) or breadcrumbs (which rather correspond to an honor paid to the evil spirit) into the sea so that Satan may feed. In Paris, one can also see groups of faithful, led by a rabbi, who go to the banks of the Seine to throw pebbles there that represent the faults of their community." Nor were the Pythagorean mathematicians free from this idea, as they considered many marine species to belong to hell.

110, VISIBILITY. In epistemological prehistory, there was no Enlightenment discussion that separated reason and experience. Back then, there was no alternative; as for some moderns, the truth was what could be seen: a buffalo, a knife, the sun, the moon, the spirit of the ancestors, and the magic of the sorcerer. Not long ago, in the northern region of Mozambique, a Makua told me, with fanatical detail, how a woman had turned a sack of sand into a sack of sugar. Not only had he seen the sand change color, from red to pure white; he had also experienced the new taste. While acknowledging that such a transformation was impossible, he insisted it was the absolute truth. Why? *Because he had seen it with his own eyes and tasted it with his own tongue.*

"Tell me, do you know what dreams are?" I asked him, not without some self-doubt.

"Yes, I dream every night," the Makua replied.

"What was the last thing you dreamed?"

"Last night I dreamed I was on a plane, flying through the clouds."

"Have you ever traveled by plane, then?"

"No. I've only seen planes from afar, flying."

"But you were there. You saw and heard the plane from inside, flying through the clouds."

"Yes."

"Then it's true that you've been on a plane at some point."

"No, it's not true."

As you can see, I resorted to the tricks of dialectic. But that's a game valid only for the children of Greece, not for others. My Makua friend was not affected by the conversation. Perhaps he was left with the same novel impression I had when I got to know them a little. —Even more thrilling are the stories told in the villages of the *African* bush. For "savage" cultures, everything that is seen is real. For the heirs of Greece, it is not: the truth is what lies behind appearances. It is said that once a critic of Plato reproached him for having only seen individual horses but never something like *horseness*. To which the philosopher replied: "That is because you, sir, have eyes but no intelligence." Even before Plato, *intelligence* meant something like the power to see the invisible. That is, the fire of Heraclitus, the inertia of Galileo, the gravity of Newton, the *will* of Schopenhauer, the class struggle of Marx, the libido of Freud. In the denial of experience, Greek rationalism was born (which is why one cannot speak of "Greek science" in the same sense we understand it today). A bit later, it was proposed that this Invisibility could also (or only) be perceived through another human faculty: faith; and in this conflicted romance, the Scholastics invested years. Many religions, from the Indian to early Christianity, concluded that everything visible was deceptive and, therefore, perverse. ("*Omnia quae visibiliter fiunt in hoc mundo, possunt firei per daemones;*" that is, "everything that occurs visibly in this world can be done by demons"). For the Greeks, behind the apparent was reason; for Christians, God or the Devil; for moderns and for the vulgar, behind everything lies sex. —Well, but both the enchanted Africans and those who only have eyes to see horses must be reminded that not everything seen is true, nor is everything true seen.

111, COHERENCE. The thought that relates and derives one truth from another was already known among the priests of ancient Egypt and only much later was called *deductive.* Attributed to Thales, it would not be surprising if the Greek had taken it from his journey to the Nile. When the Scholastics noticed that certain physical phenomena were subject to rational or Pythagorean laws, they must have supposed that this path of minor but irrefutable truths must lead to the ultimate Truth. Reason must lead to God, because Creation could not be contradictory. Someone, I don't remember who, proposed the metaphor of the wheel: starting from any of its spokes, one reaches the center. The same had been maintained by the Islamic scholars centuries before: the study of the sciences is always good (they said), because even if it begins without God as the objective, sooner or later one will arrive at Him. Because everything is a harmonious or terrible unity.

112, SIMULTANEITY. The (Western) Intellect tends to analyze the world in *pairs of opposites*, transforming it into a spectrum of intermediate grays, which ultimately results in *unification*. In turn, the dynamic relationship of the elements involved tends to be an almost exclusive relationship of *cause and effect.* For the metaphysical creature, it is at least impossible to conceive of a change produced by the action of *simultaneous* factors, by the alchemical convergence of different and opposing elements. Even when multiple factors are considered responsible for an event, there is an attempt to order them in time. Otherwise, they are seen as a darkness of analysis. (It is the same difficulty that considers the atmosphere of Gaia as the cause of life and not as the *cause and consequence*; the same difficulty, if I do not exaggerate, that sees the taboo of incest as the cause of civilization, and not as the *cause and consequence*.) Are we still not prepared to think in simultaneities? There is a very popular image that refers to the impossibility of knowing what came first: the egg or the chicken. This is due to the inability to see the simultaneous in a formation; and even more so in an instantaneous event. It is as if the modern mind were incapable of listening to a symphony (chaos) and, on the contrary, preferred the orderly sound of a music box (sequence). The creature tends to see everything in cause-effect relationships; which, indirectly, leads to scientific reductionism, the aesthetics of detective novels, and the amusement of chess. —It is possible that this difficulty cannot be blamed on mystics or the ancient Chinese, for whom reality was not only a unity but functioned, at every moment, as the result of all moments. I believe that for the *I-Ching*, the fall of a tree was not caused by a single preceding event, but by all of them. But that is already more difficult for us to conceive.

113, DICHOTOMIES. Dichotomies are celebrated in the *history* of thought, which means (I believe Lévi-

Strauss already said this) that they are a characteristic of its *nature*. Dividing the creature and the world into pairs of opposites will always be more plausible than dividing them into three. (A more promising probability would be a denominator several times greater, since the variant of unity is multiplicity, and both form a dichotomy.) The ancient Zoroastrian division of Good and Evil is the most universal of all, and since ancient Greece it has hardly been questioned. The Christian trinity, on the other hand, is a more complex concept, the source of almost all headaches between missionaries and colonized natives, and it does not refer to the world but to the Incommensurable. In the dichotomous classification, there is always a spectrum: the Universe; in the triangular relationship, one of the vertices can be more or less strong than the other two, or it can at some point be excluded. Dichotomies are famous: Good and Evil, faith and reason, Apollonian and Dionysian, left and right, interior and exterior, form and content, conscious and unconscious, culture and nature, myth and history, immanent and acquired, *yin* and *yang*, East and West, male and female, heaven and earth, light and darkness, being and non-being. If I may, I will add another pair that will surely not be novel: aesthetic and renunciant. —Triangulations, on the other hand, are less forceful. But they exist: for example, art-science-religion, since none is the midpoint between the other two.

114, HIERARCHICAL. Both logical reason and monotheism are hierarchical structures. Monotheism and primitive religions are not distinguished by the number of supernatural beings. Even in Judaism and Islam, there are angels and demons (which is why they should be called "monolatries"), but these are not independent beings as they were in Egypt or archaic Greece or black Africa. What distinguishes monotheism from other religions is its vertical ordering. Its corresponding image on Gaia is the Church or the Army; not democracy. Outside of these systems, nothing good can exist. For rationalism that contradictory periphery, the empire of the senses, was called *art.* For religions, it corresponds to the domain of the demonic, the deception of the senses, the Homeric plurality that the first Greek philosophers repudiated in the name of reason. Emerging from a stage where the multiple and contradictory were accepted, the basic condition of any proposed truth will be hierarchical unity. In ancient Babylon, alchemy was more of a magical rite that related causes and effects by a law of mimesis that could be summarized as follows: like produces like. Thus, each stone, each metal responded independently to its color or behavior. Multiplicity took a radical turn with the Gnostic proposal of the *monad.* Other monotheists, the Muslims, made the final change in alchemical practice. Consistent with the unitary conception of Creation, they invented chemistry; that is, something similar to what that science is now. The identification of alchemy with a kind of proto-chemistry comes from the pictorial and instrumental resemblance that might exist between the alchemist's temple and the laboratory of a primitive chemist. However, primitive alchemy had nothing scientific about it and much of magic and religion. Initially, alchemists ignored all observations of chemical phenomena in themselves, simply because they were not interested. They were not seeking the wealth of gold but the secrets of the spirit and the cosmos. It was the Arabs, those monotheists, who were the first to focus on purely chemical phenomena. And this was possible because Islam, an austere and vertical religion, was free from the complications of the ancient Greek and Babylonian alchemists, heirs to the magical complexities of the ancient world. Similar to alchemy in its apparent forms, chemistry responds to a radically different conception of the world. It is not knowledge of anarchic and independent effects but a body that, by principle, seeks unity and hierarchy.

115, AD-HOC. Since Plato, explaining the erratic course of the planets was an obsession for astronomers. By principle, this explanation had to be numerical and as simple as possible. Ptolemy fulfilled the first part, but the observation of unforeseen variations complicated the geocentric premise with *ad hoc* elements. With Copernicus' heliocentric revolution, this situation was not radically simplified: the premise of circular orbits also required *ad hoc* corrections. After millennia, Kepler solved the problem with a system of elliptical orbits taken from ancient Greek mathematics. Only then was Plato's metaphysical prejudice satisfied and laid to rest. Both the Copernican resolution and the older Ptolemaic one subscribed to the Pythagorean precept of a numerical nature of the cosmos. The difference between them is that Kepler's theory was much simpler, *and it had no ad hoc elements.* Newton also received the first blow when he resorted to an *ad hoc* to resolve or justify some minor errors in his theory; but his was an *ad hoc* with a double defect for science, because it referred to God. —The basis of the Platonic simplicity of the sciences lies in the elimination of all *ad hoc* elements that disrupt *unity* with independent additions. And its starting hypothesis is the exclusion of God from the functioning of His own Work. —Once, in the African city of Pemba, I ordered some Makua workers to install a lock on a door. Since they were carpenters by trade, they had no difficulty doing so. But they did it their way: the main door could not be opened from the outside.

—What's the problem? —observed the Makua—. You can enter through the back door and then open this one from the inside...

To the Makua worker, his reasoning seemed logical (or at least natural). I wanted to tell him that everything must fulfill a precise function and I don't know what else, but then I gave up on the attempt. Then I thought: "this is a door with an ad hoc, something inadmissible to our Western or even modern mind. "

116, DIMENSIONS. In the 20th century, physical reality split into two, into a micro and a macro universe. Since then, scientists have not rested in their efforts to reunite what wisdom separated. As early as 1920, the strategy of adding dimensions to the existing four began. Soon mathematicians found that five dimensions could unify the electromagnetic problem with the gravitational one. Successively, we had universes of three, four, five, nine, ten, and eleven dimensions. And finally, the twelve-dimensional universe (*F-Theory*) of Harvard professor Cumrun Vafa. Duff, another scientist, complained that "it brings all sorts of headaches that we would rather do without." Now it seems that every time new complications arise, another extra dimension is added to the theory. The theory has begun to reveal all that it has as an explanatory apparatus (*convenient device*) divorced from any ontology. It all reminds us of the Ptolemaics and their *ad hoc.*

117, ENTER. Once, in the African city of Pemba, I ordered some Makua workers to install a lock on a door. Since they were carpenters by trade, they had no difficulty doing so. But they did it their way: the main door could not be opened from the outside.

"What's the problem?" observed the Makua." You can enter through the back door and then open this one from the inside."

To the Makua worker, his reasoning seemed logical (or at least natural). I wanted to tell him that everything must fulfill a precise function and I don't know what else, but then I gave up on the attempt. Then I thought: "this is a door with an *ad hoc*, something inadmissible to our Western or modern mind. "

118, CHANCE. The greatest flaw of an *ad hoc* in a theory is not only the loss of "monism "; it also interrupts the chain of reductions, that is, *the verticality* of that unity, which is one of the conditions of materialism. Let's take any example. Why are the testicles on the outside of the human body and not inside like the ovaries? Known answer: because semen needs a lower temperature than the rest of the body. But how is such a "logical" function established? To explain it, we could resort to the *nous* of Anaxagoras or the *wille* of Schopenhauer. But both are *ad hoc* for the materialist structure, and if we were to choose them, *we could no longer continue reducing them* to simpler elements. On the other hand, we can choose a third element, as all-encompassing as the previous ones: *chance.* In this case, we opt for the Darwinian notion of chance. (Through trial and error, the testicles gradually settled into the position most favorable to their thermal conditions. The number of incorrect solutions can be counted in trillions; that's not the problem.) By doing so, we are not only reducing a complex problem to a much simpler originating factor; we are also shifting the problem into the domain of our mechanistic mindset. Mechanical nature is expressed in an apparently simple cause-and-effect relationship. But in the end (or at the beginning), the Cause can be one of two things: the Prime Mover (God, *nous*, or logos) or pure chance. If we choose the first, the problem becomes exponentially more complicated; if we choose the second, we can rest in peace, in a kind of "logical absurdity," an oxymoron more accessible to scientific reason than God. Chance is the root to which all known (or conceivable) evolutionary, physical, or biological phenomena are reduced. It is the only (physical?) phenomenon that science does not interrogate; it is the most borderline phenomenon between the complex and the inexplicable, between Chaos theory and metaphysics. We can study the probabilities of a dice game or the weather, but we will never be able to explain *what* produces chance, *what it is*, where it comes from. Not without resorting to different suspect branches of philosophy. If

Chance is at the beginning of every deduction (or at the end of every reduction), God or an ordering Intelligence is at the end. But both, God and Chance, are equally irreducible. That is, inexplicable.

119, POE. In "*The Murders in the Rue Morgue*," Edgar Allan Poe presents a highly significant line of reasoning: The narrator was walking down a street in Paris with his admired Auguste Dupin; they walked in silence for a quarter of an hour, each absorbed in their own thoughts. Suddenly, Dupin said, "He is a man of little consequence, it's true, and he would be better suited to the Théâtre des Variétés. "

"How is it possible that you knew I was thinking of..."

"Chantilly," his analytical friend correctly replied.

But how was it possible? Many times in life, we experience this: we realize that the other person was thinking the same thing as us, without any communication other than silence. But how does Dupin, an analytical hero of the 19th century, explain it? Although, for the sake of economy or due to an aesthetic prejudice, I don't like overly lengthy quotes, I'll extract one of that size because it's well worth it and has almost no waste. "I will explain it to you," said Dupin. "So that you may understand, let us retrace the course of your thoughts (...) The links are: Chantilly, Orion, Doctor Nichols, Epicurus, stereotomy, the stones in the street, and the fruit vendor. (...) We were speaking of horses, if I recall correctly, shortly before leaving C... Street. This was the last topic we discussed. As we crossed this street, a fruit vendor, with a large basket on his head, ran past us and caused you to stumble over some cobblestones that were there where the street is being repaired. You stepped on one of the loose stones, slipped, twisted your ankle slightly, seemed very annoyed, uttered a few words, turned to look at the pile of stones, and then continued on your way in silence. I did not pay much attention to what you did, but for some time now, observation has become a kind of necessity for me. —He kept his eyes fixed on the ground, looking with a sullen expression at the holes and grooves in the pavement, so I understood that he was still thinking about the stones, until we reached Lamartine Street, which was paved, as an experiment, with overlapping cobblestones. Here his face lit up, and seeing his lips move, I had no doubt that he was murmuring the word 'stereotomy,' a word pedantically applied to that kind of paving. I knew that you could not think of that word without associating it with atoms and thus moving on to the theories of Epicurus; as we had not long ago spoken on this subject, I remember telling you with what little notoriety the vague conjectures of the Greek sage had been confirmed in the cosmographies of the nebulae; I saw that he raised his eyes and fixed them on the great nebula of Orion, which I had anticipated. In the scathing critique of Chantilly that appeared in yesterday's *Musee*, the author, making unkind allusions to the cobbler's change of name upon dedicating himself to tragedy, quoted a Latin verse that we have often discussed. I refer to: *'Perdidit antiquum litera prima sonum'*. —I had already told you that it referred to Orion, a word that was previously written Urión, and due to a certain sarcasm associated with that expression, I knew that you could not forget that line. It was clear, then, that you could not help but associate Orion with Chantilly. (...)" —Later, using such determinism, Poe's analytical character solves other logical mysteries and invents the detective novel. I would dare to say more: he anticipates, at least, the style of "*The Interpretation of Dreams*" by Freud and his successors. The detective genre is characteristic of positivist optimism, a paradigm of the 19th century. Its universe is the universe of Newton, not Poincaré; its dynamics only knows *stable systems* (small initial variations produce small final variations, making predictability possible). Anyone knows that the one-dimensional image of Dupin, Poe's character, is possible and exaggerated. But a plausible exaggeration for a 19th-century scientist and a fantastic fiction for a 20th-century one. Because now we have a new paradigm that confirms the exaggeration of that reasoning: Chaos theory. That is, in any link of free associations, any small deviation will lead to different paths, opposite results. If the human brain worked as Dupin described, mediocrity and mental health would be more common than they are on Gaia, because psychoanalysts would reach the childhood of any creature with the simple use of a computer. —For any science, a theory is superior to another if it can explain the same with greater economy. We could say that more economical than Dupin's proposition would be an explanation that resorted to telepathy. But this has an inadmissible defect for science: it is an *ad hoc* still irreducible.

120, INTERACTION. Until the 19th century, physics studied the Universe as if it were an object independent of the creatures studying it. But the 20th century, from the outset, placed the creature *inside* the problem. In all of *Relativity Theory* the observer has the same importance as the observed object. Something similar also happened in microphysics but with a more radical sign: the instruments of measurement ceased to be neutral elements and independent of the observed phenomena. The phenomena observed and studied by quantum physics occur at the very moment of measurement. This does not mean that science produces artificial and arbitrary facts; it means that it is no longer possible to view material reality as a reality independent of the metaphysical creature. I first heard a fascinating idea from an uncle of mine: a beam of light traveling for millennia is an indeterminate phenomenon; only upon contact with the creature that measures it does it become an electromagnetic wave or a photon. Similarly, a flow of electrons is an undefined phenomenon: as long as it is not measured, it is both a wave and a photon, meaning it both is and is not. An electron that departs from a source F, passes through a plane via two different slits simultaneously, and arrives at a photographic plate demonstrates wave-like behavior in its movement and particle-like behavior when measured on the photographic plate. But the wave-like behavior of its movement changes when it is illuminated from one of the slits to catch it in transit. —This intervention of the "instrument" on the observed object is similar to what Immanuel Kant thought about the very act of knowing. In the 18th century, the philosopher considered it impossible to view nature in an absolutely objective way, independent of preconceptions and independent of the very nature of the intellect. It is more, it would not be possible to determine whether knowledge is a relationship of the creature with external reality or a relationship with itself. In the late sixties, T.S. Kuhn popularized the idea that a scientific truth depended on its relationship with the paradigm. The paradigm would be decisive in all movements within a laboratory: from the choice of the object to the method of measuring it; from the hypotheses to the conclusions. Now, when we study the most ancient cosmogonies, we notice the similarities between them—emergence from chaos-unity, etc. But we are even more astonished when we see that, at their core, they are also similar to the most modern scientific cosmogonies and that they share the same obsessions. Some theologians attempt to rescue epistemological virtues from these comparisons, favoring the most convenient myths. But it is also possible to conjecture that the scientific representation of the world is, precisely, the *expression* of that same cognitive structure (*"We see the universe the way it is because we exist")*. —Today, the paradigm of paradigms is beginning to take on a more psychological than epistemological tone: the birth of a new paradigm signifies the liberation from the previous one, the abolition of cognitive limits. The change of paradigms has been defined as an *archetypal*process; and in this way, we return to the human mind, to another of its old obsessions.

121, TRUTH. We can flirt with the truth, corner it, feel its breath, surround it with physical or religious formulas. But, in the end, the truth always eludes us. —Epistemology can only account for human impotence; it is not the science that studies truth but the way in which it is coveted by the creature. And epistemology is the intellectual witness of that failure. Yet, though impotent, its gaze should not be entirely in vain. After all, are we not saying that it is a witness?

XIV: The Secrets of Liberation

122, MATERIALISM. Democritus believed that the world was composed of material particles called *atoms,* endowed with mechanical movements and devoid of *nous* or ordering intelligence. Beyond that, nothing; neither gods nor realities. Therefore, knowledge was merely the result of the impact of matter on the senses, and ethics and gods were merely obstacles for the creatures. The same or similar was held by the Sophists and J-P. Sartre: beyond nothing or Nothing; to know is to *perceive* the particular.

123, HIDDEN. In the great monotheistic religions, Gnostic thought always found a place despite the proponents of revelation. In Judaism, it is represented by the Kabbalists of the 13th century; in Christianity, by the famous Gnostics of the early centuries; in Islam, by a certain Shiite current. Unlike those who uphold the authority of revelations, for the Gnostics, truth is achieved after a long path of perfection. Why should the path toward the liberation of the soul be shorter and less complicated than the path that leads to the river? (Unless there is no path but Revelation.) Like any long, ascending path, this one is divided into levels. In Shiism, the same division is achieved using the metaphor of veils, because they were Arabs and unfamiliar with hermeneutics: the Quran has four levels to unveil, each deeper and more mysterious than the last. For all Gnostic thought, as for Greek rationalism, the truth is not revealed but hidden, and its discovery implies a process of learning. The difference lies in the fact that scientific or rationalist gnosis can be collective, while metaphysical gnosis tends to be mystical and individual.

124, ORIENTALS. There are ancient doctrines that can be considered entirely Gnostic: for example, Buddhism and Jainism. Like Buddha, Vardhamana (Jina) was an aristocrat disillusioned with reality. For this reason, he renounced the world and dedicated himself to wandering the paths of infinite Asia, naked. As was known to those spirits of the Ma-Ganga, rigorous asceticism preceded meditation. Like Buddha, Vardhamana received enlightenment beneath a tree and later entered Nirvana, abandoning the painful experience of existence. I mean, he died. For his followers, the cosmos is a numerical order in which creatures, things, and gods exist, all subordinated to relentless cycles. Originating from Hinduism, this doctrine also promised to liberate the creature from the burden of existence. Even more, with the aim of escaping the *samsara*, it prescribed death by starvation, which signifies a secret and traditional form of suicide. As in all religions or spiritualist doctrines, poverty and chastity were considered virtues; not before the Law of a god but for the hygiene of the soul. Both virtues are prerequisites for any perfection. Both are renunciations. Today, the most advanced Jains possess a bowl for alms, a broom to clear the path of insects, and a muslin face covering to avoid inhaling them; not out of disgust but out of compassion.

125, HERMETICISM. Hermetic thought comes from Hermes Trismegistus (thrice great), a hybrid between the Greek god Hermes and the Egyptian god Thoth, the conductor of souls to the underworld. The known writings of this sect date from the early days of Christianity but refer to the third century before Christ. In the Alexandrian era, it was the result of the fusion of Greek and Eastern knowledge by the Neoplatonists. Like the ancient Babylonians, the Hermetics saw a correspondence between the visible world (earth) and the true world (heaven). They also taught that the metaphysical creature is body and soul, illusory matter and a fragment of the creative Logos. As in yoga, hidden knowledge is achieved by withdrawing from the sensible world so that only after multiple existences does the purified soul return to God. Now, if we change the name *Dei* to *Brahma*, we obtain a Hinduist statement.

126, DISILLUSION. In Christian Gnosticism, too, a strong influence from the banks of the Tigris and the Ganges is evident. Well, it could not be otherwise; surely this exchange of influences was due to the Orphics and the Pythagoreans. A slight historical tracing reveals it: Carpocrates, like Pythagoras, repeated the doctrine of re-incarnations; Basilides, in a Buddhist style, maintained that the true God could only be named by *silence.* But even if we lacked all these details, we could deduce it from its ideological or metaphysical content. Let us see; for those ancient Gnostics, the body was the prison of the soul, the imperfection of the spirit. Matter—the sublunar world—was the concrete expression of Evil, the work of the Devil or the Demiurge, inventor of life and death. For the liberation of the soul, trapped in this monstrous mechanism, there was only one path: as in all religious or metaphysical doctrines, that path consists of *a certain kind of knowledge.* But a kind of knowledge very different from the Greek or the Hebrew. For the classical Greeks, truth was reached through reason, and its principal instrument was dialectic. For the Hebrews, the truth had already been revealed and was entirely contained in the Scriptures. For the early Christian Gnostics, it was the same; but in a different way. Convinced that the Scriptures (no longer the world) possessed different levels of revelation, they formulated novel conclusions. In the 2nd and 3rd centuries, various sects proliferated among Christians, denouncing the demonic nature of Yahweh. According to them, only a perverse god could create an imperfect and painful world—matter. For the same reason, we can then understand why some of these sects worshipped the serpent of Genesis. As in some modern symbols, the serpent represents the will for *knowledge*, the discernment of Good and Evil, the enlightenment that would free the creature from the deception orchestrated by the Devil.

127, SOLITUDE. Heraclitus said that truth likes to hide. Gnostics and Orientals thought the same. But if the Greeks had defined a clear and optimistic method (reason, dialectic), the Orientals lacked one, and all the responsibility fell on the individual. According to the Bhagavad-Gita, the supreme and liberating knowledge resides in the consciousness of Krishna. For Buddha, it was the Enlightenment that allowed the detachment from all *karma*, but about which he could say nothing to his disciples except to point the way. In both cases, it is an individual and irrational knowledge. The study of Revelation, on the other hand, implies a certain rationality, though not much, and thus it can be collective and proselytizing. Rationalism does not seek the liberation of the soul, but Gnosticism and the revealed word do.

128, HEBREWS. For Oriental thought, knowledge is achieved after a long spiritual training. And this final achievement is the only thing that matters. So arduous and difficult is this knowledge that it tormented Buddha for years before he attained it; others, lesser but great masters, declared they had obtained it shortly before death. —Hebrew revelation does not imply this absolute internalization. Instead of Buddhist anarchy or Hindu collegiality, there was the Authority of the Father. As in its Christian and Muslim derivations, the virtue of the Hebrew lay in the immediate acceptance of the proposed truth. And in submission to authority, for as long as possible. Hebrew metaphysics, whose roots are in Pharaonic Egypt, does not despise the body and matter because they are also the works of Yahweh. —The famous soul-body dualism, attributed to Greek thought, is not foreign to any religion. In the oldest Hebrew book, the body was already distinguished from the soul, though in a more subtle way than the Oriental: the creature is of the earth and its soul the breath of the Spirit. Neither the Egyptian nor the Hebrew despised matter or the body; the destiny in Gaia and in Heaven lies in the hands of Authority, and the duty of the people is not to delve into the unknown but to accept the revealed truth. The Almighty will take care of the rest.

129, MIXTURE. Gnostic and Hermetic thought found an excellent sounding board in the Gospels. A book so antimaterialistic, so full of pain and promises of redemption, is it not the synthesis of the Hebrew and Oriental spirits? Later Christianity despised the body and matter (Paul, Saint Augustine); or, at best, had a negligent care for them. Later, in the Middle Ages, the mendicant orders resurfaced. Justified by the words of a crucified subversive, they were close cousins to those *sannyasin* who followed the Ganges in their meditations. Over time, the Oriental impulse lost strength in the Christian world, while the Greek spirit was reborn within the Church: first with scholastic theology, then with the tolerance and paganism of the Vatican. Gradually, matter ceased to be the perverse side of things. Until one day, nothing was anything else.

130, NEOMATERIALISM. Finally, the moderns stopped cursing the body and matter. But every spiritual process ends up being carried by its own inertia to unforeseen extremes. Happiness is no longer outside matter but in matter itself. Therefore, all the efforts of the creatures of Gaia are concentrated on its study and mastery. With mixed results. The Gospels, which in the early days of their own Era served to condemn gold, after the Reformation were commented on to stimulate the fever that obtained it (though wealth was already predestined by God or Calvin). And yoga, which was born in the East as a technique to separate the soul from the body, that abominable matter, is now used in the West as therapy, to return the soul to the venerated body. (Just as "religion" means *re-ligare,* "yoga" comes from the Sanskrit *yuj*, and means yoke, *yoke* or bond. But in no case does it mean a bond with the body. It always refers to a relationship with God or with the infinite *Brahman*.)

131, ANTIMATTER. Alchemy also originates from Egypt and Mesopotamia. In its Babylonian, Arab, and European versions, it sought the secret of the cosmos through the perfection of the spirit and the study of matter. Hinduism and its derivatives proceeded in the opposite way: if the body and matter are the imperfection and condemnation of the soul, nothing good can come from their study. Thus, through the excessive disdain for this world, Hindu societies achieved the same as their materialist contemporaries: the dehumanization of the creature. Because if its mechanization is condemnable, so is the abandonment of the body.

132, ABSURD. One evening in Africa, I found myself observing the crowd that was gradually sinking into a darkness without lamps. The young Makua women strolled by in their colorful capulanas, their faces painted white in search of husbands. The men, with their distant gazes, sat on the sidewalks of a ruined Portuguese town, waiting for the moment to eat their meager bread with tea. And the dirty children, pushing each other back and forth, occasionally picking something up from the ground to put it in their mouths. Then I thought (felt) that these children would grow up, suffer like their parents, and die without leaving a trace. In reality, this is not so different from the fate of almost all the inhabitants of Gaia; but that moment was metaphorical or exemplary. The young women's search for husbands gave meaning to those dull existences, while the absurd was represented by the innocence of the children. Perhaps none of them would ever attain religious or material knowledge. Of course, every people has some kind of knowledge; but I am not referring to its quality but to the awareness of possessing it: to be saved or to take advantage of it. Many of those children would pass; many of them may have already died or are dying at this very moment. And that is all. Only the awareness of possessing *knowledge* elevates the metaphysical creature above its own impotence in the face of the inexplicable. According to non-canonical writings, the Lord said: "*When you know what you are doing, you are blessed; but you are condemned when you do not know.* "

XV: Truth against Freedom

133, FREEDOM. Not only does *Muslim* mean "submitted to the Supreme "; all other religions demand the creature's renunciation of unlimited freedom in favor of an Authority or in favor of a definitive Freedom. That is why it is not strange that philosophy was born in Greece and later cultivated more in Protestant countries than in Catholic ones. Although authoritarian, Martin Luther not only liberated the Anglo-Saxon spirit from the authority of the Pope; he also (an involuntary and paradoxical consequence) undermined the authority of the Bible by reclaiming the rights of the individual. According to Bertrand Russell, "Protestants transferred the seat of authority in religion, first from the Church to the Bible, and then to the individual soul." A similar idea was expressed by C.G. Jung: "Protestant pastors have undergone the scientific training of the Faculty of Theology, which, with its critical spirit, undermines the naivety of faith." I do not know pastors better prepared than any Catholic priest; in fact, I do not know pastors prepared in anything or with something called *critical spirit;* though this is due to my own ignorance, and surely there must be some. But from a historical perspective, I believe the subversive influence of the Protestant is clear: from the *free-interpreter* to the *free-thinker* there is but a step. Only, the free-thinker, the philosopher, will never find a place in any of the Protestant sects that abound in Gaia.

134 RELIGIOUS. The religious spirit must exchange its freedom to question everything and to experience the world for the annihilation of metaphysical doubt and the experience of the pains of this world (which does not mean that freedom to choose God is unnecessary). With sensual pleasures and metaphysical doubt repressed, the religious spirit in its pure state, possessing the Truth, becomes fundamentalist and intolerant. At best, only epistemologically intolerant. In worse cases, without the experience of pleasures, it ends up throwing itself into the very pain it feared.

135, NIETZSCHE. Nietzsche fiercely opposed the Greek spirit to the Christian one, which he considered funereal and decadent. In his thought, the gods of Olympus represented the glorification of life. "The Greek gods —I read him say—, with the perfection in which they appear to us already in Homer, cannot be conceived, certainly, as fruits of indigence and necessity; such beings were not conceived by a spirit trembling with anguish: it was not to escape from life that a brilliant fantasy projected their images into the blue. In these speaks a religion of life, not of duty, or of asceticism, or of spirituality.

All these figures breathe the triumph of existence, an exuberant feeling of life accompanies their worship." The Greek gods are not the result of anguish or duty: they are the characters of a work of art; the world, the Eternal Return. —In November 1887, Nietzsche wrote to Overbeck about his desire to be remembered by a poem by Lou van Salomé that would be sung a hundred years later:

To think and live for millennia
Pour out your content fully
If you have no more happiness to give me,
Well, you still have your —suffering.

For Zarathustra, the preachers of life were, in reality, the preachers of death. "They seem like walking coffins —he said—. Their motto is: life is pain and therefore the best thing is to die. Pleasure is a thing called sin." And elsewhere: "There are some for whom virtue is a spasm under the lash. Many times we have heard their cries. [...] They do not rise except by lowering others." Many times we have felt what the German must have felt: in the presence of one of those characters proud of their faith, one feels that this life is rubbish, that the best thing is to dress in gray, throw one's testicles into the Río de la Plata and, if possible, die once and for all. In contrast, the spring spirit refuses to renounce.

136, LUTHER. In Martin Luther, the contradictions that so fascinated psychoanalysts and intrigue us were combined: the monk rebels against authority because he loves it. Although he did not intend to provoke an ism, he takes a step away from the shadow of Pope Leo X. His greatest contribution was the *legitimization* of the nascent critical and libertarian spirit. He lays the tracks for the emerging capitalist locomotive and drives it first to criticism and then to nihilistic atheism. But he cannot be held responsible for the posthumous consequences. (Something similar would be blaming Hitler's mother for World War II.) Now the Greek spirit imposes itself once again in the West and in Westernized countries, which are almost the rest. Even over the Church, the old bastion of epistemological intolerance; and at the same time that this new spirit grows within a religion, fundamentalisms resurface as a reaction.

137, LEFEBVRE. The reformers of the 16th century were opposed by the Catholics of the same century; with bloodbaths, as always happened when opinions or truths were contemporary. Not long ago, when at the Second Vatican Council in the sixties Rome recognized the validity of other religions, Monsignor Lefebvre appeared on the scene. More consistent with dogma and history, Lefebvre declared that the only path to salvation was the Catholic Church. (*Extra Ecclesiam nula salus*). And many followed him or at least agreed. "Vatican II —he said then— has given the impression that one truth could be as good as another. From this has followed a general dissolution of moral values." It is not incomprehensible that this man supported the French right of Le Pen, who preferred Franco and Pinochet over democratic governments, or that he rejected (without shame) the "rights of man" in favor of the rights of God. It goes without saying that he also rejected the right to religious freedom and dialogue with Jews and Muslims. We can accuse this man of anything but inconsistency.

138, CHANGES. In the sixties, the Church recognized (it has had to recognize so many things...) that outside its Catholic structure there are "elements of truth." Now, did those Catholics who slaughtered Moors, Jews, and Protestants think the same? In this change, we see once again the return of a more liberal and tolerant spirit. But as epistemological intolerance is expelled from traditional structures, it takes refuge and multiplies in sects of all kinds and colors, which must coexist in an unstable equilibrium or ignore each other.

XVI: Intolerance

139, IMPOSITION. It is difficult for an absolute truth not to be accompanied by some form of intolerance. Tolerance and its denial are cultural products. A hyena that steals carrion from another is not exercising either of these two faculties; it is merely responding to the predominant instinct of the moment. We could say the same of the Cro-Magnons who exterminated the Neanderthals and the same of Genghis Khan's hordes who ravaged Kiev, driven by the impulse for power, as overwhelming in the creature as its sexual instinct. Those vandals did not seek to impose any truth; the Christian inquisitors, modern revolutionaries, and new Islamic terrorists, however, did.

140, SHEPHERDS. The creatures of Gaia live in an ocean of doubts and metaphysical questions. This is a reality, but there are spirits who do not recognize it and others who cannot bear it. The former are usually hedonists or likable; the latter cling with teeth and nails to an absolute truth. It is common for a creature disturbed by the Enigma to raise a defensive wall around itself, built on two elements secretly hated: reason and logic. Among these terrorists, we find two groups: those who actually kill with bombs in the name of God; and those who would like to do so and condemn it because they have not yet done it. More than three hundred years ago, Blaise Pascal said, "Man never commits evil so joyfully as when he does it out of religious conviction." —In the West, those tasked with exercising psychological terrorism are the self-proclaimed *shepherds.* When this species goes hunting for converts to serve their own salvation, they never hesitate to instill fear and terror in the hearts of their victims. After all, the fear of the unknown is always more powerful than the kindness of the here and now. The hunter will pounce on its prey, sweating and shouting with eyes closed if it is a televised hunt. —These tragic comedians should understand that one thing is evangelizing and quite another is *indoctrination*. Have they never seen one of these indoctrination sessions? A man, with a microphone in one hand and a Bible in the other, with eyes closed and all muscles tense, repeats a phrase or a specific word while shouting. His audience raises their hands, repeats the same, and trembles in a trance. It is then that the supposed mouthpiece of God considers the message and enlightenment have reached their destination. But, truly, would God want a flock of indoctrinated spirits, that is, *dazed*? It seems that these people, from reading the Bible with fanaticism and resentment, have forgotten the sensitivity of the Master. When did Jesus shout at his disciples with such fury? A neighborhood shepherd is supposed to preach *love,* and that is what they talk about. But for those unable to receive so much, the minimum penalty includes the fires of Hell. —Of course, this kind of terrorism is legal, as it should be.

141, EXPERIENCE. Once someone told me I could not speak about religion because I was not a religious man. I paused for a moment, because in some way they were right: I am a religious spirit, but I am not a religious man because my mind knows no certainty. Obviously, they were wrong about the rest. "Sir —I wanted to reply, not without timidity—, if Catholic priests have always given marital advice and now even teach sexual conduct classes, why couldn't an atheist teach theology? "

142, PRIDE. The champions of renunciation do not conceive of themselves as sinners. Have you never heard this kind of people say they have saved their souls? And if they do not say it, they hide it, though not carefully. Have you never had the misfortune of crossing paths with someone who gazes at you from the heights of the Future Paradise? They are easy to recognize because, as I said, they do not make much effort to hide their prize; not only because there are many of them but also because they suppose themselves to be few. They carry few sins, yes, but the good ones. They possess, for example, the worst of sins: that of pride. Huizinga said that in the Middle Ages (a model of religiosity) the Devil's primary attribute was, precisely, pride. "*A superbia initium sumpsit omnis perditio.*" Pride was considered a symbolic sin, a metaphysical character: the pride of Lucifer. In contrast, greed (*cupiditas*) had no theological implication. It was, simply, a sin of this world. I understand that it must have been in this same sense that men as distant as Carpocrates and Martin Luther considered self-humiliation as a kind of path or requirement for salvation. The Egyptian recommended immorality; the German, self-humiliation as the foundation of all virtue. And it cannot be said that neither Calvin nor Luther knew what they were talking about when they spoke of pride.

143, CULTURE. Catholic priests are more tolerant people than neo-Protestant pastors. Of course, they have a long history that should shame them. Protestant pastors also have reasons to be ashamed, but they do not know as much history as Catholic priests.

144, VIOLENCE. Generally, philosophers have been tolerant creatures; *but not their followers.* For struggle, a certain kind of madness is always necessary, a forgetting of what one is fighting for. But, in fact, the atrocities on Gaia begin with a truth solidly justified by some discourse. As early as the 11th century, the Persian mathematician, skeptic, and heavy drinker Omar Ibn Khayyam had written a piece of advice that was later successfully forgotten: "Ensure that your neighbor does not have to suffer from your wisdom." In all wars, the truths that provoke them are mere spectators of the crimes committed by their followers. During the Cold War, for example, one of the guiding maxims was: "The ends justify the means." And the means of both ends were tragically the same. The victims of Vietnam or Prague knew the same: persecution, torture, and death. Neither the soldier nor the guerrilla, in the most intense moments of the struggle, finds the ideological objective clearer than the success of the combat itself. This, which is reasonable in a battle, in a chess game, becomes absurd when the confusion tends to perpetuate itself. Then, the ends are forgotten in the prolonged exercise of the means. — Epistemology discourages the use of force to prove ideas. The pretension of imposing ideas by force is a common sentiment, and its concession is a doubly irresponsible act, because ideas are often flawed or mistaken, since they originate in an organism programmed to fail without warning; and because violence is an irreversible experience. "Principles," on the other hand, are more reliable. Also for another double reason: because, by definition, they are simpler and clearer; and because they are born in an organism that, when it fails, gives warning: the heart.

145, DIFFERENCES. It is easier for creatures to recognize what is different among various elements than what they have in common. Especially when those elements are themselves. If a thousand men and women were selected by the color of their hair and eyes, by height, skin type, facial features, and some temperamental characteristic and confined to an island, in a short time we would have racial and caste divisions again. These differences, which are sometimes fruitful, are generally tragic. Something similar also happens at the level of ideas or faith. When, through a social or religious revolution, one truth is imposed over others, new divisions appear within it. These divisions, seemingly subtle, over time are capable of repeating the bloody struggles that provoked the previous differences. If the old common enemy does not reappear, the differences that were initially subtle will become radical. We know that Ulrich Zwingli, one of the founders of Protestantism, was harshly opposed by Luther. Proportionally, he was burned and quartered by the rest of the Catholic Christians of Zurich. Contrary to what is generally believed, Michael Servetus was not incinerated for his contribution to medicine (the circulation of blood had already been discovered centuries earlier by Ibn al-Nafis). He was condemned by Christians for being one of them, although *somewhat* different: respectful and believing in God,

Mary, and Jesus, he had the audacity to deny the Trinitarian ideology. Among those who sent him to the stake was Calvin, and he would have done the same with Nicolaus Copernicus if the eccentric astronomer had published his theory before dying. (Of him, the religious man had said: "Who dares to place the authority of Copernicus above that of the Holy Spirit?"). Not to be outdone, currently, in Pakistan, Shiites and Sunnis resolve their differences within Islam—also with violence. —Let us see more. In revolutionary France, the Jacobins and Girondins sent King Louis XVI and his sycophants to the guillotine. With the absolute monarchy eliminated, the enemy of the assembly and the people, internal struggles emerged. The common objective had been fulfilled, so it remained to fulfill the particular objectives. Hébert, one of the main leaders of the Commune, proposed changing the Christian rite for an exotic cult, at the time, to the goddess Reason. In the autumn of 1795, at Notre-Dame, the Hébertists performed this contradictory rite. Danton and Robespierre reacted by sending Hébert and his reasonable followers to the guillotine. A few months later, the same happened to Danton, by order of Robespierre, and then to Robespierre by order of someone else. The Great Differences were resolved at the guillotine, and the small ones as well. By then, the guillotined were counted in the tens of thousands, with an average of thirty per day, according to the truth of the moment. Some centuries later, at the beginning of the Russian Revolution, Bolsheviks and Mensheviks fought together against the despotic power of the tsars. In 1918, Tsar Nicholas II was assassinated along with his entire family. Once in power, the Bolsheviks began the well-known process of ideological purification. The same fate that befell the Whites awaited those who could not agree on which was the best Red and lost in the court of public opinion. They were then accused of being "reddish," which was tantamount to saying "white. "

146, WELL-MEANING. The Inquisition killed in the name of God; the French Revolution in the name of liberty; Marxism-Leninism in the name of equality. During the past 20th century, God, Liberty, and Equality represented absolute truths, dear to noble and diverse spirits. For each group of creatures, the imposition of their truth was essential to the destiny of Humanity. But modern Liberty opposed God, according to fundamentalists; socialist Equality opposed Liberty, according to capitalism; and religion and opium opposed the Equality of the people, according to Marxists. —During the past 20th century, blood was always shed in the name of God, Liberty, and Equality. We think that in the next century, blood will continue to flow, though it will no longer need such noble excuses to do so.

147, VICE VERSA. In matters of prejudice, political, racial, and religious persecution, *vice versa* always works. Please, let us not forget this if we wish to have something called "self-criticism." Criticism is always less effective than self-criticism, because the former produces radical reactions and the latter corrects them.

148, POST-AGE. At the end of this century, the wise do not agree on the name our time should bear. Variations have been tried, not without a desperate and proud originality that links them to grandmothers and midwives. Everyone wants to baptize the child: thus, we live in a postmodern, postindustrial, posttraditional (A. Giddens), post-European, posthistorical, postsexual, Posthonor (A. Ahmed), *postscarcity* (Ivan Illich —only among developed countries), postmortem society. Some geniuses reject the prefix "post" in favor of another that means the same: "trans." For now, the only thing that is clear to us is that ours is a "post" time. —And since we are in a "post" era, that is, *a time of returning from everything*, no one thinks there is anything absolute worth living and dying for. Now, the greatest flaw of the "postage" is that anyone can say the first thing that comes to mind. And I believe its greatest virtue is that they no longer kill for it (which does not mean they no longer kill).

149, DEMOCRACY. Even the dictatorship of the proletariat was considered "power of the people," which in Greek and Soviet was pronounced *dêmokratía*. Also, an electoral system is often the best system the rich can aspire to in order to legitimize their financial empires. Therefore, every democracy is, paradoxically, an aristocracy. What we call "democracy" in our time actually means "tolerance," so we should call it *tolerocracy* or something similar.

XVII: Cosmogony of Evil

150, PAIN. We know that pain is inherent to all forms of life. But we also suspect that evil is unique to metaphysical creatures. Or the idea of Evil. Because Evil is the metaphysics of pain, and there is only one species of metaphysical animals on Gaia.

151, ORIGIN. For many mythologies and for scientific thought, the multiple Universe originated from unity. It is the *cosmic egg* of the ancient Egyptians, it is the *Big Bang* of Alexander Friedmann. The multiple exists because the original unity was disturbed by duality. Every myth about Creation assumes the sacrifice of some god, the tension of a pair of opposing forces. This original disturbance is, in itself, contradictory, as it implies an addition *ex nihilo* to nothingness or to the first Being. Which only *seems* absurd. (Something similar was proposed in 1973 by a scientist, Edward Tryon, when he suggested the possibility that the Universe emerged from nothingness, from a fluctuation of the void.) —Parmenides resolved this paradox by denying all creation. His phrase, "what is not cannot come to be," was translated more than two thousand years later by Lavoisier: "nothing is created nor destroyed; everything transforms." A creationist perspective might solve the problem by starting from the One-creator to whom nothing is added. However, assuming a doubt, an original tension between two elements or between pairs of opposites, ultimately refutes the original Unity at some point. To explain the existence of Evil from Good (God), it is necessary for the Creator to be opposed by an external and novel element. An element coming from a kind of "perverse nothingness." A similar and less abstract thought was conceived by those Gnostics of the 2nd century: the world can only be the work of an evil spirit.

152, CONDEMNATION. At one time, the unfaithful were threatened with *nothingness.* Until it had to be pointed out that in a painful world, the idea of ceasing to exist entirely was not so terrible. It also had to be noted that far to the East, the same threat was, precisely, an aspiration. Then a change in evangelizing strategy was decided upon, and a less abstract but more effective one was chosen: nothingness was filled with the fire of Hell. It wasn't even necessary to invent it, because Vesuvius or the Greeks had already done so, as always. —Of course, the inevitable question followed: is Hell eternal? For the threat to be coherent and, above all, effective, the answer must be yes. But if Hell is eternal, two other possibilities arise: 1) God has forever lost control over a part of His creation; 2) God also governs *that part, and Evil would be one of His attributes. Someone in Birmingham observed that pantheism was incompatible with Christian doctrine, because if the metaphysical creature is part of God, the evil of the creature would also be in Him. Faced with this puzzle,* I believe pantheism could only be resolved by denying evil, as Heraclitus did. —Something else here, in 1974, Borges remarked to Sábato that in his opinion, a toothache was enough to deny the existence of an all-powerful God. This observation would be rigorously true if we assume that the Almighty is, at the same time, All-Good. If God allows even a single gram of evil to occur in the world, it is because He wants it to happen or cannot prevent it. If there truly is a struggle between Good and Evil, then God does not yet fully control His own creation. Or, as Isaiah says (45-6): *"There is no one besides me. I form the light and create darkness, I bring prosperity and create disaster. I, the Lord, do all these things."* Peter Abelard, after justifying Judas's betrayal using Scripture itself, also wrote: "Who does not know that the devil himself does nothing more than what God permits? [...] His power comes from God; his will, however, comes from himself." —The idea of an all-powerful God devoid of even a single gram of evil is impossible for the intellect. This does not prove His nonexistence, since a perfect being must be unintelligible to the creatures of Gaia. According to a logical creature, a God who is infinitely good cannot be infinitely powerful (or vice versa), because, no matter where one looks in Gaia, Evil or suffering exists. (In reality, Evil would be the consequence of an infinitesimal weakness in the Creator; because if we compare the size of Gaia to the rest of the Universe, such a minimal error would have to be concealed.) —The pantheism of the mystics is incompatible with Christianity, which denies evil in God. (The early Christians assumed a provisional Hell; not eternal like God. It was the Council of Constantinople, in the year 543, that abolished the supposed end of infernal torments.) But the idea of an eternal Hell is more persuasive and entirely contradictory: a victorious God by demolition would not leave that province of the Universe in the hands of His worst enemy. Perhaps that is why many Anglican clergy have refused to accept the idea of perpetual punishment. Already in the 2nd century, the Alexandrian Origen had warned that Hell could not be absolute because an absolutely benevolent God could not abandon any of His creatures. Of course, this statement is more sentimental than obvious.

153, LOYALTY. But if the intellect rejects the idea of an all-powerful God devoid of evil, faith confirms it. Because neither God nor faith need to be reasonable. And the more God is attacked by logic and thought, the more reasons the faithful will have to believe in Him. Because the basic premise of every believer is to stand by His side in the worst moments, no matter the cost. And if something as prestigious as logic or reason denies Him, or seeks to deny Him, even better: such a test would only leave the *true* believers standing (besides, Logic will never condemn anyone to Hell, even if it is insulted). I imagine it was in this sense that Tertullian formulated the famous phrase attributed to Saint Augustine: "*Credo quia absurdum* (I believe because it is absurd)." An intellectual stance that is more honest and more intelligent than that of those loudmouths who try to prove God through reason. Because if it is unbearable to see a scientist who believes they can overcome religious problems using the methods of their trade, it is equally unbearable to see a theologian trying to prove their articles of faith with scientific, or metaphorically scientific, proofs.

154, OMNISCIENCE. One of the most famous attributes ascribed to God is that of testing the faith of His creatures. He did so with Abraham, and the anecdote served Kierkegaard to become famous by commenting on it with arbitrary rigor. However, it must be acknowledged that the *need* to test a creature only distresses the other creatures. Especially those who make a living in police stations and courtrooms. What need does an omniscient Being have to test His own knowledge? Did God doubt what the patriarch would do? Another argument refers to

God's intention to stage a *mise en scène* that, like in Greek theater, would serve as a moralizing example. Well, but that is already a digression on the will to test the creature, which compromises the omniscience previously attributed to the Creator. —I remember one day, while resting in a small restaurant in the old city of Jerusalem, I came up with a story that I hope never to publish. The plot revolved around the apparent theological contradiction between freedom and predestination. The protagonist, following in my own footsteps, arrived in Jerusalem from Jericho. After overcoming several border inconveniences, he headed to the holy city. At one point, the road split into two, and K had to choose one without knowing which was the correct one. In the old city, K. reflected: "Two irreconcilable principles: 1) God is omniscient, He knows the future; 2) the human creature possesses free will (for which it was punished and for which it is capable of saving itself)." At the time, K.'s discovery seemed to me terribly clear and filled me with that sadness that accompanies reasoning that contradicts our best hopes. But the story did not end there. Soon, another of those imaginary beings appeared to respond to the first. Perhaps because of the apparent fatalism of the argument or because I was surrounded by Arabs, this new character was a Muslim. K. told him how he had arrived in the city after doubting which path to take. Then he recalled several Quranic verses that assert that the destiny of men is already written (On my own, I verified that in sura III-148 it is said: *"Even if you had remained in your homes, those whose death was written on high would have gone to succumb in this very place..."*) And yet, Amin, the Muslim, the fatalist, insisted on defending the freedom of metaphysical creatures.

"It is they who choose to save themselves or be lost forever."

"If it was written that I would arrive in the city today," reasoned K., "if God already knew it, then it was not I who decided to take the correct path at the Jericho crossroads."

But Amin insisted: "Now that you've told me how you got here, I know it. Now I know that you took the path to the West and not the other one that goes South. But, by knowing your choice, do I suppress anything of the freedom you exercised this afternoon?"

XVIII: On Theology

155, THEOLOGIANS. Let us imagine that known history had been different from what it was; that the Second World War never occurred and no Jews were killed between 1939 and 1945; that the *Belle Époque* was merely a pictorial movement; that in 1962 a nuclear catastrophe devastated Cuba and the United States, and now Washington and Moscow are radioactive wastelands; that six million Christians perished between 1989 and 1994 at the hands of a Zionist or Islamic plot; that a miracle vaccine eradicated hunger in India and Somalia. Let us imagine any variation on the destiny of creatures on Gaia. Let us raise up ideal states or plunge entire nations into catastrophe. It does not matter how historical or individual events unfolded. The theologians will arrive where they wanted to arrive; of course, always through reality and Revelations.

156, THESIS. No Holy Scripture has any need to respect logic or science. There, above all, miracles are recorded; and miracles are, by definition, inexplicable phenomena that are not bound by experimental laws. Any fact, real or surreal, preferably impossible, that is recorded in a sacred Scripture, can be recognized as true.

Why? Because yes, because everything *told* there is true, without taking into account any circumstance, such as the fact that the Holy Books were generally written by many men and then selected according to the judgment of many others. Now, if it is not possible to prove the impossibility that the walls of a city were brought down by the sound of trumpets, that a great river or sea split in two to let a people pass, that the dead rose from their graves, then why waste so much paper trying to prove, scientifically or with common sense, the truth contained in a canonical statement. Why waste time trying to prove something that, by sacred principle, *should not* be questioned? Is it not, after all, the *metaphysical intuition* the most important aspect of a sacred text? Would it not be more natural, or justified, to delve deeper into that inner knowledge rather than that other inclination, a kind of historical epistemology?

157, EXCUSES. Martin Luther also insulted Copernicus, of course. "This fool," he said of him, "wants to turn all of astronomy upside down; but the Holy Scriptures say that Joshua commanded the sun to stand still, not the earth." After a careful study of the Scriptures, the Inquisition that accused Galileo concluded as follows: "The first proposition, that the Sun is the center and does not move around the Earth, is foolish, absurd, false in theology, and heretical, because it is precisely the opposite of the Holy Scriptures. The second proposition, that the Earth is not the center but moves around the Sun, is absurd, false in philosophy, and opposed to the true faith from a theological point of view." Well, theology has had more intelligent and less insulting representatives than those who drafted this statement. With greater seriousness and on the same writings, Darwin was refuted in the 19th century and recognized a hundred years later. In 1996, Pope John Paul II, yielding to the persuasive Englishman, said that "while the body of man may descend from the ape, not his *spiritual soul*." Content, the Darwinians, after correcting Genesis and one step away from canonization, did not even bother to replace the word "ape" with "primate." If you cannot defeat your enemy (they say), join them.

158, FAITHFUL. In October 1996, a plane crashed into a church in Ecuador and killed thirty people. Like other objects that were not destroyed, the statue of the Virgin also suffered no damage. Just as Voltaire saw the absence of God in a tragic earthquake, the faithful Ecuadorians saw in this accident a miraculous sign. With tears in her eyes, a woman said that if it were not for the Virgin, the plane would have continued to destroy her house as well. Which, put another way, would sound very ugly. —It seems that a historical event, like the German occupation of Paris or the fall of the Berlin Wall, can change a political creed; but it can hardly do anything to the faith of a creature. Changes come from within, and events can only precipitate them. But faith in God or in His absence does not depend on *facts.* In 1989, the theologian Hans Jonas wondered what God was doing when His people were being killed in Auschwitz. I believe the answer is: He was doing the same thing He would have done if no one had died in Auschwitz. Though we will never know.

159, ORTHOPEDICS. One of the common tasks of theology is to reconcile current ethics with the Scriptures or Tradition. For this, one resorts (as Galileo Galilei already observed) to allegorical interpretation. Or to *rationalization.* Môhan Wijayaranta once wrote: “If Buddhism says that a being was born poor because their *kamma* was rooted in greed and avarice, it is not to ‘institutionalize’ poverty, but to exemplify how things happen in *samsara*: the poverty of the individual is the result of their own greed.” This is equivalent to saying that if the law states that a creature is imprisoned because they committed homicide, it is not to justify the prison system but, simply, to exemplify how things work in criminal law: the individual’s incarceration is the result of their crime.

160, SECOND. A brilliant Uruguayan theologian (almost all theologians are brilliant), Juan Luis Segundo, once wrote: "When, for example, someone claims that it is God who has ordained that the rich be rich and the poor be poor, they are speaking of a being entirely different from 'my' God. For this God seeks to liberate the poor from their inhumane poverty. It is of no use to say that we are both speaking of the same infinite being, creator and ruler of the universe. Because in one case the statement would indicate that the entire universe is governed by one value, and in the other, by its opposite." If this is not true, it is at least logical (setting aside the aforementioned divine failure to combat poverty). With these words, not only is the Hindu custom of identifying all gods and all religions (masters of "non-violence "...) dismantled; the heart of almost all monotheisms is also struck. Without mentioning them, Don Segundo swept over the doctrine of predestination and over the others as well. The God of the Christian Calvin is *another* god and not his. Well, the theological conclusion is evident: if there are at least two gods and we assume monolatry as an obligation, which of the two is worshiping the wrong god, that is, the Devil? It is also clear that an honest reasoning like Segundo's is also dangerous; at least in the hearts of religious spirits, like Calvin's and so many others.

161, HERESY. A pharaonic warning closes the last book of the Bible: "*I warn everyone who hears the prophetic message written in this book: If anyone adds anything to these things, God will add to them the calamities described in this book. And if anyone removes anything from the prophetic message written in this book, God will remove their share from the tree of life and from the holy city described in this book.*" Of course, it remains to be seen whether "this book" is the original book of Saint John or one corrected by some heretic. Because heretics have never been lacking in the history of religions, and, in fact, the same prophets, founders, and reformers were, to some degree, "heretics." —Heresy means *selection*, and it is known that in the European Middle Ages, and later, those who dared to select any part of the Dogma or the Scriptures were burned. But if one looks closely, since then every sect or modern church owes its existence to the selection of some paragraph or phrase written in the Bible. Moreover, the Catholic Church and all its derivatives are the result of a *selection* of four gospels out of more than sixty, according to the judgment of some priests who gathered to discuss in Nicaea in the year 325. The chosen writings, which were neither the most famous of the time nor the oldest, later became canonical Scriptures, while the others, now apocryphal, were censored with increasing fanaticism. — To avoid similar alterations in the Quran, Muslims, not without a certain naivety, counted the sacred book word by word. But this careful work did not prevent divisions from arising within Islam. Divisions that were sometimes tragic. Because, as in other religions, the differences are not in the Scriptures but in the readings. If one reviews the history of Christianity, almost all sects and isms owe their existence to the art of interpretation. And the interpretation of others is always a form of heresy, as it alters the original meaning. —Theology also selects, but it is also obligated to add its own commentaries and corrections. We know that these two endeavors consist of denying by affirming; if not the Scriptures, at least the commentaries of others.

162, INVERSION. Like ethics, theology is a reflection on principles that are not meant to be questioned. A fertile theology, or at least a justified one, should concern itself with the corollaries that derive from its a priori Truth. What does God want from us? Why did He create this world? Is Gaia the center of the Solar System, or at least the center of the Universe? Do the Scriptures contain the answer to these kinds of questions? Is it really important or inevitable that such answers exist in a book like the Bible? (If so, how does one deduce the Theory of Relativity using the Kabbalah or some similar apparatus?) And so on. —But that is not the common practice. I believe that since the end of the Middle Ages, the greatest perversion of theology has been, precisely, the inverse path: the pretension of confirming the unquestionable Truth based on new data from reality. Because these new data (now scientific) were presented to theologians as Unquestionable as the Scriptures. If not more so. Hence, they imposed upon themselves a deceptive, obvious, predictable, or tautological task: to prove something that is a priori unquestionable.

XIX: The Containers of the Soul

163, EGYPTIANS. In the time of Osiris, the fate of the disembodied soul depended on its previous actions, which were later classified as good or bad. Life on Gaia was singular, and everything was decided there. Each creature had a limited time within which all opportunities for salvation fit. The Egyptian people were a historical people, surrounded by a concrete past and obsessed with the perpetuation of the present. They could conceive of the future and aspired to eternity; but an eternity not entirely liberated from matter. Obsessive conservatives, they did not build the pyramids and the Sphinx so that the sands of the desert or Napoleon's spears could easily erase them. They preserved their dead and their particular histories in anticipation of a kind of dress rehearsal for the Final Judgment.

164, SEMITES. According to Sigmund Freud and other contemporaries, the primitive Hebrew religion was born from a reaction against the ancient Egyptian religion, in Tell-el-Amarna, ancient *Akhetaton*; its true founder would have been Pharaoh Amenhotep IV, and Moses one of his ministers, his successor. This reaction would have led not only to a rigid monotheism but also to the denial of a life beyond death. Whether because it could not resist this last Egyptian temptation, or because no religion lacks some kind of eschatology, the Jews did not abandon this important metaphysical terrain. —Almost fifteen hundred years later, Christ (contradicting some Jewish sects) once again emphasized the ancient hope of resurrection and the equally ancient fear of the Final Judgment. Six hundred years later, Muhammad, contradicting the idolatry and the irrepressible poetic spirit of the desert Arabs, renewed the Christian promise of a new existence. Once again, eternity depended on that confused and fleeting moment that is life.

165, RESURRECTION. Some sects that affirm the resurrection of the body reject cremation and fear the mutilation of corpses, since the body (they say) will one day rise to become the seat or inseparable part of the soul again. No religion can be expected to have logic, let alone common sense; but neither can we be forbidden from exercising these two banalities of the intellect. For example, we are given to think that a miracle that restores youth to a pile of assembled bones does not need much more to do the same with a pile of scattered bones. Nor would it be a greater miracle to do the same with a pile of dust, since, according to Genesis, that was the first thing God did when He thought of a man, and what Buddhists and Hindus fear He might do again. Undoing the process of fire should not be more miraculous than reversing the slow and unpleasant decomposition of the body. And imagining obstacles to the Divine Will is, in a way, a blasphemy or a new contradiction.

166, INDIANS. Unlike the Egyptian-Hebrew tradition, the Hindus conceived of *samsara* and sought to liberate themselves from it. After the triumph of the Aryan knights, for a Hindu, the only way to ascend the social ladder was by dying first. But their greatest aspiration was to dissolve once and for all into a kind of virtuous nothingness, *murti* or *nirvana.* A similar aspiration was that of Buddha, who also recognized two valid objectives: to engage in good *kamma,* to be reborn in heaven; or to renounce all *kamma*, even the good, to cease being reborn. Of course, according to the master, this latter choice of Nibbanic Buddhism was superior to the former, as it eradicated at its root everything that could be existence. Even happiness. This perspective, which must have excited J.L. Borges in his worst moments, is abominable to any Western religion. And it must have been so for those spirits of the early Middle Ages, as for a long time they wielded it as a threat.

167, INTERPRETATIONS. They say Buddha said: "Wherever there is shadow, there is light." Someone who heard him crossed the border and repeated it in China, and there they said that this was the principle by which the Universe moved: the *yin* and the *yang*. In Greece, a disciple of Heraclitus merely observed that if one did not exist, the other opposite would not exist either. In a European monastery, a theologian wrote that the Asian had meant that God was everywhere, and another, before dying at the stake, commented that the phrase meant that Evil was projected by Good through man, since Good had created everything. A scientist in France reasoned similarly, though he did not derive two parts from one: he said that shadow was caused by light and that this principle was not reciprocal. But just at the beginning of the 20th century, physicists proved him wrong: Buddha was speaking of "black body radiation." A few years ago, a classmate of mine copied the phrase in computer letters and hung it on a wall, replacing another that, according to her, said the same thing but was not as beautiful: "Whenever it rained, it stopped." I don't really know what Buddha meant, but I suspect that when he said it, the shadow pained him, and he blamed the light for projecting it.

168, CONTRADICTIONS. A good Hindu must not feed on another animal. According to the Jains, they must not even step on an ant. Although the body is the prison of the soul and upon death it becomes empty, it is strictly forbidden to consume the container. Nor should one kill a rat crawling through the garbage, though perhaps by doing so, one would be doing it a favor by accelerating the process of transmigrations that will one day lead it to become a good Hindu. When a tiger reaches the state of a woman and then ascends to being a Hindu, it will conceive of existence in a way that makes the final achievement difficult. Because just as a people aspiring to liberate themselves from life, they happen to be the possessors of innumerable bodies that perpetuate the sentence. It would have been less problematic to conceive of a metaphysics of nothingness, like Sartre's. In this way, they would not only preserve the tradition of abhorring existence but also the achievement, disappearance, would be inevitable. Of course, if it had been so, Hinduism would not be a religion but a philosophical doctrine. And this suggests something to us. The aspiration of the individual has always been to conquer death; this aspiration predates religions. But the aspiration of every religion is always subsequent to its cosmological conception. The perception of reality is always posed as a *problem,* which religion seeks to resolve.

169, REPRESSION. The peoples of the Ganges possess one of the most vital and sensual spirits known in history. To realize this, one need only glance at their plastic art, their mythology, and their festivals. Everywhere, the sensual, the colorful, explicit sex, *tantra*, the *yoni* and the *linga*, unbridled exuberance appear. And, on the other hand, the unsurpassed asceticism, the condemnation of bodily life as an eternally painful experience. — But these are only apparent contradictions, as sensual exuberance and condemnatory asceticism often feed off each other. Saint Augustine, for example, was a libertine before dedicating himself to asceticism. "In lust and prostitution, I have spent my strength," he once acknowledged on paper. Something similar occurs in the Islamic world. The "condemnation" of women has a historical root in sensuality. The Arabs who preceded Muhammad were not only idolaters; they were also hedonists, fond of poetry and festivals. It would be almost impossible to understand how a people who produced *One Thousand and One Nights* (one of the most celebrated exercises of the imagination), the harems of dancers and drunken poets like Omar Khayyam, also produced the Quran, the fevered Taliban, the repeated condemnation of any kind of literature, and the mummification of women. On the same sands where the art of swaying hips was once venerated, the display of lips and arms was condemned. And if they were not prescribed dark glasses, it is because in the 7th century they did not yet exist, for no part of the human body is as sensual as the eyes that gaze. And it is in this art of gazing that women in the Middle East exercise their eroticism and the audacity to seduce.

170, PHANTASMAGORIA. The custom of the wake does not have, as is often said, a merely forensic purpose (ensuring that the suspect is truly dead before burial). No custom related to the critical events of life has simple utilities. In a tradition so ancient, there must lie a symbolic purpose: to see the deceased and expose them to other family members for collective confirmation. This magical precaution will confirm the impossibility of the departed's return in a phantasmagorical form. It is not unrelated that even the most atheistic creatures clamor to bury their disappeared relatives in ritual, under inexplicable circumstances.

171, FUNERALS. As renegade heirs of ancient Egypt, the faithful and the infidels of the three monotheisms continue to preserve the bodies of their dead. According to O. Spengler, "there is a profound relationship between the way historical past is interpreted and the conception of death manifested in the funerary forms. The Egyptian denies corruption, the [ancient Greek] reaffirms it through the entire language of his culture." He then recalls that the custom of cremating the dead existed in the time of Homer, though it is even older. Ancient drama does not tolerate historical themes but mythological ones. The Hellenes opposed plastic portraiture. The myth denies what is the object of history: common existence, and does so in favor of another, ideal or superior one. And in the East, because rebirth is considered a punishment, the bodies of the dead are not preserved. The body is the prison, and like all prisons, it must be destroyed. The funerary practice, therefore, is cremation. With fire, the solid body becomes immaterial smoke, and what remains of it must be cast into the waters. This practice, besides being convenient in an overpopulated and poor country, fulfills a probable symbolic ritual: what is not erased by fire is washed and scattered by the waters. Water and fire are the agents of disappearance. Thus, like the spirit of Brahma, the creature dissolves forever into the infinite Cosmos.

XX: MATTER AND ANTIMATTER

172, DISILLUSIONED. For the peoples of the Indus and the Ganges, existence is a painful experience. Hinduism has no birth date or personal founders; it was the result of millions of beings, and it is very difficult to imagine the psychological conditions under which it emerged. Buddhism and Jainism, on the other hand, have historical births and concrete founders. Both Siddhartha Gautama and Jina Vardhamana were princes or lived as such. As was customary in modern times, revolutionaries belonged to the upper class or were educated and willing to mobilize large masses of people. As happened with other famous men, their spiritual crisis struck around the age of thirty. Princes or sons of wealthy merchants, Buddha and Jina were surrounded from childhood by the material pleasures of wealth. Yes, it is true that any of those "princes" today would enter through the service door of any modern bourgeois. But it is not the quality of the comfort they enjoyed that is important, but the simple fact that *they were aware of their privileges*. And when they left their palaces, they witnessed the worst misfortunes of this world, which is to say that they then discovered "reality." Anyone who has traveled that part of Asia can imagine it, two and a half thousand years later. The conclusion is predictable: *the world is much worse than it already seemed*. That is why it is not incomprehensible that these young lords decided to abandon their palaces to dedicate themselves to mendicancy and asceticism. Siddhartha Gautama did not belong to the religious caste of the Brahmins, nor did he lack the metaphysical framework of what is now Hinduism. Buddhism could only have been founded by a high-class Hindu, free from the obligations and rigid traditions of the Brahmins.

173, NATURE. In the East, the reality of matter was less consistent than in the West. The Eastern spirit abhors the material world. But neither the Egyptians nor the Hebrews could despise matter because, though perishable, it was also the work of God. Moses, the founder of the Jewish religion, among other material benefits, promised the faithful a piece of land; not the liberation of the flesh or Paradise. It will be with Christ and, above all, with the early Christians that this Eastern tendency to distance oneself from the material world will become evident. In the first centuries of this era, intellectuals limited themselves to studying the Scriptures because everything one needed to know was contained within them. The most important thing was the heavenly Kingdom, which is why the study of nature and the exercise of reason, two themes dear to the Greek spirit, were abandoned and despised. It was the Scholastics of the 12th century who turned their attention back to the material world and the practice of reason. (Hugh of Saint Victor understood that nothing in nature is so superfluous that it does not deserve to be investigated; understanding the physical world was necessary for mystical and religious contemplation.) The Scholastics opened a Pandora's box; they unleashed an intellectual and spiritual revolution in pursuit of confirming a faith that had until then been unquestionable.

174, DECEPTION. Heirs of the Judeo-Christian tradition, the Muslims also did not despise the material world. In fact, they considered its study as one of the many paths that lead to God. It was precisely this same ideological and dogmatic principle that saved and reproduced a large part of Greek culture; from which nothing would have remained if those Muslims had been like the fundamentalists of today. A thousand years later, Luther and Calvin prepared their own spiritual paradoxes. I believe it is unnecessary to repeat the capitalist implications of Protestantism, a theological product exercised upon the most anti-capitalist book in the West. —Matter received a different treatment in the East. For Hinduism and its derivatives, the material world was never a source of truth but of deception. Truth is achieved precisely by severing the bond that connects the world to creatures: *the senses.* This is the basis of the ancient practice of yoga, of which the West has only preserved the name and the mimicry. Under these conditions, it is easy to imagine that something like the Industrial Revolution or Marxism would never have taken place in India.

175, RECONCILIATION. In the West, when the world ceased to be unpredictable and became a more or less controllable element (if not in practice at least in superstition), it ceased to be fearsome and became an object of pleasure. It was no longer necessary to atone for moral sins to avoid being struck by lightning; one could be homosexual or incestuous or criminal if one possessed a good lightning rod. And if any of these activities is not common practice among the creatures of Gaia, it is not out of fear of divine punishment but because much of moral customs have survived this divorce. Physical pain also ceased to be fearsome: legs are no longer amputated with saws and half a liter of whiskey; now there are vaccines and anesthetics or, at the very least, sweet euthanasia.

176, BODIES. Apart from Egypt and Israel, the other pillar of Western spirituality was Greece. Let us remember that for the Greeks, the world was body or it was nothing. The Parthenon is a great sculpture. Greek architecture only considers the positive volume, the stone that is present and not the one that is missing. One must wait until the emergence of Roman architecture to see a people work with empty volumes, the great interior spaces like the Pantheon. Greek mathematics is also the expression of *being* that denies or ignores *non-being.* Its geometry deals with full figures like the circle; not the circumference. In arithmetic, the Greeks were unaware of zero because they could not work with something empty. And let us also remember that it was the Hindus who invented zero, which is highly significant. Zero could only have been invented by a people in whose metaphysics *non-being* already existed as an obsession.

177, ONTOLOGY. In the Bible and the Quran, there are no arid abstractions about *being* and *non-being.* Even the simplest ideas are expressed through a historical narrative or a metaphor—when ideas are expressed and not commands. In contrast, the abstractions of ontology were already rigorously practiced in the East; the same intellectual effort required to understand Hegel or Sartre was also necessary to follow the Buddha or the Ganges.

178, RELAPSE. Bronislaw Malinowski, in agreement with others, argued that faith and worship arise from human crises such as birth, adolescence, marriage, and death. "For you must know," says Cephalus to Socrates, "that when a man begins to think that he is going to die, he is filled with fear and concern for things that previously did not trouble him, and the tales that are told about Hades, about the punishment that awaits the wrongdoer, tales that were once laughed at, now transform his soul with the fear that they might be true." Throughout history, religious sentiment has also diminished as the threats from the future have diminished. Since the Scholastics, unconditional faith and authority gave way first to reason and then to science. With anesthesia or the lightning rod, the non-existence of God was not proven. It was simply that He was no longer as necessary. Until scientific optimism also entered into crisis and gave way to what came to be called *postmodernity*. That time of ours, saturated with sects, magicians, pastors, clowns, Taliban, and cybernetic suicides.

XXI: The Transcendent Becoming

179, HELL. For the agricultural societies of prehistory and the earliest civilizations, life on Gaia mattered more than the afterlife. What was important was health and the number of descendants, which is why sex, and the fertility of the land and women were venerated. Many later myths speak of heroes, like Gilgamesh, who sought to steal from the gods the secret of eternal youth. —When the afterlife took root in the creature's consciousness, it did so with rather dark images, perhaps suggested by the state of abandonment and decay of dead bodies. For the ancient Sumerians, the spirits of the dead had to survive in a dark land whose king was the god Nergal and whose ministers were something like demons or malevolent spirits. The poor spirits were doomed to wander eternally, feeding on mud and waste. In Homeric Greece, the inevitable fate of the dead was Hades, a land as gloomy as Nergal's, where souls (or psyche or breath) wandered as shadows, always lamenting all that was lost. And the same was true for the early Hebrews of the Old Testament. All, virtuous and sinners, would one day end up in *she'ôl*, (*sheol*, *hades* or the grave) a land of shadows and lamentations. Thus, one could say that Hell predates Paradise. In many myths of the ancient world, the god who led souls to the afterlife was the god of the underworld (*infernus*, inferior). Paradise, on the other hand, for a long time was a project or an earthly aspiration. It was so for the Babylonians and the Israelites. But a project repeatedly failed and evident to a creature more awake and discontent; which is why it had to take refuge in a time and space irrefutable by experience: the future in Heaven.

180, PARADISE. Perhaps the first representation of Paradise took place among the ancient Egyptians. Unlike the Mesopotamians, the early Hebrews, the ancient Greeks, and the Japanese, the moral conduct of the individual was decisive for a favorable judgment by Osiris. And unlike all later religions, the (re)cognition of the Truth was not as necessary (the Second Tablet was still more important than the First), perhaps because Ignorance was inconceivable. The spirit of every Egyptian had to face, sooner or later, the great judge, Osiris. In the judgment, he was accused of forty-two sins, similar to those found in the *Decalogue*, from which he had to defend himself, if his heart did not betray him, with these words: "I have given bread to the hungry, I have given drink to the thirsty, I have given clothing to the naked.." If the judgment was favorable, the dead achieved eternal happiness in a fantastic land, located to the west. —An inverse doctrine was reasoned by Calvin in the 16th century. For the Protestant reformer, no good action can save the creature; because, if analyzed deeply, every human action is condemnable. The only thing that matters, then, is the recognition of the Truth (even if it is only accessible to the intellect of the chosen).

181, MORALITY. We know that there were cultures that did not aspire to Paradise; and in antiquity, they were not exceptions but the rule. However, certain moral norms were equally observed. The Law meant order and prosperity first, and the favor of the gods later. Therefore, many peoples asked their gods for happiness on earth, not in heaven. Later, for those creatures who could glimpse Paradise, morality was not a path foreign to the gods. Not killing, not stealing, not fornicating are not enough to enter the Paradise of the new religions, as it was in Egypt. But the commission of any of these faults (in addition to ignoring the Truth) could close its doors.

182, TRANSIT. For millennia, creatures had to wander from one place to another in search of survival. Not long ago, just about ten thousand years, they abandoned that nomadic condition and became sedentary. But this new creature could not completely forget its ancient state: that of always being in transit. Only now, *going somewhere* was no longer a physical problem but a metaphysical one. But where to? Monumental and contradictory answers: Osiris, Marduk, the pyramids of the Nile, the liberation of Buddha. It is very significant that the worship of agricultural societies was related to the goddesses of the earth, while nomads venerated the gods of the sky. If for the sedentary the reality was on the ground, for the nomad it was in the stars that accompanied them; not in the path, which was mutable and fleeting. Therefore, the nomad's home was in the sky. —For so many rains, suns, glaciers, and earthquakes, the creature has been an animal *in transit*; with a disguised awareness of its transience. A being that is always (always) passing through all things. It knows this and often questions it; it denies this fleeting world or clings to it with fury. That is, it is either religious or aesthetic.

183, ZEAL. Why does God need (and demand) that above all we believe in Him? According to the Decalogue, Eastern wisdom, and the entire religious history of the West, from Jesus to Muhammad, from Buddha to Pastor Jiménez, to save the soul it is not enough to be a good creature (Servetus thought it was and was burned for saying nonsense); it is not enough to faithfully fulfill the Commandments of the second tablet: first it is necessary to re-*cognize* the Truth. In these cases, a God-fearing criminal has a better chance of receiving divine forgiveness than a harmless atheist. Why? Because for every religion, the priority is the *confirmation* of the proposed truth, the annihilation of existential doubt. And, in this sense, an unbeliever is more dangerous than a repentant murderer.

184, TRUTH. For millennia, creatures have demanded the fulfillment of certain codes of conduct for the realization of peace and happiness on Gaia. But for a long time, they did not think (Sumerians, Hebrews, Greeks, Japanese) that morality determined the creature's fate in the afterlife. The ancient Egyptians did; but their gods, or their God, Osiris, did not develop the zeal to colonize the creature's love for a specific truth. The truth as the main metaphysical urgency will emerge later when creatures confront other spiritual realities, when metaphysical security recognizes the threat of doubt and freedom. Cultural diversity leads to skepticism and fundamentalism: two phenomena of the 20th century that share the same root. All religions that demand unconditional fidelity, almost always under the threat of infernal tortures, emerged in opposition to a specific culture. Let us remember Amenhotep IV, Moses, Buddha, Jesus, Muhammad, Luther.

185, SILENCE. For obvious reasons, creatures are usually more concerned with watching where they step than with stopping for a moment and looking at the horizon. Either they do not want to look or they are not interested, which is also human. A Cuban doctor who lives on San Leonardo Street 335 in Havana read my book *H.* and wrote me a letter saying: "For me, the meaning of existence fits in a grain of corn." I believe you, Javier; I believe you.

186, DEATH. The desire for *non-being* in the East and the desire for *eternal-being* in the West both express the anguish of death. Eternal life means being safe from death. Obvious; but also ending the cycle of reincarnations is to suppress the torturous and repeated experience.

187, RENUNCIATION. With renunciation, the fear of becoming is exorcised. For the religious consciousness, this world is transient, and the best thing is to give everything in exchange for something permanent. Saint Teresa formulated it thus:

Life, what can I give you
To my God who lives in me,
If not to lose you
To better enjoy Him?

The degree of renunciation measures the religious spirit. And its pathology as well. In ancient times, for example, the Jains prescribed suicide to free themselves from the body that bound them to the world. And the same is done today by religious sects in the developed world. A proud variation of this type of suicidal renouncers are the voluntary martyrs. Fearful of what lies beyond, they hasten to abandon the here and now. With the renunciation of one, access to the other is paid for.

188, FEAR. According to the Old Testament, God gave Abraham the long-desired son at an impossible moment. Then He asked for him as a sacrifice, *to test his faith.* However, it must be assumed that Abraham's decision to kill his son was due to a clear and precise order from the Supreme. That is, at no point is his faith at stake, as is often claimed, but rather his *obedience.* The patriarch has faith, but he acts out of fear. I understand that for this statement I will be crucified by several neo-inquisitors from the village that I know. But let us remember that, in its origins, acting out of fear of the Lord was considered the greatest virtue of a creature. That now they are ashamed of it in the name of Love, is another matter. According to Genesis (22-12), the angel says to Abraham: "*Do not do it, for now I know that you fear God, since you have not withheld your only son from me.*" This action, which the Danish theologian Søren Kierkegaard called an "ethical suspension," would today be condemned as attempted homicide anywhere in the world. No matter which god is invoked in defense. No matter how Abrahamic the judge may be. The example of Abraham is clear: here it is the religious spirit that speaks. With it, it should have been made clear that *the First Tablet stands above the Second.* —Now that hierarchical order is inverted. According to this new order, anyone who hears God's command to repeat Abraham's feat will be unanimously condemned. Even by those religious individuals who now praise the patriarch's attempt; perhaps because the "ethical suspension" has been lifted.

189, UNCRITICAL. At times, the fear of the Supreme is explicit, as in the Old Testament or the Quran. Each surah begins with the same expression, unequivocal and unchanging: *"In the name of God, the Most Gracious, the Most Merciful* "; in every church, it is repeated *"Lord, have mercy on us."* Ignoring it implies, according to each religion, a terrible punishment. Today, no pious religious person would dare to criticize even one of the crimes recounted in the Bible as feats, motivated by God's order and not by geopolitical interests. Few religious individuals, if any, would accept the idea that the Bible is imperfect; or that in its writing, at some point, the uncertain hand of a human might have intervened. Because questioning one part would mean questioning it all. (Muslims consider the Quran to be a part of God, therefore it is a perfect and immutable text; the Kabbalists thought the same: the Torah is perfect, therefore every sentence, every word, every letter is significant and unchangeable). —We know that fear is the most powerful uncritical force. And that, therefore, the path is to interpret: where it says *white* it means *black.*

190, ELEVATION. The fear of the Unknown was followed by the fear of the Almighty. Since one cannot converse with an inexplicable phenomenon or one without intelligence, one does so with a Being capable of hearing our pleas and interpreting our good deeds. And who, moreover, is omnipotent and omniscient, the enigmatic repository of all answers inaccessible to creatures. But although in the past the primary bond was fear, no good creature can be denied that their relationship with God is based on pure love. After all, metaphysical creatures are historical beings, and therefore mutable or perfectible.

191, PROCEDURES. If for Egyptian and Mosaic religions salvation was a legal problem, for Buddhism it is a psychosomatic one. Nietzsche had already noted this when in *Ecce Homo* he wrote: "their religion, which I would better describe as hygiene, to avoid mixing it with such deplorable cases as Christianity, made its efficacy depend on the victory over resentment." And further on: "this is not how morality speaks, this is how physiology speaks." An attentive observer will note that no doctrine is more opposed to the philosophy of the German than

Buddhism. Immersed in a reality dominated by the cycle of reincarnations, the repeated experiences of illness, old age, and death, Buddha reacted by denying the experience of being. Nietzsche, on the other hand, challenged that very existence *to be.* Beyond good and evil, he sought to embrace both the joy of living and the pain. Buddha did not; he sought to extinguish pain but also happiness, because one feeds on the other.

192, EXTERMINATOR. For Buddhism, pain is inherent to all forms of life. In the end, even pleasure and happiness signify pain, because they bind the being to material life; that is, to the cycle of reincarnations. Passions and desires lead to action, and through this occupation, the creature cannot attain Enlightenment. 2500 years ago, Buddha said there were no gods nor a creator God, as the Brahmins claimed, but rather a physical-metaphysical continuum, eternal and infinite. This primitive misfit believed the Universe was composed of countless solar systems like ours, full of life. Now, if pain and life can repeat themselves eternally, and to make matters worse, there is no God to help us, understand us, or judge us, the best thing is to end this absurd chain of rebirths. And for that, the creature is alone. It is obvious that, for the Indian spirit, death alone is incapable of achieving definitive liberation. It can only send us back to repeat the process. (Schopenhauer agreed: the world is illusory, and simple death cannot end it. Much less a passionate act like suicide. Because the will, *wille*, was to Schopenhauer what *karma* was to Buddha.) Animals are forbidden from modifying nature. Only the creature, then, can do so. And it will do so by using that which, apparently, most distinguishes it from its lower relatives: *the knowledge of truth*. Buddha not only rejected revelations from tradition; he also disdained cosmogonic speculations as distractions from the true goal. Enlightenment had to be achieved through knowledge but, ultimately, everything depends on the individual, on their personal experience. Pain and death are multiplied by an infinite factor, and the goal is nullification to zero. Dissolving into Brahman or Nirvana. The West, on the other hand, reacts to death by denying it; with a certain optimism, since it assumes there are two lives but only one death, and it is ineffective.

193, PREPARED. Judeo-Christian-Islam inherited its eschatology from ancient Egypt. Every future here on Gaia will one day be past (and trampled), but beyond lies eternity, the incorruptible. Then, this moment became the only real thing in an apparent life, and the only thing that could matter to the creature. Yahweh rewarded and punished in cash; but later, faced with the disobedience of His creatures, He decided to send His Son with a clear message: *We'll settle the accounts in the end.* As in Hinduism, living is preparing for death. The difference lies in the fact that Hindus give their souls countless opportunities for salvation. Judeo-Christian-Islamics, on the other hand, make eternity depend on a single moment, fleeting and confused; that which we call life.

194, RENUNCIATIONS. In the beginning, sacrifices consisted of renouncing a part of what one wished to preserve (a bull, the best of the harvest; though not all bulls nor the entire harvest). Over time, to ensure the absolute enjoyment of all desires in the afterlife, repressed in the here and now, the detachment was carried out on the same scale: it became total and unrestricted. Sex, the body, the pleasure of all things sensual, and all that was most cherished by primitive creatures were stigmatized. But the act of renunciation is not only pathological; it can also be therapeutic as well as wise: The Bhagavad-Gita says, for example: *"Only the person who has renounced all desires to please the senses can find true peace.."* Of course, psychoanalysis disagrees.

195, REWARD. What is lost on Gaia is gained in Heaven. According to Jesus, it is easier for a camel to pass through the eye of a needle than for a rich man to enter the Kingdom of God. From a dynamic perspective, a rich man always has more reasons to fear than a poor one.

And if in fact this is not the case, it is because societies are organized to benefit the former and harm the latter. But any change or disorder can mean a loss for the rich. No poor person would struggle to adapt to the conditions of a rich person's life, but we know that the opposite is almost intolerable and often leads to suicide or madness. Therefore, a creature aware of its privileges has more reasons to fear time or entropy. Like Siddhartha Gautama. Renunciation is the foundation of the religious spirit, and in proportion to it is the reward. —Not only has Christ's advice to not worry about tomorrow been forgotten in favor of capitalist ethics. So too has the metaphor of the camel and the needle. Or almost; in Europe, a Christian millionaire had a needle built with an eye large enough to allow the passage of a camel he brought from the Middle East. Less primitive, Protestant theologians demonstrated that the rich did not need to enter the Kingdom *because they were already in it.* This reassuring idea is also known as the doctrine of predestination and was deduced from the same Scriptures that initially seemed to say the opposite.

196, PREDESTINATION. The doctrine of predestination is as old as the idea of an Almighty God. But during the Reformation, it was also a theological consequence of navigation. Before (and after), Moors and Jews could be infidels and heretics on their own responsibility, as they knew the Books. But not the savages of the distant periphery. They were the responsibility of a cruel or at least negligent God, as they could not be accused of rejecting something they did not know. —The doctrine of predestination contains theological opposites: religion and irreligiosity. After the fatalistic reasoning, the logical conclusion would be the abandonment of ritual and good deeds, since nothing can be done to change one's fate, and it would even be an affront to try. And yet, predestination is as powerful a doctrine as it is ancient. Why? Because although nothing can be done to change destiny, one will never know *who* the chosen are and *what* their fate will be before death (though the renouncers will always claim it for themselves along with good or bad fortune). Faced with this terrible doctrine, the creature is left with the experience of religious anxiety or metaphysical indifference.

197, TRUST. In opposition to the Christian metaphor of the needle and the camel is Calvin's doctrine of predestination, according to which a creature's fate on Gaia has already been predefined by the Omniscient before birth. Therefore, wealth and good fortune in a creature can only demonstrate that it belongs to the select group of the chosen. The psychological process that leads from this doctrine to capital accumulation and obsessive work was already described by Erich Fromm. This idea or form of predestination served to legitimize a new state of European society in the 16th century; *but it was religiously weak*, less cohesive. It is understandable that it was within these societies that secularism first developed, followed by atheism—with their corresponding effects of action and reaction. At the same time that work, capital, and humanism favored the "domination" of nature, a new psychological condition regarding time was consolidated. Men became overly optimistic, and the fear of pain and scarcity became more manageable. (The history of anesthesia itself is allegorical: when it was discovered to alleviate pain, it was already being used as a laughing gas in circuses.) The modern creature has partly mastered its fear of becoming on Gaia, and for this, it has developed not only medicine but also social security systems, insurance policies of all kinds, and provisions even in cases of death. In some corners of Africa, the elderly and sick are abandoned by the riverside. And in not a few rivers of Asia as well. In the modern world, the System takes them to a hospital already paid for by a mutual fund or the government. The modern elderly know that, in the worst-case scenario, their pain will be numbed with a pill. Physical pain, because neither the medical system nor the insurance fee will answer their existential questions.

Similar to anesthesia, the spiritual alternative is often nihilism.

198, LOSS. In *The Decline of the West*, Oswald Spengler refers to cosmic terror: "Only the man who is already a corpse internally —he says—, the inhabitant of the great final cities, the Babylon of Hammurabi, the Alexandria of the Ptolemies, the Baghdad of the Islamic world, the Paris and Berlin of today; only the pure intellectual sophist, the sensualist, the Darwinist, loses or denies that terror, interposing between themselves and the unknown a 'scientific conception of the world' without secrets or mysteries." In his time, Albert Einstein wrote: "The most beautiful and profound emotion we can experience is the sense of the mysterious. It is the source of all true art and science. He who has never felt this emotion, who has never paused to reflect and been captivated in fearful wonder, is as good as dead." More recently, the Norwegian Jostein Gaarder wrote: "To marvel at existence is not something one learns; it is something one forgets. "

199, GOD. If you did not exist, you would still be the main protagonist of history.

XXII: The Sin of Existing

200, AWAKENING. The myth, before being a question, is an answer. Like philosophical thought, it is not devoid of aesthetic conditions, such as that of unity. The myth represents an unconscious response to questions like "Where did this mountain come from? Where did we come from? Where are we going? Where will this mountain go when we are no longer here?" Conversely, philosophy arises from conscious activity (critique, reflection). Before formulating its answers, it begins by posing the questions, or at least pretends to. Between myth and philosophy lies Greek tragedy. Not only because of its moment of appearance; tragedy internalized the world in the metaphysical creature. The ancient gods or demons who guided, disturbed, or doomed the hero became states of the soul first, and mental phenomena later. Thus, they became desire, passion, love, anguish, question, and mystery. Myth, tragedy, and philosophy are intellectual products of the creature moved by nature first, and by itself later. —The myth does not become religion because, on its own, it does not demand any renunciation from the creature, nor the obligation to remain unquestioned. Depending on how the myth is taken, it will become religion (Semitic) or tragedy (Greek). Tragedy continues a tradition but does not respect it: it questions and interrogates it. Its attitude is defiant, rebellious. It is characteristic of the aesthetic spirit of the Greek people. The tragedy and the art of this people demonstrate their boundless audacity before the world. It is an adolescent spirit, an uninhibited people capable of probing and expressing without fear or shame their entire inner nature. So much so that they have supplied modern psychiatry with an infinite collection of symbols: Oedipus Rex, Sirens, Furies, the phallic woman, satyrs with erect penises, maenads, and Dionysian hysteria. The Greeks were the only creatures capable of fornicating with the gods and not dying in the act. That is why the children of such audacity were called *heroes*.

201, BEING. In *The Birth of Tragedy*Friedrich Nietzsche says: "the same instinct that gives life to art, as a complement and consummation of existence destined to continue living, was also what brought forth the Olympian world, in which the Hellenic 'will' placed itself before a transfiguring mirror." And further on: "...inverting the Silenian wisdom: the worst of all for them is to die soon, and the second worst is to die at all." For any religion, the worst of all is the opposite. For the metaphysics of the Ganges and the Himalayas, of course. And for Christians as well. I believe the statement of Jesus (according to John 12:24) is unequivocal: "Truly, truly, I say to you, unless a grain of wheat falls into the earth and dies, it remains alone; but if it dies, it bears much fruit. He who loves his life loses it, and he who hates his life in this world will keep it for eternal life." —Of course, if we don't like it, we can interpret it differently.

202, ART. The aesthetic spirit possesses the will to *exalt* the world, the need and the value of experiencing the world through the senses. But that longed-for world will always be above common reality. This almost always translates into the *search for lost time,* for a time always different from the present. In the transcendence of the present lies the magic of literature, imagination, and the evocation of all art: cinema, painting, music. Even dance, which has as its main "instrument" the most powerful agent of the present time: *the body.* In every dance, we can note a common attitude: the movement of the feet. In every dance or ballet, the feet always strive to lift off the ground, seeking the body's weightlessness.

203, RIVALS. In their most intense moments, religions have always condemned the practice of art. Judaism and Islam rejected the sensuality of images. Even Muslims went so far as to censor more ethereal arts like music and poetry. The Quran says (sura XXVI; 224): "*It is the poets whom the misguided follow in turn.*" As a good revolutionary and reformer, Muhammad acted in opposition to the fundamental elements of the despised order; like Moses, like Luther. Precisely, one of the passions of those desert Arabs was poetry. In Okadh, a market in Hedjaz, poets from all over Arabia would gather once a year to compete in a kind of festival. The best *kasidah* (poems) were written in golden letters in the temple that later became the Kaaba. The Bedouin spirit, like the Greek, loved the beauty of the world, adventure; it cared more for the present than the afterlife. And it was against this independence of spirit that Muhammad fought, in favor of a new Muslim creature, which means *submitted.* Four centuries later, the poet Omar Ibn Ibrahim Khayyam defied Muhammad and the renunciation of the Muslim. He exalted the world, women, happiness, and wine. Perhaps there is a verse that summarizes all his hedonistic skepticism and all his irreligiosity:

As swift as the river's water
or the desert's wind, our days flee.
Two days, however, leave me indifferent:
the one that left yesterday and the one that will come tomorrow.

The only day that matters to the Persian poet is today. But his first two lines reveal that the tragedy of today is becoming yesterday, while the last two rebel against the awareness of tomorrow and the memory of what is lost. That is, in the face of existential observation, he does not choose religious renunciation but its opposite: the challenge of experience. —For its part, Christianity was no less severe with similar spirits. Although during the Renaissance the Catholic Church promoted plastic art as it did, this was due to the strong Hellenization in which it was immersed. Never before had the clergy been further from religious dogmas. At that time, neither the Pope nor the cardinals condemned the audacity of Copernicus; they were so Hellenized that they let it pass with a smile; a tolerance that the Protestants condemned as heresy. And perhaps never before had corruption been so brazen within the Church. (Let us remember that in the time of Leo X, a murderer or an incestuous person could buy the Pope's forgiveness with a few pounds.) But it was not only because of this type of corruption that the Church fell into crisis but, above all, because the "religious factor," renunciation, was diminished by the humanism of the time. A thousand years earlier, Saint Augustine, the African father of the Church and Martin Luther's favorite, had written in his *Confessions*, "To love this world is adultery against you [God]." Luther's reform arose in opposition to the Hellenization of the Renaissance Church. At that time, art burners like Savonarola entered the scene. Andreas Carlstadt, one of Luther's followers, separated in his thought the body from the soul; and considered the former and the entire world as an impediment to salvation. Immediately after, he condemned all artistic expression, plastic art and music, because they distracted the spirit through the senses. In England too, there were Savonarolas after the Anglican Reformation, thanks to whom much of medieval English art has been lost forever. —Christianity is the only one of the three monotheisms that matured among non-Semitic peoples. It is the only one of the three that included in its dogma the worship of a female figure, the cult of the Virgin Mary as the great Mother Goddess; and also the worship of images. But the passion of those early Renaissance popes for painting, sculpture, and music represented a digression too intolerable for the religious spirit. Which is human and impious.

204, SENSES. For Heraclitus, the senses could only perceive diversity and not unity; appearance, illusion, and deception, but not the truth unified by reason. For Hinduism and its variants as well; the senses are not capable of perceiving true reality. Therefore, they can only be an obstacle in the pursuit of Enlightenment. One cannot perceive Krishna if one attends to the senses. Like Socrates, Buddhism prescribes, above all, the elimination of passions, the voluntary indifference to any desire. The senses can only grasp the material world, and it is because of this distraction that man becomes confused and lost. In Calvin's time, one of the therapeutic measures to combat the irreligiosity of the Genevans was the prohibition of the colorful Renaissance attire. Priests dress in black, brown, or similar tones; nuns wear exclusively gray and more decent colors. The goal is (always) to repress sensuality, because sensuality and the senses bind the creature to the material world. In opposition to the renunciation of the religious spirit is the aesthetic or spring spirit. For the doctrine of Eternal Return and for Sartre's existentialism, the world is the exploration and apologia of all its possibilities. Therefore, art is the only thing that can fully justify the life of an anarchic, rebellious spirit.

205, WORK. Hinduism prescribes mendicancy as a virtue. With the metaphor of the camel passing through the eye of a needle, Christ made it (almost) impossible for a rich man to enter Paradise (for which he would have been tortured and crucified twice in the 20th century). All religions aim to contain the materialistic ambition of men. Generally, the path to supreme truth is free of money and the obsessive occupations that lead to it. The Bhagavad-Gita prescribes the near-absolute forgetfulness of any mundane task. Other religions, like Islam, legalized trade and some inferior activities, but this is only tolerance or necessity; like polygamy as a consequence of war. But the Scriptures have always warned of the dangerous forgetfulness or distraction that threatens the worker. With a different spirit, Nietzsche observed the same: "Have you noticed that modern industriousness, scandalous, stingy with its time, self-satisfied, is something that educates and predisposes, more than anything else, to 'lack of faith?'" —According to Huizinga, already in the 14th century in England, poverty began to be disregarded as a virtue and work was sanctified (a human activity not devoid of renunciation). Later, Anglo-Saxon reformers decriminalized gold; but if any of them had foreseen the consequences, they would have burned themselves alive in the square of their town. —The doctrine of predestination led to compulsive work and the religious austerity of saving, which in one word is called *capitalism.* Paradoxically, Calvinism ended up legalizing capitalist ethics when both Calvin and Luther despised this world and even more so the *shopping centers.*

XXIII: THE CHALLENGE TO BECOMING

206, AESTHETIC. With renunciation, the religious spirit suppresses a part of the world; it renounces taking all it can take and places a transcendent and eternal reality above the precariousness of the body. For the aesthetic spirit, on the other hand, the world is a work of art, magnificent or absurd, which it longs to explore and experience. Its principal domain is *being*, amoral experience. Where the religious person experiences mystical ecstasy, the artist experiences aesthetic ecstasy. Both claim eternity, but while the former denies the material world, the latter confirms and exalts it. Even by destroying it.

207, HELLENES. The Greeks neither conceived nor needed the zero in their mathematical or architectural formulations. The zero could only originate among the Hindus, whose metaphysics accounted for *non-being*. An aesthetic religion, if there ever was one, was the Greek. The spokesman of the gods was Homer, a poet. In his poems, no Authority like Yahweh is expressed or highlighted, but rather the beauty of their gods and heroes. The doctrine of Eternal Return, celebrated by a German philosopher who loved Greece, is an unequivocal expression of this spirit. To Zarathustra, he made him say: *And this moonlight, and this spider climbing, and you and I, gathered under this portico, musing on eternal things. Have we not been here before, necessarily? Will it not all be an eternal return?* —The pagan wants to live and therefore does not fear taking it all and throwing his challenge to life. The doctrine of Eternal Return was already in some way implicit in all of Eastern metaphysics: there are infinite Shivas, infinite Brahmas, infinite Buddhas. When the *bodhisattva* throws his bowl into the river, he does not throw one but infinite bowls. But Nietzsche and his doctrine oppose any religion; he refuses to renounce the world and multiplies its possibilities to infinity: what is now will be again. That is to say, what we are seeing is eternity. Nietzsche opposes not only Christianity but also Indian metaphysics, because the cycle of repetitions that perpetuate life and death is not abominable. On the contrary, it is a cause for celebration. (Nietzsche hated Christian renunciation and was not a declared anti-Buddhist because he was not born in India or Nepal.) Good and evil, even pain, are preferable to nothingness or Nirvana. The metaphysical consolation (he says, analyzing the Hellenic capacity for suffering) that true tragedy leaves behind is that, despite all changes, life is indestructible and pleasurable. The Hellene is that man endowed with deep feelings and a great capacity for suffering. The Hellene has penetrated with his gaze the senselessness of history and the cruelty of nature, "and is in danger of longing for a Buddhist denial of the will. Art saves that Hellene, and through art, life saves him for itself. "

208, FAME. Jacob Burckhardt said that the longing for fame was a characteristic and novel trait of the Renaissance creature. Let us say that now it is no longer novel, but it remains characteristic. With fame, men prolong and multiply their own existence in the world. If the Renaissance creature was "pro-Hellenic" by vocation, we are so because we were distracted. For them, for the Hellenes, and for us, fame is a form of immortality, and only heroes or stars achieve it. —The longing for fame is a childish remnant of the ego. It does not seek the love of the mother but the attention of the world. It was the glory of the Greek hero, the confirmation of the solitary Renaissance creature. And, more than anyone, it is the populous solitude of the modern or postmodern creature.

209, NIETZSCHE. The fact that Che Guevara and Marcel Proust were asthmatic does not mean that the illness in each was an irrelevant detail, one that does not explain such different personalities. It only means that in a historical process, the same cause can produce different and even opposite events. But it produces them. —While reading Nietzsche, it is not easy to forget the torments that pursued him or to think: a creature strengthened by pain no longer anguishes over the unpredictable tomorrow. I understand that one cannot reduce the thought of a creature to its psychological conditions. That would be like affirming that Archimedes' principle is only valid for bodies submerged in a bathtub since, according to legend, it was there that the Greek conceived it. However, considering the circumstances, we can understand why a thought arises in one creature before another. Why was Nietzsche a declared "anti-compassionate "? —Well, let us think that morals consist in the abolition of Darwin's laws, in the censorship of the strongest. (Morality, I have come to think, is the consciousness of the species.) It is a statistical fact that today, the most cultured or economically successful creatures do not reproduce more than those below the poverty line. Modern societies have operated an inversion in the savage order: creatures reproduce according to the law of *cultural selection,* which consists of the sexual or reproductive triumph of the "less fit." But the cultural refutation of Darwin does not begin with religious compassion but much earlier; it is as ancient as the last five Commandments. The Confucian principle of not doing to others what one does not wish for oneself is a very old social pact. It can be said that it was one of the first syntheses of the last commandments, even without translating into the positive like the Christian suggestion to love one's neighbor as oneself. Confucius did not have to invent it, but he ensured it was repeated and respected. Translated into the psychology of the primitive creature, it meant: *do not do to the weak what you do not want the gods to do to you*. This formula, which is simple and basic for any society, is called *compassion.* Nietzsche, without gods and without fear of more pain, was a deliberate anti-compassionate. A philosophical translation that would have restored the Darwinian principle in favor of the Superman and to the detriment of humanity.

210, SADNESS. Why does tragedy exist? Why do creatures listen to sad music and become moved? Perhaps because it is in this way that poetry is capable of reversing an inexorable defeat (death, abandonment) into a triumph of the spirit. The devastating solitude of the Inexorable, through the beauty of devastation; the body that falls to its knees and the defiant gaze against the pushing wind. —Art unjustly called depressive cannot depress; on the contrary, it strengthens. And that is why it is called art and not masochism. Tragic poetry is the aesthetic recognition of sadness. Because there is no true depression with beauty. There is none.

211, COURAGE. The guild of depressive geniuses is well known among psychiatrists. The list of famous cases is long and almost entirely signed by artists. Some attempt to explain this phenomenon as a cause or consequence of more developed intellects; all of which does not prevent the existence of another, more justified guild of suicides: the mediocre. But I understand that the aesthetic vision of the world demands from it an intensity that cannot be sustained for long. Like copulation, according to Borges. However, these spirits have their own antidote: the challenge of *being*, inherent to art. The aesthetic challenge can be an existential attitude, if not the best of existentialism. With it, a solid stance toward life is established. Reality remains tragic; it does not change its sign but changes its meaning.

212, LIFE. Fray Luis de León admired the poetry of Saint Teresa, and the saint wrote verses like these:

Life is gloomy
Bitter to the extreme;
Anxious to see you
I desire to die.

Perhaps someone might ask, "if religion condemns suicide, why does it not condemn the religious desire to die?" I believe the answer is simple: the condemnation of suicide is the condemnation of the Second Table, of the social and psychological order; the desire to exchange this world for the other is the metaphysical aspiration of the First Table, of every religious center. —Well, it is true that Saint Teresa used poetry to express herself. But *she used it*, she did not cultivate its original nature (we must distinguish aesthetic ecstasy from mystical ecstasy). Because poetry is the domain of this world. Exalted to the heavens, yes; but exalted, not overturned for its renunciation but for its confirmation. Both poetry and its principal instrument, language, are made to express life; not its negation. It was no coincidence that the Buddha named his deepest knowledge with *silence.* (In Sanskrit *mūni* means, at once, "wise" and "silent.") It was not out of ignorance or indecision that Jesus did not answer Pilate when he asked what the truth was, after the Nazarene had told him that he taught it. Nor was it chance that Saint Teresa resorted so often to the oxymoron: "I live without living in myself/ And so high a life I await/ That I die because I do not die [...] For with life/ one cannot live. [...] Oh, what captivity/ Of great freedom! [...] Let my joy be in weeping,/ My rest in alarm/ My peace in sorrow/ And my calm in turmoil. [...] Let my life be in death [...] In darkness my light [...] It is death that causes life." —The oxymoron violates language to express something that language does not know. Because language and poetry only recognize life.

213, SEA. Borges said that he preferred the plain beneath the hooves of horses to the sea of poets. But one must consider that the sea is responsible for more than one verse. In Europe or America, almost all poets have sung to the

nearby tempest
of the waves
unreachable stillness
of blood and silver
passion of men
on the sand
serene eternity
of the skies;

and for a reason, Chile has as many good poets as people gazing at the sea. Ecuador also has my friend, the poet Freddy Peñafiel. In contrast, Bolivia... How does a Bolivian become a poet without a sea and with a lake called "Titicaca "?

214, LOVE. The religious spirit praises the past and aspires to the future, which is not the future of this world. For its part, art is realized in all times that are not the Present, but are all the other times of this world. In contrast, deep love, like vulgar hedonism, is fully realized in the Present. Love is the most prestigious redeemer of the Present, because it does not seek to deny or change it. It is the only moment when the Present has someone to celebrate it. Because love is one of those few states in which one is happy but also obliged to recognize it.

215, POETRY. It is understandable that the foundations of all poetry are time and love. Sensual love is of this world, which is why it is celebrated by art and cursed or concealed by religion. The aesthetic spirit loves the intense experience of existence and sees the world as a work of art. It mourns the passing moment because it is a loss. And to avoid thinking it is irreparable, it demands or imagines eternity, an eternal return that restores all that is lost.

You must remember this
A kiss is just a kiss
A sight is such a sight;
As times goes by.

XXIV: An Aesthetic Century

216, DIONYSUS. If the 19th century was scientistic, the 20th was a century dominated by the aesthetic impulse. During these years, the pretensions of "art for art's sake" were confirmed; the most defended thesis that art should have no other reference than itself: it must be *self-contained.* Abstract art emerged, according to which a painting is paint, a sculpture is volume, music is sound, a novel is a combination of syntactic techniques, and poetry is, or should be, the mere sound of vowels and consonants. The new and prestigious art form is cinema, and it develops under the purest aesthetic impulse of life for life itself. — Ortega y Gasset saw in the new art of his time and in the popular rise of sports the same attitude: self-containment and corporeality. The same could be said of other phenomena of our time: tourism, which represents, like no other, the aesthetic spirit and its endeavor to *experience* the world; and rock'n roll, whose attitude is characterized by experimentation and provocation, sometimes violent. The defiant attitude of rock toward the experience of the world translates into defiance and rebellion against society, but its root lies in the aesthetic spirit in its rawest forms: *"sex, drugs, and rock'n roll."* —

Even the two world wars are expressions of an aesthetic impulse. If in previous centuries God had been replaced first by reason, then by science, the 20th century had postponed Him for the sake of experimenting with the world.

217, WARS. The great wars of the 20th century were consequences of social, political, and economic conditions. True, but let's not stop at that famous all-explanatory trilogy. Let's not forget other no less important aspects; there are also religious and mystical factors (as in Hitler) and the aesthetic spirit that characterized the century. Modris Eksteins, in *Rites of Springs (The Great War and the birth of the Modern Age)*, showed or demonstrated that war, the soldier's action, the annihilation of social orders, and the experimentation with the world were experienced as an aesthetic realization. We don't only have the testimonies of those who didn't go to war; there are also the confessions of the combatants, which are almost as important as those of the others. Even surrounded by death, war was an aesthetic, monumental event; like Nazism. An unparalleled spectacle. The same experience is repeated in the last Gulf War. War is lived (by those who didn't die) as a plastic, Hollywood-like spectacle. Aviators don't distinguish between reality and simulated flights, between a blue spot on the screen that disappears and thousands of people dying. That's why one pilot enthusiastically said: "This is really exciting; I'm ready to do it again." The transcendent meaning of the action has been lost in pure, childish experimentation.

218, PURITY. After an exhibition of paintings that Sábato held in Brazil, a critic accused him of contaminating his canvases with "literature." (If I remember correctly, something similar had been said about his literature: his novels were full of ideas, and his ideas were contaminated with passions.) To say that a painting is full of literature would be a valid observation; but to disqualify it for that is amusing and disappointing, as well as a bad habit. What are the other paintings full of? Pigmented oil? —In reality, an affirmative answer is not uncommon. Even great artists and theorists of the 20th century claimed that a painting is, above all, flat patches of color. Because abstraction was overvalued; not just any kind of abstraction: only that which left color and form standing, regardless of whether what was expressed was a triangle or a crucified corpse. The paradigms of this particularity were Kandinsky and Piet Mondrian, and the exceptions were surrealism, expressionism, and the so-called "metaphysical" art of Chirico. Once, Picasso said that with time, a painting would come to soothe a toothache. For his part, the critic Wilhelm Worringer, in 1908, not without enthusiasm, compared art to a good armchair that served as a rest for the tired businessman. So great is the trust in this project of ocular orgasm that it is still encouraged in art schools today. —So, if art is only form, what are the paintings of Lascaux, ancient Egypt, or Fra Angelico? Perhaps impure or imperfect arts. Thus, Delacroix would be a bad painter because his works are full of romanticism and patriotic sentiments; Van Gogh is too expressive; Munch too existentialist; Grosz confuses social critique with painting; the Mexican muralists should cleanse their walls of politics. What would so-called "sacred" art be if we removed everything that is not form and color? It would be what the Bible is to an atheist: literature. Would they then say that the Bible is an impure book because it includes an extraliterary element like God? Imagine someone proposing the purification of the detective genre by removing all references to the common themes of police reports. —Well, literature is not religion, it is not politics, it is not philosophy. But what would remain if we removed all that? Perhaps that project of Gertrude Stein, a cubist novel: "One is one, one is one... "

219, SCENARIO. Paradoxically, as art seeks to "purify" itself, it increasingly expands and becomes contaminated with the rest of human activities. Art begins to surpass its own traditional limits in the 19th century. Perhaps a prototype is William Morris; perhaps the great provocation came from the industrial machine that multiplied the experience of the creature in the material world. Soon the aesthetic experimentation of the world will extend to the rest of the human habitat. Until it transforms into a way of life—challenge, revolution, change, amorality. Dada, surrealism, Bauhaus, sports, pop art, rock'n roll. From the very fact that art occupies the entire life of a society derives the idea of its own death. Because it is difficult to appreciate what is everywhere, like air or evil. —But let us also see that the idea of the "death of art" can only arise from a superficial conception of art. If we consider that art is not an instrument (like a stagecoach or a telegraph), but the expression of a part of the spirit that cannot stop expressing itself, we will realize that for art to die, the spirit of the creature must first die. Which is also currently possible. But in that case, I would not worry so much about art.

XXV: Greek Precocity

220, AUDACITY. The Ionians, free from the limits of mythology and authority, burst into known history with a strange, novel, and absurd concept: nature. On the same theme, they later made no less admirable variations. Not all denied the existence of the supernatural, but no individual spirit was decisive in the new cosmic mechanisms. In any case, they remained part of nature. The ordering intelligence (*nous*) of Anaxagoras, the *logos* of Heraclitus, were no more anthropomorphic elements than Einstein's Old Man without dice. —As in all the world inhabited by creatures, in Greece there were also gods. And many; but nowhere else were these deities so permissive. At the same time, in the domains of metaphysical absolutism, in the Middle East, free thought and individual imagination were condemned. Neither in the Torah, nor in the Gospels, nor in the Quran was there ever someone who had something good to say and, at the same time, was entirely responsible for their own ideas. Nor in the ancient Egyptian, Hindu, and Babylonian texts, if we forget Buddha and Confucius. All sacred books were written by *intermediaries*, prophets who spoke in the name of another Being and whose virtues lay in respecting a tradition; even when, like Jesus, they were operating a revolution within the very tradition they respected. But the innovation of the first Greek philosophers, post-Homer, was not only the theme (nature) but their audacity, metaphysical and epistemological: they did not lean on ancient texts, known traditions, or fearsome authorities. On the contrary, they criticized and rejected the established. Even what their own colleagues had upheld minutes before, in the best style of the 20th-century avant-gardes. Each could boast of their own enlightenment and accuse of blindness those who did not understand how the world worked.

22, IMAGINATION. Until Socrates, philosophers were almost exclusively concerned with cosmology. The difference between any of those cosmologies of the 5th century B.C. and the latest in vogue is only one of information; not of inspiration or genius. The Greek people, in addition to being admirable, are perplexing: they are the real characters of a modern science fiction story. Thales of Miletus, with a very scientific style (genius or plagiarist or both), observed that every living being needed water and from this deduced the primary element from which everything emerged. (The same reasoning would have been followed by Akhenaten when observing things under the Sun; but the Greek did not worship water.) Another Greek, Anaximander, conceived the world surrounded by an infinite space, filled with other planets like Gaia. For Heraclitus of Ephesus, the Universe was composed of a single element: fire, which in turn was subject to rational laws. "This order of the world," he wrote to our astonishment, "the same for all, was not made by god or any man, but it always was, is, and will be; an ever-living fire, kindled in measure and extinguished in measure." The difference between fire and energy is minimal; one is the metaphor of the other, or the other is simply a modern abstraction. If we replace the image with the idea, instead of an archaic statement, we obtain a thoroughly modern one. Noticing the presence of calories in cold water, as Joule did, is less heroic than noticing the presence of fire itself in hot water, as the Greek did.

222, PRECOCITY. Those original geniuses of Greece who invented philosophy and modern thought are unjustly more known for their errors or metaphors than for their successes. Empedocles is remembered for his four elements; Parmenides for denying motion; Heraclitus because he could never wash his hands twice in the same river. But all those ideas that consecrated Darwin, Freud, Saussure, or Lévi-Strauss are overlooked. Almost no one recognizes the Freudian precocity of Plato or the structuralism of Heraclitus. Moreover, I know of no author who has observed the Darwinian discovery of Empedocles (though this may well be due to my irremediable ignorance). Or yes, because Aristotle made some reference.

"Those beings in which everything happened as if they had been born for a specific purpose," commented Aristotle, "were preserved for being adequately constituted by chance; those in which this did not occur, died and continued to die, as Empedocles says regarding the 'bovine creatures with human faces.'" More recently, we could consider Parmenides or Zeno. I refer to that absurd idea or dialectical product that an arrow shot into the air does not move. Now scientists affirm the same but in a more sophisticated way. The ancient wooden arrow is now the "arrow of time" and points to the second law of thermodynamics. And, like the other, it does not move. Time has a direction but does not flow. Paul Davis defined it thus: *"The correct way to picture the arrow of time is by analogy with a compass needle or weather vane, which point in a direction but do not move towards it.* "

223, GODS. How did the Greeks arrive at such audacity? We know that even to understand a rupture, one must turn to tradition, to that rejected past. In that past dwell the Olympian gods, all forming a semi-anarchic state. Or at least a democratic one. The Greek gods were diminished by the defects typical of "creatures of a day "; they were, moreover, products of the powerful aesthetic spirit of their people. They often ascended to the stage where they were admired or mocked. By the time of the last of the classics, Euripides, these supposed authorities no longer weighed on him, while Aristophanes mocked them without fear of torture or imprisonment. The Greek gods were immortal, but they possessed all the defects that humans could have, which made them beautifully tragic. Their virtues were more aesthetic than ethical. What united them was not fear but admiration. The cults expressed emotion and joy, not repentance or atonement. The gods could help the creatures, *but they were not responsible for their destinies.* Any misfortune could befall a good man or a bad one. In *The Republic* of Plato, Adimantus says: "The gods have destined calamities and a miserable life for many good men or contrary fortune for those who are not." It is difficult to find in other myths, contemporary to the Greeks, the same intervention of creatures and demigods. In this sense, the myths were similar to a *modern* film: the fame of the protagonist, the hero, was the ultimate state to which mortals aspired. Fame was the way to prolong existence in the moved memory of other creatures. —Meanwhile, in other myths beyond the Aegean, the creatures were passive, extras or supporting actors for whom the greatest virtue was *due obedience.* To doubt and act on one's own was condemnable: there could be nothing new under the sun because the truth had already been revealed. This obligation to submit and not doubt meant metaphysical security, but it would never have encouraged the emergence of philosophers as in Greece. And although unlikely, it would not be impossible for one of these intellects to have seen the light in Palestine, but they would have been condemned to public silence or to silence themselves. —Saint Augustine, Origen of Alexandria, Thomas Aquinas, Luther, Kierkegaard are only understandable if placed in the time they lived. Like almost all theology, they are the hybrid result of a religious faith accustomed to the intellectual exercise inherited from Greece. The Greek gods, powerful but not invincible, influential but not determinative, imperfect, prolific in existential conflicts, encouraged or allowed the critical spirit of a skeptical people. No Christian or Muslim would ever dare to question a single act of God. Such is the respect that God radiates that not even atheists mock Him. The worst that could happen to Aristophanes would be poverty or death. But not eternal punishment. And that this was, in one way or another, an invincible fear, is demonstrated by those Christians who accepted torture and death with fanatical resignation (not to mention some modern fundamentalists). Therefore, it is no coincidence that theater, tragedy, fiction, comedy, and politics were born or passed through the Greeks. To create and to think freely, a great deal of spiritual audacity is necessary. A great deal.

224, ESCHATOLOGIES. For the ancient Greeks, life beyond death held no more importance than this one here. Or they simply did not believe in it. Similar to the

Sumerian vision, the afterlife was gray and as undefined as an ungrateful dream, though not nightmarish if the dead grew accustomed to it. Only exceptional beings like heroes could be rewarded with something better. But in any case, they were not taken very seriously. Somewhat later, with the first philosophers, this disinterest was refined into condemnation. For Democritus, the world was composed of atoms in eternal and mechanical motion. Therefore, all knowledge was the consequence of the impact of these atoms on the senses. Upon death, the "soul" disappeared, and the atoms of a body passed on to form other bodies. And in all this, there was no purpose. Protagoras said it was impossible to affirm the existence or non-existence of the gods; the sophist Critias, that the gods were merely the invention of the fear of those who acted wrongly. The world was built of visible matter and nothing more; and, thanks to this recognition, men could then free themselves from religious constraints. —It was not until the 6th century BC that in Eleusis, a town near Athens, two new gods appeared promising eternal life: Demeter and Persephone. It was then that a kind of Paradise and a kind of Hell began to emerge on the eschatological horizon of Greece. Of course, it is not difficult to guess where such gods came from.

225, REACTION. At the end of the sixth century, the mystic Pythagoras taught that the soul survived death to return in a new birth. The soul could descend into any other animal, which is why the consumption of meat was despised by the Pythagoreans. Herodotus commented that Pythagoras had taken this idea from Egypt, but it is clear that such an idea must have only been passing through there. With the rest of the Greek philosophers, metaphysical and ideological diversity multiplied. There was a time when the creatures of Gaia began to question all the ancient mythological explanations about the Universe, and from this audacity, philosophy was born. But since it arose from the critical spirit, whose main instrument is doubt and questioning, it was not long before its opposite reappeared on the scene: the religious spirit. With the imposition of a truth and the obligation not to question it, metaphysical doubts and tolerance were pushed away. Thus, in Greece too, the spilling of thinker's blood occurred. The leading intellectuals of Athens were assassinated. Socrates was not condemned for corrupting the youth, simply put, but for doubting too much, that is, for being irreligious. —Once again, it was demonstrated that death and censorship are often useless against great creatures. Because the ideal of the last two thousand years has been, at least in the West, to think like Socrates and feel like Christ. Two condemned to death who could not be silenced by human laws and justice.

XXVI: The Unnecessary Intervention of God

226, TRAVELS. Travels have been fruitful and catastrophic in history. Thales of Miletus, one of the first great philosophers, traveled through Egypt and Chaldea when these two superpowers were the First World, and from there he likely took the idea or inspiration that water is the origin of all things. Deductive thinking, the foundation of Western rationality and attributed to this same man, was already known and practiced by the Egyptian priests. Pythagoras also undertook a long journey through the Middle East, and from Mesopotamia he took his famous theorem. Or, at least, those people already knew it before he discovered it. (I believe Pythagoras took something more from Egypt, if Pedro Guirao was correct when he wrote: "...the way of expressing oneself through symbols allowed Pythagoras to leave his thought in the penumbra, thus compensating for the deficiencies of the Greek language, which does not allow for the hieroglyphic writing of the Egyptian priests.") —A little later, at the beginning of the 12th century, Adelard of Bath undertook an extensive study trip through southern Europe, Syria, and Palestine. This young Englishman took from the Arabs what they had taken from the Greeks. And without intending to, he sparked an epistemological revolution that did not deny God but sent Him on vacation for a while.

227, ADVICE. In the 7th century, Muhammad uttered the phrase that modern fundamentalists most like to ignore: "*The ink of the scholar is more sacred than the blood of the martyr.*" Immediately afterward, he advised: "*Go seek knowledge, even as far as China if necessary. Knowledge, even if it begins without God as its object, ends with Him in the end.*" The Arabs took this precept to heart and put it into practice. During the entire time that Europe had forgotten and despised non-Christian cultures, the Islamic world devoted itself to studying and collecting Greek, Chinese, and Hindu texts. Shortly after this intellectual exercise, they began to produce their own contributions until no people surpassed them in science and philosophy. Now, through some mysterious process, Algerian traditionalists warn that those who live by the pen will die by the sword. And they also put it into practice.

228, MODERNUS. Upon returning from his journey, Adelard had to confront the dogmas that predominated in England at the time. But he managed to introduce a paradigm that is still upheld by famous scientists like Stephen Hawking today: God had created Nature in such a way that it could be studied and explained without His intervention. I believe this idea was that of the monk Peter Abelard. "One cannot believe," he said, "what one does not understand." And elsewhere: "In matters that can be discussed by reason, the judgment of authority is unnecessary." However: "The use of dialectics in theology cannot lead to the teaching of truth in a field that no mortal can reach through their own reflections." Therefore: "Authority should be trusted only while reason remains hidden." Contrary to what William of Ockham first, and Kant later, would understand centuries later, he thought that: *"There is a continuity between the world of reason and that of faith."* More radically, Adelard of Bath reproached the thinkers of his time for having been dazzled by the prestige of authority. For them, he wielded the slogan "reason against authority," and he called himself *modernus.* "I have learned from my Arab teachers to take reason as my guide," he once said. "Undoubtedly, the birth of plants is willed by the Creator. But this does not happen without a reason." He revisited the four elements of Empedocles, the four responsible for the growth of plants. Like most Greeks, he taught that the movement of the stars obeyed numerical laws and that it was no mystery that Gaia was suspended in space. Gaia is heavy and tends to fall; but it is spherical, and the lowest point of a sphere is its own center. Therefore (he reasoned) if I were to throw a stone through a tunnel that crossed the planet along one of its diameters, the stone would tend to stabilize at the center. And God did not intervene in these details.

229, BESTIARIES. A genre unique to the Middle Ages was the bestiaries. There, no rational explanation of nature was presented; rather, they assumed powerful analogies. They sought to match each type of animal with its human character. In their intention to confirm the Scriptures through examples from nature, they placed theses before demonstration. The theologians who reacted against the rationalization of nature must have intuited the impossibility of deducing moral values through such a neutral path. On the other hand, it was even more difficult to explain miracles since, by definition, a miracle was anything that escaped rational laws. The miracle is the most direct manifestation of a Will independent of the laws that govern the Universe. Reason says that a peach tree can only produce peaches, but God can make it bear pears or apples. To this argument, William of Conches responded that God could make a calf from the trunk of a tree, but He had never done so. To assert that a peach tree will never bear apples did not mean denying the existence of a Creator, but this idea placed Him in a gnostic distance. That is, through reason, the creature renounced direct contact with God; between Him and His creation stood a Nature full of endless laws, dense and inherently unknown. This threatens the memory of the Supreme and deepens the solitude of the metaphysical creature. Perhaps for all these reasons, in the 9th century, Peter Damian warned that philosophy was an invention of the devil. "*God cannot be the object of rational investigation,*" he said, not without reason.

230, HYPOTHESIS. Isaac Newton managed to discover that his cosmological theory produced some irregularities in calculation; minor ones, but when accumulated, they threatened the solidity of the entire system. Since he did not dare to speak of errors, much less of imperfection, he attributed these details to the sporadic intervention of God. That was the last time in the history of science that the Creator was involved in His own work. Since then, assuming His intervention in the functioning of the Universe became, in fact, an intolerable Imperfection; both for the theory and for the Creator. A little later, in 1796, the French astronomer and mathematician Pierre Simon Laplace formulated his theory of the Solar System. In reality, what he did was perfect the Newtonian paradigm by cleansing it of the sporadic interventions of a correcting Being, ultimately assumed by Newton. When Napoleon asked him where God was in his theory, the scientist replied: "*Sire, God is an unnecessary hypothesis.*" In the same century, John Stuart Mill declared that science was incompatible with a willful God. Since it was no longer possible to dethrone the quantitative paradigm and it was somewhat frightening to dethrone God, a completely new God was invented who seemed the same: only a God is possible (Stuart Mill asserted) who governs the world according to invariable laws. This new God, the God of G.W. Leibniz and Spinoza, had created the Universe with its laws and then retired to rest. But to rest seriously, which means it was not He who was responsible for violating the hydrostatic laws in the Red Sea. —Einstein himself said, in 1947, that the idea of a personal God (willful) could not be taken seriously. Which, in short, all the Holy Scriptures deny, from Moses to Muhammad.

XXVII: God and Science

231, ATHEISTS. If theology is a branch of thought that starts from a precept —God— to return to it in its conclusions, science is that discipline which starts from the assumption that God, if He exists, does not intervene in the functioning of His own work. That is to say, all science starts from a particular metaphysics: the elimination of God as a working hypothesis. This particularity has led many creatures to a fantastic conclusion: atheism is more scientific than theism.

232, MATERIALISM. Materialism, from the moment it is a representation of the world, is also a metaphysics. A paradoxical metaphysics, since it pretends not to be one. A creature bathing in the rain is not doing metaphysics: it is bathing. But from the moment it conceives its body and the water falling on it as a closed set of atoms, it is representing a form of being. And that, besides being scientific ontology, is materialist metaphysics.

233, PLATONISM. Perhaps there is no semi-educated person in the world who has not heard the comment about the mysterious similarity between the pyramids of Mexico and those of Egypt. For some addicted to the mysteries of weekly magazines, this resemblance means "irrefutable" proof of extraterrestrial intervention. This idea of irrefutability, I suppose, comes from the superstitious notion that only a flying machine is capable of connecting Egypt with Mexico, bypassing the ferocity of the Atlantic. But let us remember that the greatest separation between Khufu and Chichen Itza was not in the Atlantic but in the three thousand years that passed between one construction and the other. Now, how would one of the scientific disciplines respond to this enigma? Answer: the pyramids in question are the expression of the human mind at a certain age. Because pyramidal constructions represent mountains (perfect ones), a primitive sacred element among creatures. Mountains, pyramids, and *ziggurats* rise toward the sky. In Mesopotamian cultures, mountains signified "the threshold to the beyond "; among the pagan peoples of Palestine, it was a mound, elevation, or *ramah*; for the Hebrews, it was Mount Sinai; for the Greeks, Olympus. *It is then assumed that what is true are not the particular elements but the common ones.* — Since the 19th century, various theories and disciplines (Lamarckism, Darwinism, sociology, psychoanalysis, anthropology, structuralism) have studied the religious phenomenon as an expression of the human mind. Carl G. Jung and Joseph Campbell also studied myths and dogmas as if they were the necessary reflection of an archaic structure of the brain. Although they did not wish to refute God, they translated Him into psychological formulas. Since then, god (with a lowercase g) has become one of the pillars of the human brain. Dreams ceased to be the bearers of external messages, as in Homer or Joseph, to represent the narrative of a millennial history perpetuated in copulation. The *tetrakis* (the Pythagorean number four) would have reached every creature just as the sign of the god engraved on the jaguar's skin reached that character in Borges through "that hot labyrinth of tigers, spreading horror across the meadows and herds to preserve the design." There is a thought by Jung that I believe sums it up in an unparalleled way: "The form of these archetypes might be compared to the axial system of a crystal, which predetermines the crystalline formation in the mother liquid without itself possessing material existence." —It is a pity that, not without remorse, the scientist later confuses an epistemological observation with one related to psychology: "A scientific theory," he wrote, "will soon be surpassed by another; the dogma endures for countless centuries. The God-Man who suffers is at least five thousand years old; and the Trinity may be even older. "

234, IRREFUTABLE. As Popper said, a hypothesis is scientific when it can be refuted. Since God lacks this virtue of refutability, He is not only excluded from the sciences (which is logical) but also, due to an excess of professional zeal, from metaphysics, which is absurd. According to Islam, science would be something like a secular path leading to God; but according to atheists, that path ends in the atom and the number.

235, COSMOGONY. Reflecting on the origin or nature of the Cosmos has always fascinated the creatures of Gaia. It is difficult for this type of thought to be devoid of strong emotional charges because, in one way or another, reflecting on the Cosmos is secretly touching the destiny of the human creature. And not without prejudices or fears. —Every time a new star or galaxy is discovered, the existence of God is called into question. As if the creation of a mountain were easier for an Almighty Being than the entire Universe. But astrophysical cosmogony, the most prestigious of our time, will forever remain unfinished; because that is the destiny of all scientific knowledge: provisionality. The cosmogony of the Big Bang, if it does not incorporate God as responsible, becomes a mere Big Pop. Which is probable and only probable. For their part, evolutionary theories and geology can deny the Creation in seven days, but they cannot simply deny it. As long as the original Enigma persists, God cannot be refuted. At least not scientifically. God will disappear when science can answer the ultimate Question without resorting to God.

236, ILLUSION. If God is the consequence of human Ignorance, all the more reason to believe in Him. Because if all human science is relative and weak, Ignorance is powerful and invincible. If God is an illusion, scientific materialism is no less so. But with one disadvantage: materialism is a double illusion: it is an illusion based on the illusion of positive knowledge of the world, which has already been revealed as relative, limited, and provisional. God, on the other hand, contains what we sense but cannot possess: the Truth.

237, SUCCESS. Just as religion has lost all its battles with science, science has been unable to prevent the rebirth of religion from its own contradictions. Which is nothing short of a resounding success.

238, TIMES. For religious thought, the past was always better. The mythological past, because the creature is a "fallen being "; the historical past, because there are no longer prophets or creatures are always worse; the theological past, because authority increases with the antiquity of thinkers, so much so that Galileo was refuted with another pagan named Aristotle. This attitude toward time is also reflected in clothing: modern priests dress as they did in the 12th century; the Protestant group of the

*Amish*not only dress like their 19th-century grandparents but also refuse to ride in cars, and thus, in the United States, they travel using four-wheeled carts pulled by a poor horse that cannot comprehend human arbitrariness. For scientific thought, the opposite is strictly true. For any modern or postmodern scientist, their knowledge is superior to that of Archimedes or Galileo. Unlike the two, for art, there is no such imbalance between past and present; profound art tends to operate within its own time: eternity or immanence. Almost no contemporary writer, for example, would dare to look down on Homer or Shakespeare.

239, SEPARATION. Thomas Aquinas, among other scholastics, sought to reconcile faith and reason. William Ockham decided that this endeavor was not only impossible but also unnecessary. Since then, since the 13th century, the condemnation of scientific thought has been the exclusion of God. (With the notable exceptions of Newton and Descartes. The Frenchman made God the center of his thought; the Englishman resorted to His services to correct some defects in his system). Just as a theology without God would cease to be theology and become atheistic philosophy, a science with God as a hypothesis would cease to be science and become theology. There is, or should be, no possible contact between physics and metaphysics, according to Kant; any scientific hypothesis, no matter how absurd, will be preferable to the recourse of metaphysics to explain matter. No scientist, no matter how religious, would accept the Aristotelian assertion that a stone falls because the Spirit of the Lord propels it downward. If that same scientist one day discovered a stone resting on the ceiling of his house, he would seek to explain the phenomenon by resorting to the known laws of physics or by seeking new ones. These laws may revolutionize science with a new paradigm, but at no point will they involve God in the matter. Then, if someone questions him about how his cosmological conception reconciles with God, he will respond the same way the heretics Abelard of Bath and the priest William Ockham did.

XXVIII: The Birth of Modern Science

240, CHANGES. Where did the humanist challenge of the 15th century arise? We can think of four important causes: a1—The critical impulse of scholastic rationalism; a2—The revival of the aesthetic spirit of ancient Greece; b1—The development of agriculture in the 13th century due to new technical discoveries; b2—The migration from the countryside to the cities, where one is further from the unpredictability of time and closer to other creatures and their commercial relationships.

241, AESTHETIC. By the end of the Middle Ages, intellectuals were entangled in the issue of faith confronting reason. In the mid-14th century, William Ockham, inaugurating the *via moderna*, resolved the conflicts of the pair with a divorce: the kingdom of God had to be separated from material reality. For the former, there was faith and theology; for the latter, rational analysis. The rigorous and abstract rationality of the scholastics was followed by the no less pagan imagination of the Renaissance. Dante and the scholastics focused on nature and abstraction; Petrarch preferred his own self. From the Aristotelian, the shift was made to the Platonic, as Greece continued to think for a

Europe that was not yet capable of doing so. The liberation of the imagination of the Neoplatonic humanists advanced. Then a respectful paradox arises: Plato, who influenced the new Christian spirituality at the beginning of the Middle Ages (Plotinus, Saint Augustine, and the *Logos*), a thousand years later, ends the same era when the aesthetic dimension of his thought begins to be considered. A new era called the Renaissance emerges, dominated by the challenge of experimenting with the world, by art and technology. Luther's Reformation meant, above all, a strong rejection of this Hellenization of the religious spirit. He rejected the Hellenic mentality and also the scholastic one; because for both logos and physics, matter and spirit, were elements of the same reality that had to be integrated into the same intellectual formulation. With the subsequent fundamentalism of the Reformation and the Counter-Reformation, the religious spirit regained its ancient nature, while, for its part, Greek imagination was once again liberated to fertilize art and the sciences.

242, SCIENCE. Ptolemaic stubbornness was the result of an anthropocentric prejudice: the creature is the center of the Universe. The heliocentric hypothesis was already known at the time, but it was cast into oblivion for humanist reasons first and religious ones later. Not only because Aristotle and the Scriptures suggested it, but also because it was theologically convenient. But the Renaissance is not solely the consequence of scholastic rationality; the new aesthetic spirit of the Neoplatonics also played a role. Initially, the Copernican hypothesis was not much more useful than the patched-up Ptolemaic calculation, but its simplicity made it superior. Explicitly, Copernicus, Kepler, and Galileo acknowledged Pythagoras and Plato as their inspirations. (When Kepler wrote to Galileo, he recognized those two Greeks as his true predecessors.) The principle that the world is organized according to numbers belongs to Pythagorean mysticism and was only taken seriously again, albeit with a different spirit, during the Renaissance. "The book of the Universe," wrote Galileo, "is written in the language of mathematics." The idea of the Sun as a divine and central element comes from the Neoplatonics of the time and inspired Kepler to explain why the planets moved in ellipses at different speeds: the Sun exerted a magnetic attraction on the planets. And none of this would have been possible without aesthetic prejudices like the harmony of celestial bodies, without the audacity of Greek imagination. Copernicus's god, the creator of the Great Harmony, is, in essence, a Greek god and not a Christian one. The scientific revolution of the Renaissance astronomers was, above all, a provocation of the aesthetic spirit. —Still immersed in this Hellenic spirit, the Church, which allowed Michelangelo to paint the Sistine Chapel, also tolerated the cosmological audacity of

Copernicus. The reformers, and later the inquisitors, condemned both offenses. Calvin, entirely devoid of Hellenic sensibility, condemned both the colorfulness of the Renaissance and the audacity of decentralizing the Universe's focus from the human creature.

243, PROVISIONAL. When Newton formulated the behavior of universal gravitation, everyone agreed on what the Universe was and how it worked. The absolute Truth was synthesized in the formula:

$$F = k \, . \, (M \, . \, m) \, / \, d^2$$

Using this same theory, the astronomer Edmund Halley predicted the appearance of a comet for the year 1758. Of course, the comet appeared and was baptized with the name of its prophet. Experience and observation confirmed all of Newton's predictions. Why doubt, then? After all, it was a mathematical formula. —All was well, until a few centuries later Dr. Einstein formulated his own. Then Newton's absolute, three-dimensional space collapsed like the apple. There was no longer a gravitational force emanating from bodies but a space-time that curved to swallow them. Newton's theory became a very particular case of the new General Theory, which, like the previous one, was confirmed by observation and experience. The cosmological vision of the Universe changed once again. Radically, as it had so many times before.

244, SYSTEMS. Thought can produce philosophical systems, but philosophical systems cannot produce thought. They only produce dogmas. In this sense, it could be said that Hegel was the most famous anti-philosopher of the 19th century, as his effort was always to create an ordering method that would allow philosophy to be taught scientifically, just as geometry is taught and learned. Nietzsche stood in total opposition. I believe Nietzsche represents the true philosopher and the opposite of the true Hegel.

245, POSITIVISTS. Disillusioned with the changes and revolutions of philosophy, the positivists proposed science as the model of Truth. Except that later, just as the 20th century began, the sciences also revealed themselves to be as unstable as the abhorred history of philosophy. Although fruitful, the history of the sciences began to show its true nature (the nature of the metaphysical creature), full of revolutions and parricides. This phenomenon affected not only the natural sciences; it also shook the foundations of divine mathematics. —For centuries, scientists were certain that the world was *res extensa* and that, as Descartes reasoned, the distance between the walls of a glass filled with vacuum was equal to zero. In the 1920s, another scientist, Mr. Arthur Eddington, observed that the solid table on which he was writing was more empty space than matter. In fact, it was only a billionth part matter, and what he saw as a table was nothing more than an "effect" of the new phenomenon on his senses. If I may exaggerate, I would say that Eddington understood that the world was an illusion, like the illusion of Buddha or the hallucinated George Berkeley. —Now, Platonism in the deepest cosmology and the beautiful Pythagorean principle, *both, the metaphysical foundations of all modern science*, are no longer possible. Because the Great Harmony does not exist; there is no music of the spheres but dissonance of explosions; there is no order but chaos; the world no longer expresses itself through numbers but the opposite: it is numbers that express themselves through nature (and that's when they pretend to be more than a formal science). By the 21st century, science has come so close to philosophy that it is almost impossible to distinguish a theoretical physicist from one of those philosophers who dealt with cosmology, in Greece or in 18th-century Europe.

246, KNOWING. To know means to retain the experience of an object or a phenomenon when it is no longer present. In reality, the only things we can know positively are our own emotions: love, hate, euphoria, fear, the idea of an object (*res pensante*); and other direct experiences of the spirit: faith and mathematics (*res infinita*). The world (*res extensa*), on the other hand, is far from our complete grasp. (I believe Husserl would have named these three concepts with three other words: *noema*, *eidetic intuition* and *pole*.) —The Greeks formulated a premise that is fundamental in all scientific and theological thought: truth likes to hide. The true cannot be seen with the eyes. In reality, this idea may be due to an inverse reason: the world cannot be known, and what the metaphysical creature aspires to is to solve the enigma *by creating* a representation of the world that allows it to dominate it. That representation, therefore, is not visible but lies behind an intellectual operation. In the same way, a citizen must learn the traffic rules of a city to understand why people and vehicles move in one direction and not the other. But the rules are not the city, nor a univocal and necessary truth, but a way of dominating it. In the same way, we learn to interact with a computer screen, we learn to control it. We drag an icon from one place to another, open it, close it, cover it with ten windows, send a file to the trash, empty the trash, check it, pull out a pyramid, a geodesic, rotate it. But all those symbols, with their shapes and colors, are only a representation of *another* reality, the invisible reality of the hard drive. —What we can know of the world, apart from our direct experience in it, are our own representations. These representations can be scientific, religious, or they can belong to the more scattered set of superstitions. But in no case are they truly "positive" knowledge, as is always claimed, but indirect. And it is never devoid of a metaphysical basis. Any scientific formulation about the atom will always be a "false image" of something we cannot know directly. A false idea but of great utility. Bohr's atom, for example, with its electrons orbiting in a restricted number of paths, was compatible with quantum physics and allowed for the verification of experiments and the prediction of results. But, in its time, it was set aside by scientists who replaced it with a more convenient image. We can know the mathematical formula W = V.I because, in its entirety, it takes place within us. We can also know the relationship that links it to the experience of electricity. But in no case can we say that we know electricity. Something similar has happened to me while working with building structures. Every time I face a calculation of stresses and resistances, I have the sensation of conversing with a shadow. I know that if the shadow does not move, the body that projects it will not move either. That shadow is the theories, the numbers, and the mathematical formulas; and the body, the invisible reality that I presume to dominate but do not know. I can only know the legal artifice of the formulas, with their theoretical reasons, and then I verify that the structure behaves as expected (or is it the formulas that behave according to what was previously seen?); but I can know nothing of that "intermediate reality." —We can perceive the world (immediate knowledge), and this perception will depend on our senses and our spiritual nature: a tree is very large or very small, it is shade or a threat. It is never a neutral object. We can say that when a tree becomes a neutral object, we cease to know the tree in favor of a representation of it: then it is an artistic or scientific representation, a drawing or a botanical diagram. —A great scientist does not study the world but the forms in which that world can be represented for its domination. And to dominate does not only mean to control it but to make it comprehensible. We will never be able to know *what* the world is by relying on data and scientific theories. (With data and theories, we can know certain representations of the world: we can know Newton's world, Planck's world.) But with scientific progress, we will increasingly have better representations of that unattainable idea. And we will consider them more "true" the better they integrate into a principal image. A guiding image can be a paradigm. But the starting image is the materialist and Pythagorean metaphysics, according to which the Universe is a collection of matter and energy, ordered by numerical laws. As Heraclitus said, fire kindled and extinguished according to measure.

247, LAWS. How many would dare to question the Pythagorean principle that nature expresses itself in numbers? Why does a stone and all stones fall according to the formula $S = ½gt^2$? Well, on a cosmic scale, this is not entirely true. There are many things that in our small world are invariable and beyond that change. Like time, for example. But let's look at it from another perspective. Let's consider what would happen if stones fell according to one formula and others according to another, depending on their color and the time of year. I think in that case we would live in an upside-down world, but we would still find mathematical formulas that summarize the "unstable" behavior of those stones. As long as it is not possible, the problem will remain a scientific enigma, just as the indefinite behavior of light has been. Since we would also be moving within a particular and limited point of the universe, these mathematical laws would apparently be invariable. Then we would say, as we say now and have for thousands of years, that nature expresses itself in numbers. Will it occur to us to think that it is the numbers that express themselves in nature?

248, CHAOS. The so-called "chaotic" systems refer to the *sensitivity of initial conditions.* This recent trend in thought does not mean that science has given up searching for an *order* in diversity; it means that this order is so complex that it is impossible to dominate it with mechanical laws, just as the optimism of the 19th century believed it possible. In the Boltzmann-Gibbs model, where a particle collides within an ordered field of disks, an initial precision with an error of one billionth is necessary to predict the direction of the particle after 12 collisions. An infinitesimal initial deviation would, after three movements, yield completely contradictory results. This *sensitivity* is what differentiates chaotic systems from stable systems, which are the systems that optimistic science dealt with. Using a metaphor, one could say that it is here that mathematics increases its "entropy" (increase in information necessary to define an order). Currently, physical reality presents itself as if resisting mathematical simplicity. That is, the book of Nature is not written in numbers, as Pythagoras and Galileo affirmed. On the contrary, it seems that it is the metaphysical creatures that force it to do so.

249, ADVANTAGES. A sorcerer also relates causes and effects. In the use of plants and attitudes, he sometimes achieves an effective treatment. Ten men with the same demon are cured with the same treatment. Of course, our scientific mindset will deny the animist representation of the sorcerer by resorting to other explanations. We will assume that the explanations of a doctor or a psychoanalyst represent the truth for two reasons: because they convince us and because they achieve better results. But this only proves two more things: that our intellect is prepared for scientific effort more than for superstitious credulity, and that science achieves greater domination of phenomena. But in no case does it prove that the metaphysical principle that sustains it, materialism, is the truth of the world.

250, POWER. Every scientific formulation is inevitably accompanied by a cosmological image or representation that science itself eventually demolishes over time. We can never affirm whether a scientific knowledge is true, definitive, or not. What we can say is that it is effective and overwhelmingly useful knowledge. —The only progressive constant we can observe in the history of science is the *power* derived from it. (What matters is how the intellect manages to dominate, to integrate, the scattered data of an increasingly vast and complex reality.) Every investigation, even the speculative one, is oriented toward those forms that can be "dominated" by the intellect. Epistemological revolutions and paradigm shifts show us, time and again, that a Truth can become false or can be replaced by another. Ptolemy's universe has nothing to do with Newton's, and Newton's in no way corresponds to Einstein's. Yet, all three cosmological representations have been enormously useful in their times; and even in ours. This indicates that it is not *truth* that is the primary engine of science but *power*. The former comes from the intellect; the latter is the unequivocal product of the *will* of the species.

251, CERTAINTIES. The most prestigious form of knowledge in the last three hundred years has been the scientific. As in other eras, this way of thinking and seeing the world led to unquestionable certainties, to eternal truths; as in other eras, they ended. —When Kepler managed to explain with simple formulas the elliptical motion of the planets, he wrote: "I have written the book; to be read now or in posterity, it does not matter. I can wait a century for a reader just as God waited six thousand years for a witness." Later, marveling at the mathematical clarity of his theory, Isaac Newton exclaimed: *"O my God, I think Thy thought after Thee!."* Which means not only that even the great ones once lost their famous modesty.

252, KNOWLEDGE. The worst of the ignorant is the one who does not know it. Creatures aware of their own ignorance possess the only and wisest possible knowledge. —If I remember correctly, something similar was thought by Nicholas of Cusa six hundred years ago: ignorance made conscious reveals a truth that pretended knowledge cannot access. In a proverbial way, we could formulate it like this: he who sees what he lacks sees more than he who only sees what he has. I believe Cusa titled this idea, humble and proud, thus: *De docta ignorantia*. —I mention the Latin to avoid returning once again to Greece.

XXIX: The Decalogue is Split in Two

253, SEPARATION: In many religions, the daily actions of the faithful are rigorously regulated by norms and codes of conduct. To be a Hindu or a Jew, it is not enough to believe in reincarnation or Yahweh; one must also *live as such*. An Orthodox Jew is not a Jew or is not Orthodox if he eats a *cheeseburger* or pork; and a Hindu is not a Hindu if he eats any meat. Christ, on the other hand, set aside the formality of obligatory rituals to internalize religion in the individual. He separated Heaven from earth. The clear distinction between the law of men and the Law of the Father is summarized in the phrase: "Render unto Caesar what is Caesar's." Even this same attitude is repeated in the recurring use of metaphor: where it says "seed," it means possibility or destiny; when it says "lamb," it means man or fidelity. The metaphor is uncomfortable because it demands interpretation; laws and dogmas only need to be followed.

254, THEOLOGIANS. In the 12th century, Peter Abelard confirmed the independence between the act and the intention. Like Freud, he recognized the immanent desire of every creature or its own desire to bypass the Commandments. And he did not call that sin. Sin (he wrote) consists in *consenting* to the desire to forget the prohibition. "It is not written," he said, "that we should not want to bear false witness, or that we should not consent to it. Simply that we should not bear it." And elsewhere: "Nor should the prohibition be understood as referring to the action, but to the consent." The medieval monk does not blame the demons and absolves the guilty for their nature. This distinction between Heaven and earth is explicit in Luther. Some have seen in his reform a return to the Old Testament; but in some aspects, it is clearer that it was a regression to primitive Christianity. His doctrine of *the two kingdoms* recalls Babylonian and Hermetic ideas, but above all, it signifies the ancient separation of the material world and the kingdom of God. During the Peasants' War of 1525, Luther made it clear that "the freedom of the Christian cannot be confused with social and political liberation. "

255, STATE. Christ translated the last five negative Commandments into a positive synthesis. The obligations not to kill, not to steal, not to lie, not to fornicate were synthesized into the precept "Love your neighbor as yourself." An ethical translation that implies an even deeper internalization. Almost all of us are horrified by the mere idea of killing a person. But from there to a democratic and indiscriminate love, there is a distance. If we were capable of such greatness of heart, social conflicts and exploitation among creatures would at least be rare. Nevertheless, this interhuman love was differentiated and far below the supreme love for God. And it is precisely this hierarchical order that maintains Christ's preaching as a religion and not mere humanism. An inverse order would be the order of the modern State. For any government, the last five Commandments must take precedence over the first. And this is called tolerance and secularism.

256, LEGAL. At the same time that the bourgeoisie and modern states emerged in Europe, morality once again separated from religion. Naturally, for this divorce to have occurred earlier, it required *legitimization.* Ethical legitimization, like religious legitimization, consists of a discourse that relies on some basic, non-negotiable principles. In the case of ethics, they are summarized in the Second Table; for theology, it consists of the a priori acceptance of the First Table. Ethics and theology are *rationalizations* that seek the confirmation of moral and religious axioms. Often, these attempts at confirmation result in contradictory refutations: in the name of good, evil is professed; in the name of God, it ends up denying Him. —It is not uncommon to find in the same Sacred Books justifications for slavery and all kinds of crimes and genocides, both racist and ideological. The Russian historian V.I. Avdiev, after enumerating various examples, concluded: "Biblical teachings, reflecting the views and interests of slaveholders, recommended applying the cruelest forms of forced constraint to slaves." —More recently, capitalist ethics also needed ethical legitimization; in its case, the discourse came from religion itself: the Protestant Reformation. Later, philosophy fulfilled the same role: the combative ethics of Marxism-Leninism and the consumerist ethics of the postmodern neoliberal state. For one, property was theft, so owners were imprisoned and killed; for the other, property is success, so those who lack it are despised and trampled upon; when they are not killed for it.

257, FREEDOM. The consequences of the doctrine of predestination on the emerging capitalist ethics have been psychoanalyzed to the point of exhaustion. But there are other elements at play; at least two: Freedom —different ethical habits could be the basis of good Christians with faith; Tolerance —authority became secular and more permissive. In the modern world, except for fundamentalists, the creatures who say they believe in God are, above all, secular. The believer and the atheist are no longer distinguished by their daily habits but only by their inner convictions. The Church, the institution of Truth, left power to the state, the institution of Order.*The priority of Order was inverted.*The principles of Equality and Fraternity were already in some way included in the Decalogue, so it can be said that the French Revolution contributed the most novel of the three Masonic principles: Liberty.

258, RIGHTS. With the French Revolution, the Rights of Man became famous, soon to include Woman as well. The spiritual atmosphere of the time was dominated by the secular literature of the Encyclopedists. In the modern encyclopedia, there is no privileged knowledge or truth. It is not a sacred book but a skeptical one, because it presents the known truths of its time without taking sides. It represents a heroic advance of the informational spirit, the systematic and indifferent organization of information (because when one seeks to deny any kind of hierarchy, one resorts to alphabetical order; whether to organize names or things). —After the Revolution, it would no longer be transcendental Truth that mattered most in the life of a society, but the simple and "insignificant" truths of each creature, coexistence, social justice, and material progress. Law and the here and now are what matter, and it is expected that these problems will be resolved before moving on to the clouds. —When morality becomes independent of God and falls into the hands of creatures, it ceases to be a set of perfect norms and becomes something debatable and perfectible. They are no longer prohibitions but prescriptions. "Thou shalt not fornicate" transforms into "you have the right to fornicate if your husband allows it." The biblical condemnation of homosexuality becomes a vindication. The ancient dictates that demanded women's submission to men are progressively annulled.

259, PLEASURES. Ancient tribes considered their customs and their own language to be the best customs and the clearest language. Every society in every era considers its own morality superior to the past or to an emerging new morality. When an old man says that "there is no morality anymore," it means that a new one has been born; that is, a new *consciousness of the species* has formed, just as ideas and paradigms form. They can be good or bad ideas, there can be healthy and sick consciousnesses. But, generally, the past generation always discredits it, while the new one will defend it for its virtues. —Now that creatures consider liberal ethics more just, many cut to the chase by denying the rest of the Scriptures. Now postmodern thought aims at the progressive and unlimited increase of individual freedoms and, above all, the share of pleasure that belongs to each one. It is the triumph of basic instincts (sex, consumption, and preservation) over the transcendent. Metaphysical creatures have ceased to be the kings of Creation and are now just any beings seeking their sustenance in a lost point in space. Life is no longer sacred nor a preparation for a higher state. It is something that emerges and disappears without any meaning. Therefore, one must not "commit the worst of all possible sins: not being happy." The ethics that crown the millennium are closer to ancient Greece than to later eras. Minorities discuss, demand, and obtain their rights. Homosexuals are accepted by the Church as they once were in Greece. The paradigmatic virtue is tolerance, though it does not mean it is also the practice. The entire book by theologian Hans Küng, in his search for a "global ethics," is, in some way, the recognition of the Second Table as the only common factor among peoples. At no point, as Christians once attempted, does he propose the suppression of metaphysical diversity by the imposition of evangelical Truth.

XXX: The Devolution of the Species

260, FUNCTIONALISM. Jean-Baptiste de Lamarck published his *Philosophie Zoologique* in 1809. Despite its name and its origins, he proposed a theory that contradicted the official version of the Church. In it, nature appears as a relentless intelligence: species evolve in response to the needs of their environment. It was easy to understand, or imagine, that giraffes stretched their necks when food on the ground became scarcer than in the trees. After all, men had observed for millennia how a muscle demanded by a certain effort would eventually develop and adapt to the new effort. But, on the other hand, it was much harder to explain the stripes of the tiger and the nearly infinite and ingenious camouflages that exist in nature. This theory, scientific and mistaken, has an admirable metaphysical translation: Schopenhauer's concept of *will* . With this, one could not only explain the long neck of the giraffe and the hump of the camel; also the colors and patterns of plants and animals, responsible for the survival of each species. But this theory also had a flaw: it was not scientific. That is, it was not a *refutable* proposition. If I may exaggerate, I would say it also has another flaw: it is tautological ("the bull has horns because it seeks to gore," etc.).

261, BLINDNESS. Between 1831 and 1836, another traveler gave birth to a theory that would enjoy a long and prestigious life. A close relative of Lamarckism, this theory would, at its core, be radically different. If Lamarck's famous statement was that "form follows function," the Darwinians formulated something like a semantic inversion: function follows form. (A story that repeated itself with rigor in the architectural thought of the 20th century.) From then on, Nature would no longer be an intelligent will but a mechanism, *blind and stupid*. In Darwin's theory, a woman or a bird is the consequence of millions of genetic accidents, perpetuated by inheritance. This series of accidents would not only have produced admirable and perfectly adapted bodies, like the tiger, but (and above all) a series of countless variations that turned out to be failures. But each of these imperceptible variations ended in oblivion. Others are called Neanderthal man or Arsinoitherium, who in turn were the pride of an unstable nature. Now, when someone contemplates the white camouflage of the polar bear, the false eye drawn on the tail of a fish, the optical effect produced by the stripes of the zebra in the confused eyes of the tiger, they can only say, "how wise nature is." Until Sir Charles Darwin appears to prove them wrong: in reality, nature is stupid, sir. For although each species lives as a perfect and beautiful machine, this is only due to the fact of having hit one good variation in a million bad ones. Like someone who gradually becomes rich by betting for free in the lottery, for years.

262, COSTEAU. Once, in a television interview, the famous oceanographer J.I. Cousteau was asked if he was religious. "Yes," replied the Frenchman, "because I cannot believe that all the wonders around us were created by chance. *No, ce n'est pas possible*." I share your sentiment, Monsieur.

263, SEX. Why is the entire animal kingdom sexual? Is it inconceivable for nature to evolve and sustain itself without the necessary intervention of sex? It is estimated that sexual reproduction began 2 billion years ago. Until then, the norm was asexual multiplication (mitosis). Bacteria and fungi copied themselves. They did not evolve, but they also did not age. If something did not kill them, they could live indefinitely. Not only was life possible, not only was the individual immortal; changes and evolution were also possible, and this is demonstrated by the very appearance of sex in an asexual world. So, why was sex invented? To accelerate evolution? —Suppose that, upon reaching a certain age, women reproduced on their own. As in cloning or as in one of those cases of virgin mothers recorded in medical history. Perhaps evolution would be slower, because all the genetic information of the male would always be lost, because the inevitable novelty that arises from a random combination would not be possible. But what does that matter? Of course, to evolve, one would have to wait for infrequent genetic accidents, something like an imperfect cloning. But what's the rush? We can well suppose the total nonexistence of males in the animal kingdom, and still, life would be possible. Or at least imaginable, which is already a lot. So, why and for what does sex exist? And why, precisely, is it the most important phenomenon in the life of the animal kingdom? —Darwinian logic considers sex in its theoretical formulations to explain the evolution of species. But sex is not a fundamental hypothesis in this evolutionary theory or its variations. I would almost say it is a consideration *a posteriori*. Even if animals reproduced like cells, evolution would be explained by this theory: the weakest would not reach reproductive age; only the fittest would. There would still be *struggle for life,* though it would no longer be a *struggle for female.* —I would dare to say that it is not nature that serves the sexual relationship, but the opposite: it is sex that serves nature to fulfill itself. The only flaw in this theory is that it is a metaphysical theory.

264, EVOLUTION. A being that reproduces itself generates two identical beings. Or almost identical, because even then, from time to time, some accident, some meritorious deformation, would be possible. Thanks to these minimal imperfections, the simplest beings evolved and, who knows why, managed to invent sex. In turn, sexual reproduction accelerated evolution, because the random combination of intercourse makes perfect copies impossible: the child resembles the father or the mother, but is never the image of either. But there is still another novelty on the anxious path of evolution and, as one might suspect, it is related to the metaphysical creature. More precisely, to its inner history. I am referring to the famous taboo of incest. Because exogamy, unlike racism, leads to the random combination of different traits. And that is one of the pillars of evolution.

265, MYOPIA. The Argentine epistemologist Gregorio Klimovsky, after analyzing Darwin's theory, concluded with an unexpected observation: "The visual characteristic called myopia, commonly considered a defect, would be favorable in urban environments, as a large number of tasks in cities are bureaucratic in nature, and myopia facilitates the apprehension of what is close and therefore concentration on work. The opposite would occur in rural areas, where attention must be paid to what is distant; here myopia is an unfavorable characteristic, while hyperopia, in contrast, is favorable. If human evolution, in terms of lifestyles, continues as it has until now, one could make the Darwinian prediction that, in the distant future, city dwellers will be myopic, while those in rural areas will be hyperopic." Klimovsky makes an observation worthy of Lamarck, but not of a Darwinian. Between the hypothesis (H1, as epistemologists mean it) and the Gregorian statement (E1), there is an intermediate step called deduction (D1), which means: myopic individuals, in a state of free competition, are the most fit for office work, and thus they manage to reproduce better than those with sharp vision (*survival of the fittest*). In other words, those sedentary, chubby individuals with thick glasses attract more women than any athletic sportsman with good eyesight. And, in this way, their characteristics are reproduced more. Well, I don't know what the women living in Buenos Aires might think, but to me, the conclusion seems fantastic. Yes, there is still a justification for the epistemologist's conclusion, from a Darwinian point of view: the sedentary, chubby individuals with bottle-thick glasses (H1) are more fit for executive work; that is, they earn more money than the rest. Money attracts women (H2), and therefore myopic individuals reproduce more in large cities (D1). —I understand that some women might feel offended by H2. But I refer them to a conclusion made by Helen Fisher, a female anthropologist: "From a study conducted in thirty-three countries, we concluded that women are attracted to wealthy men, a trait that developed millions of years ago... "

266, ACCIDENTS. Let us consider the relentless simplicity of the theory of evolution, and we will see that it has only one flaw: *it is correct.* —The Hindu doctrine of reincarnations is the only one capable of metaphysically justifying animals; they are variations in transit to something superior: human knowledge and subsequent liberation. In evolutionary theories, on the other hand, not only are tigers and birds the result of an innumerable series of accidents; so too are creatures and their productions: the theorem of Pythagoras, Buddhism, Schubert's Unfinished Symphony, and all conceptions of the Universe (that is, the Universe itself). Everything would be the consequence of a quasi-infinite series of coincidences ranging from a protozoan to Paul K. Feyerabend. It is assumed that all life originated from a chemical soup, a magical and unique alchemical conjunction of imperfect RNA. It would be interesting, moreover, to find out how it was that from that original combination emerged both a fly and Professor Isaac Newton. Both, according to Darwin and all the dissenting subcurrents of evolutionism, are products of successive survival successes. —But even this type of mechanical evolutionism can be saved from absurdity. Obviously, a metaphysical dimension is always necessary: an *evolutionary gnosis*; that is, the spiritual achievement of Gaia's most problematic creature.

267, MODESTY. At the same time that Darwin's theory triumphed in the world, the modesty of some creatures made them turn their faces away every time they passed by its existential implications. Sensing the catastrophe, many religious spirits bowed their heads; others hurled dogmatic and ineffective insults. The most optimistic uttered the famous phrase: "nature is wise," as if behind every physical phenomenon lay the *nous* of Anaxagoras. Others saw in the evolutionary path a kind of *deliberate project* , and formulated some respectable theories. I think it is understandable that they preferred to think this way, rather than accept that they were surrounded not only by a *mechanism* but also by a blind and stupid mechanism. Or at least no wiser than roulette or the lottery.

268, ARGUMENTS. In May 1997, Pastor Henry Feyerabend gave a series of televised sermons in Portugal. Among other things, he declared: "*We descend from Adam and Eve. Just as an ear of corn does not produce bananas, neither did the monkey give rise to man.*" Perhaps one day it will be proven that the theory of evolution was wrong and that Pastor Feyerabend was correct. But, in the meantime, he should refrain from arguments that may sound striking on television or in a newspaper headline, but which have the flaw of demonstrating more ignorance than wisdom. And less intelligence as well. In this brief statement, the televangelist not only shows that, out of ideological modesty, he never read Darwin or *New Scientist,* but also that he does not know how to construct a syllogism, which is already serious for a theologian. —To claim that creatures descend from Adam and Eve *because* the Scriptures say so is understandable. The problem arises when one attempts to argue using intelligence and lacks it.

269, COINCIDENCES. The doctrine of coincidences is a characteristic of the thought of the last century. Well, there are the principle of indeterminacy, the theory of Chaos. But all these are details compared to that great cosmogonic accident called the *Big Bang.* I believe that never before had human intelligence gone so far in stripping all Meaning from existence. Even things and numbers are beginning to lose their meaning. —The metaphysical creature is the product of two miracles or cosmic improbabilities: life and consciousness. Has it perhaps reached its "dead end," as happened to other species? Maybe the 21st century will restore to the creature some of the transcendental value it once had. This would be possible if the concept of *gnosis* is introduced into the paradigm of evolution. Then we might even say that the gods also descend from monkeys.

270, PROJECT. The immense variety of species is due to the element of *chance* that infiltrates another constant and deterministic one: the inheritance of the genome. In living beings, genetic information can vary infinitesimally, but the inheritance from one generation to the next is always maintained. —The emergence of life is the result of a "coincidence" with a probability close to zero. This still does not mean a miracle as we would like, because on an astronomical scale there are no exaggerations; everything is possible. But, in a Universe that inevitably degrades or destroys itself, that exhausts its energies at every moment, life is a *unique* event: it does not dissipate like radium; it regenerates. Life, from the humblest insect, differs from the rest of matter by its miraculous capacity for preservation and progression. For one eagle that dies, a hundred may begin to fly, and for a hundred, ten thousand. And for life, they are all the same eagle reborn. Inheritance plus chance form a mysterious project called *life.* As if the Universe had produced a tiny luminous point in the immense darkness, to save it from aging, to reverse the laws of cosmic Irreversibility. At least for a second before definitive death.

XXXI: The Insignificant Universe

271, FALL. Once the world was populated by spirits. Everything visible (a tree, a river) had its own life. At that time, the creatures' capacity for abstraction was very limited, so the gods took the forms of kangaroos, cats, lizards, winds, hurricanes, night, and the Sun. Later, combinations of these forms. In time, more complex religions appeared, and the gods ceased to express themselves directly in nature, doing so instead through symbols and writing. Thunder and wind became *things*, while the gods ascended to more complex and profound heavens. Far from the creatures of a day, the gods perfected themselves into God. And God, because He was perfect, insensible, or irresistible to the senses, chose the symbol and the metaphor to communicate with those fragile and transient beings who had remained on Gaia.

272, SHAME. In the time of Christ, creatures prayed in public places, perhaps with the same inhibition seen today among Arabs. So much so, in fact, that at times they did it to boast of their faith. For this reason, Jesus advised his disciples to pray in secluded places (Matthew VI. 5:14 and Luke XI. 2:4), like someone making a donation to someone in need and taking precautions so that no one finds out. Today, Jesus' suggestion is followed, but for a different reason. Many creatures on Gaia have faith in God, *but they are ashamed of Him.* With scientific modesty, they pray in secret or make the sign of the cross as if they were fixing their hair or shooing away a fly.

273, GODS. The cosmogonic conception of our time, like previous ones, is a belief formulated on some kind of eloquence. In our case, it is a scientific eloquence. The theory of the *Big Bang* and all physical laws can do without God, but they cannot deny Him. The situation has already occurred in the same terms in ancient Greece. Now, without those gods and with a God who has fallen silent, the higher truths are delegated to scientists. In turn, these scientists, who are closer to their own impotence, postpone the answers to an abstract entity called the Science of the future. That is, when they are optimistic.

274, REGRESSION. As in the 19th century, the primitives only believed in what they saw. Today, the relationship of creatures with the material world—a sensual relationship—is more important and more intense than a couple of centuries ago, perhaps as much as in the Stone Age. Though also more empty. In this sense, we can say that we have regressed to what was once called "the night of time," though ours is a night illuminated by neon lights. The consumerist character of postmodern societies is a clear manifestation of this curious regression. According to the most cheerful surveys, the greatest hobby of the inhabitants of the evolved world is "going shopping." And for this reason, the *megamalls* gather more faithful than Mecca or the Vatican. Buy something today, something else tomorrow. The difference between this attitude and that of a child clinging to their mother's skirt to demand a new toy is negligible.

275, KNOWLEDGE. Today, the super-networks of communication are wonderfully perfected and produce a suspicious behavior: *surfing* the Internet is a popular habit, and there are countless courses to do it better and faster. But one must surf to nowhere; otherwise, one is committing an informatic heresy. —Hans Küng says that our world is over-informed, but the individual no longer knows what to do with so much information. If I remember correctly, Eduardo Galeano expressed something similar in an interview: "The *means* have replaced the ends." It seems that the greatest difference between the modern creature and the ancient one is not only in their greater knowledge of matter but in their greater ignorance of their own spirit. And what is worse: in their indifference. Now, if Stupidity is very well informed, no one should think that it can be combated with ignorant wisdom. In the times of barbarism, the great difference was made by books. In the Age of Computing, it is the same, because it is the same as the first but with more information and affectation. —It's fine, we also cannot prove that well-informed stupidity is condemnable (sometimes stupidity is not bad; it is just that: stupidity.), because it may well be the paradox that, given our natural impotence before the Enigma, stupidity is the wisest state. In that case, yes, we can say, with infinite joy, that we have reached the pinnacle or the Fourth Miracle.

276, EXTERIOR. Where the gods once were, now there are artificial satellites and the Hubble telescope, scrutinizing the *Finitebutunlimited* quasi-void. Also in this sense, we retain a primitive mentality: we look through millions of light-years seeking existential explanations. As if the Truth were located in a spatial beyond that surrounds the material world. Not in an insignificant being like the metaphysical creature.

277, INSIGNIFICANT. In such a way, creatures have become accustomed to being labeled "insignificant" by scientists and materialist philosophers that it no longer offends them. In some cases, the doctrine that classifies the creature as an *insignificant being* has achieved such success that they were often suppressed as a farmer does with ants. They forget, I presume, that all that immensity of stars, with their fourth and eleventh dimensions, with their numerical laws and their colors, with their truths of five hundred years and their truths of a single day, are, first and foremost, *formulations* of those insignificant beings. —According to a prestigious astrophysical cosmogony, the Universe and the creature are the result of a Big Bang whose sidereal echoes can still be heard and measured. The fantastic thing is that *that is all.* As incredible as the creation of the world in seven days or the destructive dance of Shiva.

278, EPISTEMOLOGY. Reflecting on the latest representations of the world on Gaia, Richard Tarnas wrote: "The great irony [...] is that it is just when the modern mind believes it has most fully purified itself from any anthropomorphic projections, when it actively construes the world as unconscious, mechanistic and impersonal, it is just then that the world is most completely a selective construct of the human mind." Which, in other words, means: As the human mind strips the Universe of human characteristics, it begins to consider it as a construct of the human mind itself. That is, as the world becomes dehumanized, it reveals itself as a purely human product. It is as if the most lucid creatures of Gaia have stopped seeing their own reflections in the mirror to see the mirror itself.

279, MEANINGS. As a child, I had the habit of randomly reading the *Cumbre* encyclopedia. Back then, those twenty red volumes were something like a poetic summary of the human adventure. A kind of Great Novel, composed of chapters with an unquestionable yet enigmatic and almost always incomprehensible, partial, and unfinished relationship. I would open it at random and find heroes, mountains, crimes and loves, prophets, formulas, and passions. Spenser, Sperry, Spitzberg, Stalin, Stalingrado, Storni, Stuttgart, Subconscious, Submarine, Sudan, Dream, Suez. But I also remember a night without this aesthetic support. I took one of those hardcover volumes and saw some of the absurd phenomena that make up a materialist universe: Dilthey, Flood, Dimensions, Denmark, Dynasty, Money, Dinosaur, Diogenes, Dionysus, God, Diplomacy, Airship, Disney, Dniepro-petrovsk.

XXXII: Toward a Trivial Being

280, TRIUMPHS. Not only has the creature's conception of itself and its universe lost almost all meaning; its works also reflect this orientation. As many battles have been won for living better as have been lost for conferring a transcendent meaning. All that is called "advances in ethics" or "liberation" means nothing more than greater enjoyment of sex, the body, and distraction. All of this signifies a resounding success of the aesthetic spirit and, in some cases, a success of hedonism. But as the barriers that limit the most immediate desires are torn down, the creature is increasingly conceived as a self-indulgent object. Each day, the creature ceases more and more to be a transcendent being through its own achievements. Each day, it moves further away from the Fourth Miracle.

281, WOUND. All or nearly all creatures consider contraception a medical and social achievement. However, when they first faced this possibility, they resisted accepting it. Today, the same is happening with cloning. In principle, cloning a human being would be no more harmful than manufacturing aerosol deodorants. The experiments of genetics do not contradict the last five Commandments in any way. But cloning has been declared an "immoral practice," and it disgusts almost all creatures. At least for now, because it is possible that their ethics will change before their practices do, just as Michael Jackson changed his nose before turning to a psychoanalyst. That would be consistent with the current state of affairs. But why do people still react with horror to cloning as they once did to contraception? I believe we should not look for moral reasons here before spiritual or psychological ones. Because the only concrete thing so far is the rejection, the *disgust* it provokes. —Both cloning and contraception represent new wounds in the metaphysical nature of the creature. Apparently, we are moving toward its own objectification at the expense of its ancient search for transcendence. Thus, the creatures feel the blow by wielding moral values that are very difficult to rationalize. —But let us see that the cloning of human beings will one day reveal the difference between body and spirit. Not long ago, in 1997, a Russian scientist proposed cloning Lenin. What can be gained from such an experiment? I believe we can anticipate the results and say that *the perfect copy of Lenin will not be Lenin.* It is most likely that the reborn Russian revolutionary will start selling McDonald's on Nikitskaya Street, or open a Rockefeller branch in the former Leningrad. Of course, in any case, it will be an *impetuous yuppie* with a strong will to succeed.

282, SPIRITUAL. Someone once informed me that Western society is one of spiritual values. I understand that not all of us can think and feel the same way, but it would be prudent to point out that if this is a spiritual society, it doesn't seem like it. —According to a survey at the end of the century, ninety percent of Americans claim to believe in God. I would like to know more precisely if they themselves consider American society to be more spiritual than materialistic. Could it be that God is just one of many comfort and security items? Besides being *free* and harmless in case of nonexistence. Let's not confuse things; claiming that Jesus was an exceptional and even superhuman man is a way to please both atheists and Christians alike.

283, NECESSITY. Hans Küng says: "The crisis of the leading power is already a moral crisis of the entire West, including Europe: the collapse of traditions, of a global sense of life, of absolute ethical criteria, and the lack of new goals, with all the psychological damage that derives from them." These points made by the German theologian are dialectically refutable, one by one. But they make it clear that we need a new truth, even if it's a lie.

284, MACHINES. When the computer *Deep Blue* checkmated the chess champion, the press, with the superficiality that often characterizes it, announced the triumph of the machine over man. But not over the man Kasparov, but over man in general. Now, the fact that IBM's computer defeated Kasparov does not mean that machines can think; it only means that chess is not thought. Comparing the metaphysical creature to a machine is obscene, something very characteristic of this era, since the only thing Kasparov and IBM's computer have in common is that both can be bought. For now, I'm not worried that machines might one day think. What does worry me, deeply, is that creatures might stop thinking. Perhaps because deep down I'm optimistic about the functioning of the human brain. Despite everything.

285, POVERTY. Poverty, like all human adjectives, is a comparative condition: it is measured in relation to its opposite, wealth (I think Heraclitus might have said this). The only absolute attribute of poverty is hunger. The other categories are relative conditions. Therefore, the assessment of poverty through numbers is largely unreal. Most poor French people could be considered rich in Nepal or in 9th-century France. However, these relative poor consider themselves absolutely poor. —And in some sense they are, because in our time poverty is doubly significant. It not only deprives the creature of the means of consumption but also makes consumption the only goal.

That is, spiritual poverty makes material poverty a miserable creature. And often violent.

XXXIII: The Suicide Club

286, SUMERIANS. The sacrifice of domestic animals in Neolithic tombs was a common practice. This was possible thanks to magical thinking. Not only was a dog sacrificed to accompany its master; plates and vessels were also broken, symbolically killing these inanimate objects. More precisely, 5,000 years ago, when a Kurgan chief died, he was accompanied by his servants and wives. The Sumerians took a similar step 4,500 years ago. Like the Greek Hades, the Sumerian afterlife was an undesirable place; there, spirits were condemned to wander in a cold and swampy land, populated by malevolent spirits. Since no one achieved happiness after death, the ancients focused on life on Gaia. When they worshiped their gods, the only hope that motivated them was the achievement of health and wealth. In any case, the religious translation of moral sins among the Sumerians consisted of punishment in this world. As was common then, Sumerian kings were considered almost gods. Therefore, upon death, they could not abandon such high ranks. Following the kings or being sacrificed to the gods was a privilege. In the royal tombs of Ur (of Abargi, Sabud, and Queen Shub-Ad), several dozen ritually sacrificed corpses were found. Queen Shub-Ad's tomb contained 74 attendants. Typically, the entourage was composed of maidens, guards, servants, and drivers with their draft animals. They are all courtiers and not condemned slaves, as was once assumed. Beyond these facts, we must retain others that are no less significant: the privileged companions prepared themselves for a long journey to a state superior to the common. For this fantastical voyage, they meticulously arranged the space and dressed in luxury and good taste. They did not neglect any accessory that might hinder their journey. When everything was ready for the marvelous experience, they poisoned themselves with opium and hashish. Not only was the drug meant to spare them the pain of death, but, according to scholars, the very position of their bodies indicated that they did so with a certain pleasure. Surrounded by luxury and solidarity, they embarked on their journey to the celestial planets. Since then, the club of happy suicides has continued this tradition, especially among Protestant sects in North America: Jonestown, Guyana, in 1979; Waco, Texas, in 1993; and the European sect of the Solar Temple on several occasions.

287, SECTS. The sect that best reproduced the archetype of the Sumerian suicides so far was *Heaven's Gate,* in San Diego, California, in March 1997. On that occasion, 39 people died, led by Marshall Applewhite. As throughout history, the powerful triggering sign was the passing of a comet, Hale-Bopp (it will take 2400 years to worry the creatures of Gaia again, if by then they haven't all committed suicide). Consider these facts: A1, The setting was a luxurious mansion valued at over a million dollars, in one of the wealthiest neighborhoods in the United States; A2, Its members owned a prosperous computer company, *Higher Source.* A3, The space and belongings of each were carefully arranged. Everyone had five dollars and some change in their pockets, as well as a valid passport; A4, They were known as computer experts, for their responsible work, intellectual, intelligent, and kind. They designed the San Diego Polo Club's website for ten thousand dollars; A5, The suicides poisoned themselves with vodka; B1, Tom Crow, who decades earlier had worked in music with Applewhite, said that "at times he showed curiosity about Eastern mysticism "; B2, Applewhite had written in 1995 that bodies are merely the container of the soul. The soul can evolve (he said) to a higher state where it receives a new physical form to house it. The final stage is liberation from the human realm; B3, One of the men had been castrated (elsewhere two are mentioned); B4, Shortly before, they had published in *USA Today: "Men refuse to evolve ";* B5, The human body is again mentioned as a container; B6, All had very short or shaved hair; B7, The idea of learning and evolution is recurrent (*Beyond Human*); B8, With the suicide, they hoped to move to a higher level. "*We simply take off the virtual reality helmet* —said one of them with a powerful cyber-metaphor—*; we take off the vehicle we have used for this task* "; B9, The group had considered moving to India or Nepal; C1, The comet was the sign they were waiting for; C2, Since 1970, Applewhite had said that "*to be saved from Lucifer, humans must renounce the pleasures of the earth* "; C3, Applewhite's father was a minister of the Presbyterian Church. He too had studied to be a minister of the same church, but later dedicated himself to music; C4, The documents the group disseminated through *Internet* described a world interpreted from the Gospels. The idea that Evil predominates in the world was affirmed; C5, Applewhite considered himself a messenger to Gaia with a biblical mission. —Well, we see that the data from group A reveal psychological and symbolic conditions very similar to those we find among the Sumerian suicides, 4500 years earlier. Group B is unmistakably identified with the Hindu and Jainist tradition. And group C refers to a Christian-apocalyptic vision of the world. The suicides of San Diego represent the ancient drama in a contemporary language. The destiny of the creature, the nature of the soul, the justification of life and death spoken in a language of *science fiction.* Men and angels integrate into a cyber-cult, for whom reality is no longer apparent but virtual; where souls seek evolution as before, but now relying on spaceships hidden behind an old comet.

288, DEPARTURE. Before embarking on their journey, the San Diego suicides recorded a video tape. At different times, the camera zooms in on each of them. While smiling and joking, they say things like: “We couldn’t be happier doing what we’re about to do. I’m really excited. Uncertainty was never a problem for us.” A woman says: “It’s simply the happiest day of my life.” A man adds: “People who think I’m crazy are deeply mistaken.” In reality, no; according to postmodern ethics, no one can say they did anything wrong: “live and let die.” Everyone is happy in their own way, and criticism is not accepted.

289, CHANGE. Changing states is denying the previous one. In the face of a painful event, we fall into unconsciousness if we’re awake; or we wake up if we’re asleep.

XXXIV: Postmodern Pride

290, COMPETITIVENESS. After the fall of the Berlin Wall, talking about "class struggle" became an anachronism. In its place, the no less ideological doctrine of "free competition" took root, which is nothing more than the *light* translation of the old Marxist crutch, since the famous Competition is not simply posed at the level of individuals but, above all, of social classes.

291, FREEDOM. It's useless to speak of Freedom as if it were a single issue. It might be for a horse; and perhaps it was for Plato. But for creatures who are not just flesh and bone nor just Ideas, Freedom is at least a diverse set of liberties. Political freedom depends on the political system; economic freedom depends on each individual's power. Freedom of conscience sometimes depends on nothing, but almost always depends on an ideology or a religion. —To say that we are all equally free, thanks to democracy, and that each individual's success depends on their own talent, is not only an American dream and another government demagogy; it's also an insult to the submerged classes and a greater insult to intelligence, which is not always in power. "Free competition" is a scam or a postmodern illusion. Anyone who has lost their innocence knows that nothing is more effective and immediate than political or familial connections. Both are social privileges, even if one is democratic and the other post-dynastic. Of course, as soon as one becomes a bit critical of "reality," its unconditional defenders come out with their famous argument: "And what's the alternative?" A question that usually leaves half the world speechless, since it's always easier to imagine what exists than to be a bit more original; and because, at times, the answer is too obvious: the alternative to a corrupt democracy is a non-corrupt democracy. For example, those who have no *link* in the powerful sectors of society must simply settle for their intelligence, which will be of little use if they also have the bad luck of possessing some non-negotiable ethical principle, such as not climbing over their coworker's shoulder. Later, when this type of creature reaches old age, poverty, and some sense of failure, they will be compensated with a shovel of dirt in the face, in the form of the beautiful phrase: "where there's a will, there's a way," not without first or later referencing the case of a known millionaire who made it from nothing, with the sole resources of their work and honesty, irrefutable proof of the virtues of our egalitarian, liberal and merchan*theistic*system. One case in a million fools goes without saying. —We all celebrate freedom (now, in a Platonic sense), but let's not be deceived by it. That is, let's not be deceived by its appearance, by that optimistic abstraction that the "successful" throw in the face of the dispossessed. One could say that in a totalitarian system, the most democratic thing is censorship. But the faults of others should not make us proud; on the contrary, others always take pride in our virtues. Let's look at the plank in our own eye. When, in a liberal society, was freedom ever democratic?

292, PRODUCT. Now, the media, universities, and human enterprises of any kind only speak of quality and effectiveness. "Demand a good product" is the new mantra repeated five times a day everywhere. When someone utters it, all discussions about ethics and morality cease completely; and the faithful kneel until their foreheads touch the ground. The modern cult of work has given way to the cult of product excellence. Demanding a good product (potatoes, hamburgers, bibles, water heaters) is the ethical obligation of any good citizen. The access codes are: Quality, Productivity, Sustained Increase in Purchasing Power. Any mortal who questions these basic principles of consumerist ethics will be condemned for mutiny. Because the stock markets of Tokyo, Hong Kong, New York, or Buenos Aires are so sensitive that they cannot even tolerate a single word of doubt from a businessman or bureaucrat about the health of the system. It is enough for a minister to stop praising the numbers here or there for the stock market to slump and panic to spread across the world. Panic or hysteria that, in normal times, is represented by the steady comedy of the aforementioned financial temples. Therefore, the condemnation is justified.

293, XXI. Not long ago, in small Switzerland, two banks merged: UBS and SBS. The new bank is now the second largest in the world, after Tokyo-Mitsubishi, with assets of 658 billion dollars. When the merger was finalized, 7,000 workers were laid off, but this is just a detail. Associating banks, companies, and concentrating capital is in the nature of the new world, just as dispensing with human workers is. Therefore, it would not be absurd to assume new associations of money. It is estimated, for example, that if four or five of these large financial institutions were to come together, the total capital would amount to more than two trillion dollars. The figure reached means they could buy or control (it's the same thing) the entire economy of Germany, almost all of South America, or a third of the United States. Currently, the fate of the world's countries depends on the decisions of these seven apocalyptic monsters. It is enough for them to arrive in a region of the world and then withdraw to disrupt the economies of the strongest countries. And this is just a sample. Over the next century, a terrible triangle will be fully drawn, at whose vertices will oppose the free concentration of *Capital*, the displaced and *Poverty*, and *Democracy*, which will be the target and the instrument of the other two opposing vertices.

294, POWER. Once, power was concentrated in priests and pharaohs; then it was in kings and emperors, as in Syria or Rome; once, power was in the people, or in a class of the people, as in Greece, which was not a proletarian minority but an aristocratic one; then it was in the Church and later in the States. Now, power is in Money and, as always, poorly distributed.

295, PILATE. It is curious and suspicious that, in the past, the Church and even Protestants considered, or simply taught, that the power of rulers has a divine origin, when the Gospels insist precisely on the opposite. Especially in the Apocalypse, power means Evil, the deception of the force that governs the world. Positioning oneself to the left of power is the most authentically Christian way to relate to it. However, this apparent contradiction is a traditional form of theological coherence. —In a recent and extensive twenty-four-page book, the former Uruguayan president Juan María Bordaberry expounded all his living thoughts on democracy. For Bordaberry, this system that brought him to power in 1972 is to blame for all the immoral vices of our societies.

For now, the only concrete thing we can say is that the greatest flaw of the system this gentleman criticizes is that it is capable of granting power for its own destruction, as happened in 1973. According to this politician and extensive thinker, we must "*recognize divine sovereignty as the origin of power.*" —From the ancient pharaohs to Juan María Bordaberry, passing through all the kings and despots of history, the creatures who held power have always believed it to be of divine nature. And for this reason, all of us who believe in the democratic value of the individual soul must remain heretical and disrespectful. And if we are democrats and cautious, when we manage to bring a party to government, we must return to the opposition. Because power is not divine but perverse by vocation, and that is why it must always be criticized.

296, SYMPTOM. Competing does not seem bad. At least, the opposite cannot be affirmed. But when societies become monothematic, when the material product of their labor is the greatest goal and the basis of all ethics, it is then that they are manifesting neurotic symptoms. Surely, they will not face immediate risks of disappearing or sinking into chaos, but they are exposed to an unnoticed process of idiocy. —A utilitarian mind (the wave of the latest creature) may view this perspective with enthusiasm: the education or training of their children for economic purposes. And thus, childhood is increasingly shortened, pressured by the urgencies of a savage future. And in part, it is understandable. How many misfortunes await those who do not follow the mad in their madness! But where can humanity go with highly competent beasts? Every day there are more demands for efficiency and fewer for reflection. Because reflection *never pays* unless it is market reflection. Fine, but let's imagine what will happen if we hand over the administration of a racetrack to the best horses.

297, DIRECTIONALITY. Everyone talks and writes about the dead of communism; and that's fine. But the other millions of beings who die in the world are forgotten, not under communist regimes but enjoying the free market and the directives of the International Monetary Fund. (On this, I refer you to the books of my friend, the English writer Joseph Hanlon.) The economic and social crises that hit Latin America, Africa, and Asia do not affect ministerial averages or financial empires; they hit, as always, directly in the stomach and head of the poor democrats. —To justify the ethics of "competition," it is argued, not without tenderness, that greater production will combat hunger in Africa or India. (The intention reminds me, I'm not sure why, of those who proposed a dictatorship of the proletariat as an intermediate step toward anarchist liberation.) But, except for sporadic attempts, the consequences of overproduction have not reached these places. More than that: we know that now the poor are poorer and more numerous than before. In 1997, according to UNICEF, 1.3 billion people survived on less than a dollar a day, and of them, 650 million were children. Between 1988 and 1993, in Latin America, those living below the poverty line and under neoliberal doctrine increased by twenty percent. We also know that every hour, 1,500 children die of hunger in the world, while almost two million dollars are spent every minute on military armaments (I ask for a moment of silence in front of a clock). And we also know, among the little we can know, that the world's largest arms seller is the country that shows the most concern for global disarmament. If that same country, the most polluting in the world, refuses to reduce industrial waste because it affects its economy, what should we think about its intentions to eliminate global conflicts? —Meanwhile, the rich countries live neurotized by the famous intestinal movements of the Stock Market. Because if the Annual Growth does not exceed Rising Expectations, worse for the hungry of the world who beg for alms and kill for it.

298, ECONOMY. The idea of indefinite Progress is from the 19th century and was supported by the unconsciousness of the planet's limited resources. But in a short time, the exploitation of nature by the market and industry decimated and polluted the forests, prairies, rivers, and skies of Gaia. A minority fraction of the planet's inhabitants consumes the majority of its resources under the shortsighted vision that they consume what they produce. But let us remember that there is almost no production without exploitation. On the other hand, the world's largest polluters refuse to reduce their waste, arguing that it would affect their economy. Traditional industry exploits and pollutes the biosphere to deadly extremes. And consumption does too. The consumption of goods and services is desperately encouraged by governments as a way to activate the economies of underdeveloped countries and as a way to sustain the living standards of rich countries. No minister would think of recommending austerity to their voters, one car per family instead of two or three. No, because that would affect the economy and growth. But what *growth* are we talking about? On a planet with limited resources, isn't it an ethical duty to save excess? Why is a family with one car less rich than one with two? Is it because the GDP or per capita income might decrease, shaming us before the international community? If there is some measure of a new ecological consciousness, why isn't there a consciousness of austerity? Of course, I'm asking for a lot in times when money and ostentation are the main Commandments of existence.

299, SOLZHENITSYN. Upon returning from exile to Russia, Aleksandr Solzhenitsyn was no less complacent with the new reality. "No," he said, "all hope cannot be placed in science, in technology, in economic growth. The victory of technological civilization has also instilled a spiritual insecurity in us. Its benefit enriches, but it also enslaves us. Everything is about interests (we must not neglect our *interests*), everything is a struggle for material things; but an inner voice tells us that we have also lost something pure, elevated, and fragile. We have ceased to see the purpose. "

300, UNDEREMPLOYED. In 1998, according to reports like CEPAL, young people with more years of education do not achieve the same social and job stability that their less-educated parents did. In response to this, ministers around the world chastise them for their insufficient preparation to enter "an increasingly competitive world." In countries like Japan, being incompetent is, at the very least, equivalent to treason against the nation. The result is statistical: the teenagers who survive do so in a *suicidal state* (not to be confused with "harakiri"); and so does the country. In Latin America, we don't go that far; incompetence is simply high treason against the market, and the market itself takes care of delivering justice. —I believe the biggest problem in the coming years will not be unemployment, because economists or advertising agencies are already taking care of that. The biggest problem will be underemployment, because it is the main resource to reduce unemployment. Full-time jobs will be reduced in favor of part-time ones, to the dissatisfaction of everyone.

301, SUBJUGATED. Africa and Latin America are so preoccupied with Europe and the United States that they are unaware of each other. I am tired of hearing in their countries that Americans are not very intelligent; then, invariably, they add that they have us subjugated and exploited. Well, which is it?

302, VILLAGE. Every time politicians and uncritical supporters of the system talk about trade and communication, they convince us that we are in the Global Village. But when they talk about hunger and misery, we are expected to distinguish between the first world and the third. "We must go where the world is going," warn the wise men of the government, refined in the art of eloquence that is professional politics. Then "world" means, as always, those minimal territories that make up Europe and the United States. The existence of an Anglo-Saxon locomotive and a single railway line is assumed; the rest of us can either cling to it or fall behind. To deviate is never an option.

303, COMMONWEALTH. An Anglo-Saxon cannot read more than a hundred pages if the writing is not adapted in the form of a *thriller*. This could be a scientific investigation about the Sphinx of Egypt (see *Keeper of Genesis,* by Bauval and Hancock) or about the location of Christ's tomb. If Copernicus had been born in an Anglo-Saxon country in the 20th century, he would have resorted to mystery to delay for 900 pages of *paperbacks* the idea that Gaia revolves around the Sun. —A person who has the fortune or misfortune to be born in an Anglo-Saxon country will be condemned to live and think within the geographical limits marked by their own language. If they are a cultured man, they will likely ignore all those thinkers who did not express themselves in their language. If they are a tourist or an emigrant, they will go to one of those countries that were once part of the British Empire. If they are an encyclopedia editor and not the one for the Encyclopaedia Britannica, they will surely have no place for names and words that do not have an arbitrary pronunciation. —In our time of computing and global communications, the only thing that has been internationalized is misunderstanding. Misunderstanding between peoples, between religions, between genders. Info-misunderstanding and misunderstanding-net.

304, CONSERVATION. The life of a modern creature was justified if it was capable of living in such a way that each day was the result of the summation (or product) of the previous days. All of Western culture and all that is Westernized is the expression of that Egyptian will: nothing is lost; everything is conserved. There were cultures for which forgetting and eliminating certain knowledge was a necessity. In some, like ancient Japan, temples are destroyed every twenty years to renew the spirit that inhabits them. But, for the modern mindset, nothing was ever worthless. Not a single verse written on an ancient Sumerian or Babylonian clay tablet. The French encyclopedia of the 18th century expressed that same will without euphemisms. Everything had to be the sum of something prior, because that signified knowledge, progress, and accumulation. The modern creature suffered from a phobia of loss and demonstrated it by preserving: dead objects or living animal species (the latter in the name of nature, when it has been "nature" itself that has been extinguishing millions of species long before the creature assisted in that task. Though natural extinctions were never as dangerous for Gaia). Every human object was also filled with memory: from a museum to a harmless transistor, since it carried the memory of Volta, Edison, and all the technicians at the *Bell Telephone Company* who ultimately produced it. —Perhaps things have changed a bit, because now the obsession is not to accumulate but to consume. And in this attitude, the abandonment of linear time for its opposite, circular time, is also expressed. If there are no other forms of time.

305, SIMPLICITY. In 1951, Karl Jaspers wrote: "The high risk and endeavor of personal reflection, the condition of all truthfulness, has degenerated through the path of the theory of ideologies. [...] Thus, the method of increasingly penetrating knowledge of the truth has ended in the baseness of psychoanalysis and vulgar Marxism." —Let's see, for example, that Marxism was such a complex intellectual construction that to popularize it, it had to be reduced to clichés like "religion is the opium of the people" or "property is theft." Like all reductions, these maxims were never clear without their corresponding commentary and in the long run ended up being an inefficient caricature. Moreover, it was never very clear why a creature should make so many altruistic sacrifices if there wasn't even a God. On the other hand, how did capitalism take root so easily in such different societies? Capitalism never overcomplicated itself; its greatest ideological strength lies in its simplicity. In this sense, it is like Islam; for a Muslim, a basic precept suffices: *Allah is One and His messenger is Muhammad.* For capitalism, the basic precept is: "*Time is money*" or "Saving is the foundation of wealth." Every day a million; and every day is worth the sum of the previous days. All of which implies that to be a Marxist, one had to be an intellectual, a self-sacrificing rich person, or at least an exploited poor person; while to join the capitalist club, it is enough to be honest or to let oneself be driven by greed. Capitalism has proven more effective than socialism at generating capital. The question remains whether it is effective for everyone or only for the winners, because we know that in the race for money, more flaws than virtues are needed.

306, TECHNOLOGY. On the Mozambican island of Ibo, drum dances were common. As in other places, the musicians were replaced by records and cassettes. Because they may sound good or not, but they are always cheaper. One night I attended a dance on the island, between the sea and some bamboo walls. As long as there was fuel for the small generator, the Quimoa youth danced to Madonna's music and other products someone brought from the other world. Is it necessary to repeat that technology is not devoid of ideology? Is it necessary to warn, once again, about the cultural genocide of capitalism?

307, MARKET. The Market has two flaws: one is its invisible hand; the other is its lack of conscience. *The Market has no conscience of any kind*; neither social, nor ecological, nor ethical, nor cultural. The Market does not distinguish a whale from incest, drug trafficking from cultural cannibalism. In fact, crime would be one of its ideal states, since crime, aside from promoting the economic progress of many countries (the "invisible hand" of the market not only sets prices), is the culmination of its unrestricted liberation. Of course, no politician, or almost none, would propose the absolute liberation of the Market; many would lose their positions in the Administration. But everything indicates that it is accepted as a necessary evil of Progress. We cannot ask more of them; they are so preoccupied with responding eloquently that they no longer hear questions. —Well, the Market is not the Devil, but it is a beast. For example, if frivolity sells more than culture, it is ethically just, according to the Market, for frivolity to prevail. And in fact, the media thrives on that proportion. The greatest virtue of the market, we know, is strength. But would anyone sleep peacefully knowing that we are governed by an invisible entity as unconscious as a rhinoceros? Of course, we could say that the dictatorship of a creature is worse. Agreed, but isn't this kind of mercantile omnipresence a form of dictatorship? Don't even the most optimistic say that this Order imposed by the Market is inevitable? So much so that even the opponents and the "leftist" governments resign themselves to the order inherited from the fatality of the times. Well, but what to do then? Let's see, if the rhinoceros is as powerful and irrational as it seems, shouldn't we domesticate it? That is, even if it seems utopian, we must place a yoke on it so that it is guided by a Conscience or, at least, controlled by one. It seems obvious that this "conscience" takes the form of the State. I understand that it sounds like Planning, but let's not be swayed by prejudices. It's not about teaching the Market what it already does very well; it's about not allowing it to tell us metaphysical creatures what we must do. Those who associate the word "control" or "intervention" with communism and other witches of the 20th century can start thinking of something else. Because, gentlemen, the alternative is not to let the beast loose inside the bazaar.

308, PROGRESS. The greatest danger of material progress is its visibility. And the visibility of its effects is the consequence of all optimism. Any spirit that manages to associate itself with it will be internationally revered. No matter how demonic it may be. Even communist regimes had their moment of glory when their numbers added up and the Soviet Union was a world power, both here on earth and in the sky. When communist regimes fell, they did not fall due to their moral shortcomings; they fell due to their economic flaws. And that is precisely what they are reproached for as the main argument. Wasn't it the same story with the rise and fall of Nazism? It seems that justice only arrives with economic failure. What will we say of this anachronistic end of the century when it fails? Must we wait until then to say something?

309, SUCCESS. In 1967, Sukarno was deposed by Suharto and the economic crisis. The new Indonesian dictator improved the numbers and remained in power for thirty years (a critical figure for great dictators). A new economic crisis was necessary for the IMF and the people to question the ethical virtues of his government and force him to abandon power in 1998, amid a national revolt. Similar stories are scattered across the world and throughout history, which shows that there is nothing better for abusing power and a prostitute than economic success.

310, FAILURE. The failure of the Socialist Paradise on Earth does not mean that socialism is impossible but that Paradise on Earth is impossible. This is demonstrated by the failure of the Anti-socialist Paradise, which is not only possible but also fashionable.

311, GOLD. Gold, which in our culture is the symbol of the material and its implications (greed, impurity, ambition), in another time signified purity and the immaterial. Those were the times of the most ancient alchemy, of Buddha and other beings now unrecognizable or belonging to fantasy literature.

32, INSTABILITY. The sea, the silence of dusk, the plains, the mountains... The contemplation of nature always attracts the metaphysical creature because it signifies its origin and its contradiction. The reality of the creature is always, or almost always, marked by change, the uncertainty of the future (there is no happiness that is not threatened by the future; not only Buddha had to understand this). Nature, on the other hand, has always been there. The twilight, the same waves dragging themselves over the sand, unchanged for thousands, millions of years, represent for the agitated spirit of the creature peace and eternity. —Now, the greatest difference between the ancient world and the new lies in the fact that the latter is more exposed to great crises. Because the world surrounding each creature increasingly depends less on nature and more on other creatures and the systems left behind by those no longer on Gaia. Even nature itself begins to depend on this unstable being. The serious issue is that the creature makes mistakes on a grand scale. The errors of nature, on the other hand, are almost infinite but occur on an infinitesimal scale, so it is later perceived as infallible; for example, in the form of sporadic genetic mutations that are later corrected by death. It could be said that nature perfects or readapts itself through *approximations,* while creatures do so through crises and revolutions.

313, CRITIQUE. History has shown that it is always healthier and more effective to critique the present than to design the future. Warning of a problem does not oblige us to donate the solution; it obliges us to seek it.

XXXV: Civilization, Refuge, and Threat

314, LAW. The secular and atheistic vision that prioritizes action over thought, formal goodness over inner conscience, is summarized in the formula: "think and feel as you please, but act according to the norms." The Mosaic commandment not to harm one's neighbor was translated by Christ into the duty to love them indiscriminately. According to John 13:34, after announcing Judas' betrayal, Jesus of Nazareth summarized: "I give you a new commandment: Love one another." This democratic love had a modern equivalent in socialist altruism. Later, savage neoliberalism returned to the Mosaic root: it is no longer necessary to worry about others as long as you do not harm them; they will not harm you either.

315, SOPHISTS. Creatures can only be united by an ethic of survival, which is insufficient because it is trivial. An atheist who condemns a crime or drug trafficking has a moral reason to do so. A religious spirit has two. Let us remember that the philosophy of sophists like Protagoras or Critias began with a valid epistemological stance, very similar to the postmodern one: all mythologies are false or at least unprovable. *Therefore*, creatures should only concern themselves with their own success, and for that (obviously) everything was valid. For money, the sophists taught this truth to the most important sons of Greece, which led it from the Acropolis to the plains of chaos.

316, REFLECTION. Governments around the world invest even what they do not have in scientific and productive research. That is, when they invest well. In other words, professionals take care of the production of things, but ethical reflection on the results is always left to amateurs. On Gaia, ethical reflection is cultivated in sports programs or passionate electoral debates.

317, CULTURE. In 1978, the Argentine writer Ernesto Sábato recalled a phrase by Goering: "When I hear the word culture, I reach for my revolver." Under this principle of involutionary power, the Nazis burned books and people, all as a Paleolithic way of suppressing culture in Germany and losing honor, progress, and the war. Something similar was achieved by the military dictators in the Río de la Plata a few years later. Another Argentine, the Nobel Prize winner in Biology Cesar Milstein, recalled in 1994: "I remember very well that a minister of the military government said that in Argentina things would not be fixed until two million intellectuals were expelled." Indeed, in the 1960s, when Milstein and a group of eminent scientists were expelled,

Argentina was intellectually on par with Australia and Canada. Since the brightest minds were expelled or forced to resign to cooperate with the best universities in Europe, in the Río de la Plata things have been fixed as those in power wanted, though they suffered from a well-known complex.

318, INSTRUCTION. The virtue of the military lies in discipline and the fulfillment of superior Orders, in the repression of any emotional impulse that might compromise victory. It would be universally healthy if, on the first and last day of classes, military schools taught that *there is no such thing as due obedience when it comes to violating Human Rights.* And by the way, that golden rule should be abolished, according to which a genocidal maniac like Pinochet or Videla or that other monster who decided the massacre of Vietnam has a better chance of being forgiven than a chicken thief. —I remember that when, in Latin America, one of these gentlemen took power, they did so swearing in the name of God, the Fatherland, and the Nation. Later, they were judged and forgiven, or only forgiven, in the name of God and the Fatherland and the Nation. Now, if God has truly decided to pardon these poor sinners, we can say, without fear of being wrong, that Hell does not exist. Or it exists and is here on Gaia.

319, COMMUNICATION. If Latin American governments did not have such a formidable backing as military force, *they would surely* take the trouble to communicate and make themselves better understood by their people. —It's fine, armies are there to protect States, and if those States are democratic, their existence is justified. Fine, but in our Post era, democratic States are increasingly a formality of parallel and subterranean Powers; a formality of financial Empires, drug trafficking, arms trafficking, speculation, and the illusions of the people.

320, MORAL. I remember that in high school we had a subject called "Moral and Civic Education," when our government was neither civic nor educated. In that subject, we were taught about the moral virtues of *our* army while in the barracks, Human Rights and animal rights were being violated. For different reasons, many of us knew it. And perhaps that's why many of us are cured of "patriotism "; we distrust "patriotic symbols" and distance ourselves from all the sermons that explain to us what "morality and good customs" are. We can no longer believe in speeches, in parades, in the honor of arms, in "my flag," in the index of caudillos, in the neatness of suits, in grave faces, in the eloquence of numbers, in the realism of businessmen, in the witches of the town, in the success of opinions. To lie to us again, they will first have to invent something clever and original. It won't be easy for them, because now we are made of distrust.

321, EXPERIENCE. We cannot blame everyone who supported the dictatorship during the dictatorship; the real culprits are those who defend it now that it has passed. Because we cannot expect someone to have enough clarity in the midst of events. The precariousness of the well-known phrase "I know what I'm saying because I lived it" is demonstrated by the contradictory wisdom of two people who lived through the same events.

322, MASSACHUSETTS. On May 5, 1920, Nicola Sacco and Bartolomeo Vanzetti were accused of a murder they did not commit. The judges who sentenced them to the electric chair did not want to hear a witness who told the police that Sacco and Vanzetti were not the men he had seen on the night of the crime. They also did not want to consider that at the same time of the crime, Sacco was in the office of the Italian consul, nor the confession of the real killer even before the sentence. Webster Thayer, the presiding judge, did not acknowledge the xenophobic motives of the verdict, but at least he declared that "*The defendants in the murder are guilty of socialism.*" I think it would be excessive to recall other patriotic examples from the forties or sixties. Of course, in the United States there were also communists. But they all disappeared, because it was a democratic country.

323, PARADOXES. Those who do not believe in paradoxes risk being trapped in the deceptive logic of obvious things. For example: *there is nothing more dangerous than security*. This paradox was successively confirmed by epistemology, by political and scientific ideologies. — And by military governments.

324, ARTIGAS. When Artigas triumphed in the *Battle of Las Piedras* in 1811, he uttered one of his most famous phrases: "*Mercy for the vanquished*" —which in his original Spanish must have been a less affected expression. This phrase was often repeated in the schools of the dictatorship, a historical period characterized by the inverse exercise of Artigas' order. This means one of two things: a) those military men had an anti-Artigas education capable of erasing the imprint of childhood schooling; or b) childhood schooling education was useless.

325, BALANCE. Once the *raison d'être* of the army was the *domination* of the other. Then it was for *defense.* Now the word that justifies them is a synthesis of the previous pretensions: *armies exist to maintain "balance."* In structural calculus, this is known as "unstable equilibrium." But at what level is this equilibrium that leads them to arm themselves more every day? To maintain it, armies demand more resources from their governments every day. And if times are bad because no new conflicts arise, they invent them. If Chile buys a nuclear submarine "because Argentina is not reliable," Argentine generals demand that their government level the playing field. And if India, democratic and malnourished, boasts of having obtained the atomic bomb, Pakistan conducts its own nuclear tests until it achieves and demonstrates the same destructive power and the same intelligence. —We know that wars are not won by suppressing the enemy's weapons but by eliminating the enemy itself along with all the civilians living nearby. But why is an equilibrium of armed countries better than an equilibrium of disarmed countries?

326, NATURE. It is no coincidence that most basketball players are tall men, nor that most cross-dressers are homosexuals. Nor is it a coincidence that the majority of those who hold power are ambitious people. In other words, it is no coincidence that the world is governed by people who should not govern it.

327, THREAT. For the past two hundred years, the creature's intelligence has shone brightest in the exercise of science and technology. With these, it multiplied the possibilities of two ancient powers characteristic of its nature: destruction and preservation. For destruction, it invented and organized imposing mechanisms of death; for the preservation of life, it perfected medicine and various health systems. But, unfortunately, this is not a balanced relationship in its possibilities. What medicine builds in ten years can be erased with a single act of war. A plague can be eradicated after a tremendous global effort, but no holocaust can be remedied by any science or technology. This means that intelligence makes the creature, every century, every day, more dangerous to its own existence. Therefore, the affirmation of an ethical consciousness becomes more urgent every day, and one way to measure it is through the renunciation of the individual or a group for the benefit of the rest of humanity. —For a million years, creatures expressed their violence with sticks and stones. We cannot erase millennia of violence from our spirit; but as our intelligence becomes more powerful (and that means danger), so must our culture, our outer history, rise to the same level. We know that a dictator or a soldier wielding a weapon of mass destruction resembles a Paleolithic god, and that is why demanding a better consciousness seems entirely utopian. But we can never give up on such a demand.

328, PROSELYTISM. Proselytism is a characteristic of the Western mind, and if its origins are not in Christ, they are at least in Christianity. It would be too obvious to note that these origins are historical and religious, if we consider the New Testament and the Judeo-Roman and Roman-Christian relationship of the early centuries. First came the universal claim of the Church over truth and morality, and then one of its products: the ethical and ideological universalism of modern atheists. Oswald Spengler had already observed, almost a century ago, that "Everyone pronounces an imperative—'you must'—in the conviction that something must be changed in a uniform direction" [...] "On this topic Luther, Nietzsche, the popes and the Darwinists, the socialists and the Jesuits agree" [...] "He who deviates is an infidel, an enemy to be fought." Then, Spengler recalls that it was not always so: neither in India, nor in China, nor in the ancient world; neither Buddha nor Epicurus wanted to change the world like Nietzsche. —Perhaps there is no longer sexual and ideological proselytism. Or what is promoted (because a living society always promotes something) is the opposite: "be different." But diversity is appreciated at the same time as it is nullified. Postmodern discourse praises sexual and cultural differences, but in fact does not renounce uniformity. The market, technology, and laws cater to a much more restricted and uniform human type than the ancient one: visual codes, ideas, languages, music, a single currency, television, an infinitely diverse offer and uniform consumption, the process of education and health, transnational monopolies. All children must go to school, all must be vaccinated, all must contribute to the pension fund, all must pay their taxes, all must register their fingerprints, *all must...* There will be fewer and fewer opportunities to step out of the system without falling from it, without becoming a *homeless* person or a leper. The system is designed to protect us from violence and disease, but at the same time it abuses us and tends to destroy the freedom it claims to empower. Will that be the necessary price that societies will have to pay from now on? Paradoxically, the diversity of our time is so great that it identifies with uniformity. Because it is only an apparent diversity. —I have always thought that, just as living organisms in their evolutionary process tend to associate into an increasingly complex body (like the original unicellular organisms), so too do the consciousnesses of Gaia tend toward a Global association. When I read James Lovelock's Gaia theory, I understood that there lay the biological metaphor of this idea: the planet (Gaia) *as a living unit*. This, which in principle would mean peace and security, also frightens. Especially considering the current state of affairs. Though such pessimism may well be due to the fact that, in addition to being metaphysical creatures, we are also discontented creatures.

329, SILENCE. To live for a while in a first-world country, it is not necessary to know the language. Although *it is still* necessary to speak some English, over time one can do without any spoken language. That is, if machines are not mostly voice-controlled. Even today, the life of a foreigner includes: an *tourist information* electronic kiosk at the airport, to choose a hotel and plan the itinerary for the next thirty days; a hotel without receptionists, accessed with a credit card and a six-digit code that opens all doors; a hypermarket where one can pick up and leave an infinite number of items and pay with the same credit card without needing to utter a *merci* or a *thank you* to the cashier; a *self-service* station to grab a drink and fill up with fuel, after a dialogue with a payment machine; a *fast-food* restaurant where the menu is chosen with a number or a code; a long list of *tickets* extracted from the corresponding machine to access any means of transportation or entertainment; and a long etcetera of codes and electronic signals. —Each day it becomes less necessary to speak and more necessary to speak less. I must admit that, although I have always been an obsessive conversationalist abroad, even with language difficulties, I have always felt very comfortable in this impersonal and anonymous relationship of postmodern cities. Even here, in my own country, I always choose shopping centers where the interaction between customer and seller is minimal or anonymous. But I am not a good example for anyone, and from every point of view, my taste is both legal and suspicious.

330, CITIES. The age of an object can be measured by the presence of Carbon-14; the more of this element, the older the object in question. The age of a particular stage of the Modern Era can be measured by the amount of science and technology involved in it: the more recent the year we consider, the stronger the presence of science and technology in the lives of creatures. Similarly, the age of a city can be deduced by its violence: the more modern and evolved a city is, the more violence it suffers. Along with the decrease in Carbon-14 and the development of material intelligence, the insecurity of each creature has increased. And if it is true that in a small town there is the same proportion of criminals as in a big city, it is also true that the inhabitants of a small town do not fear for their lives as the Neanderthals did in the Paleolithic era, or as the evolved inhabitants of our civilized world now fear in big cities like São Paulo, Johannesburg, or Los Angeles. —The loneliness and mutual ignorance of big cities lead to the loss of group consciousness. Anyone can see that the violence of cities is often directly proportional to their size; but fear and insecurity are proportional to the square of that size. That is, as creatures crowd together, they become isolated beings; as the size of civilization increases, so does the size of savage behavior.

331, COMMANDMENTS. All peoples should, from time to time, rewrite the Ten Commandments. Not to replace Moses' Ten (because that would be impossible as well as ridiculous), but to better observe our changes. Since our time is no longer that of Moses, we cannot expect the dictatorship of a new leader. Now there is only a democratic or vulgar way: a collective survey of individual opinions. So here, in passing, is my own classification:

I

1— *Thou shalt not kill*, under any circumstances, because there is always a reason to kill.

2— *Thou shalt not covet thy neighbor's partner*. That is a good reason to ignore the first commandment.

3— *Thou shalt not bear false witness against thy neighbor*, for justice is blind.

4— *Thou shalt not steal*. If you do so out of necessity, make sure it's not a necessity you've created for yourself.

5— *Thou shalt help thy neighbor* to survive and to fulfill the rest of the commandments.

II

6— *Thou shalt be tolerant;* for when you become a fool, you never know it.

7— *Thou shalt not believe thyself the owner of the Truth.* If Truth existed, it would not have such a poor owner.

8— *Thou shalt not consider thyself better than others.* Only then can you consider that you are not among the worst.

9— *Thou shalt seek the truth both on earth and in heaven,* for that is thy destiny and thy eternal condemnation.

10— *Thou shalt seek God,* for no Commandment is worth anything without Him.

As we had seen before, the order of the tablets is, or *tends* to be, inverted. In the biblical *Decalogue*, the first tablet refers to the metaphysical (II), while the second repeats ancient moral principles (I). As if it were a typographical paradox, we see that Hebrew writing developed from right to left, so the stone of the second tablet had been placed at the beginning of our Western reading, while the first was at the end. It's as if the West had understood the order of Hebrew writing, just as the Russians copied the Roman alphabet from a wet piece of paper.

XXXVI: The show must go on

332, AMERICA. A year before his death, the science communicator Carl Sagan wrote: "In surveys from the 1990s, two-thirds of all adults in the United States had no idea what the 'information superhighway' was; forty-two percent didn't know where Japan was; and thirty-eight percent were unaware of the term Holocaust. But over ninety percent had heard about the criminal cases of Menéndez, Bobbit, and O. J. Simpson; ninety-nine percent knew that the singer Michael Jackson was suspected of abusing a child. Perhaps the United States is the most entertained nation on the planet, but the price we pay is very high. "

333, CORRECTION. Our modern standard of living is superior to the ancient one, but every day we need more time and more concentration to survive as such. At 25 or 30 years old, we finish our formal education, and by 40 we might achieve some economic stability and a defined role in society. By then, we will have only learned to compete, and we will likely continue to do so for the rest of our lives. —Now, how is the lack of transcendence in our order compensated? To forget that all our efforts ultimately end in nothingness, and to forget the collective fatigue produced by such efforts, the cult of entertainment was born. Not long ago, a European economist or businessman proposed reducing working hours. What seemed like a sporadic outburst of humanism soon revealed itself as a new service to the system. This economist or businessman argued that if creatures worked too much, they couldn't have fun, *ergo* they couldn't consume (it remains to be seen where those who have no time to live put their money). And that's bad, very bad. Which shows that the economist or businessman wasn't as crazy as he seemed at first.

334, TELEVISION. The cult of the *product* demands a complementary *ad hoc* that allows us to forget the emptiness of effort. But in turn, the system charges for entertainment. The list of pastime institutions is vast: shopping centers, sports or political spectacles, videos. And the irreplaceable television. For some reason, this democratic vehicle has become the paradigm of vulgarity. Most of television is the representative of a suicidal manifestation, it is the *culture of anti-culture.* Because if the basic requirement of any form of culture is memory, for television it is forgetfulness. A person can watch hundreds of movies and thousands of commercials in a year; after suffering or enjoying a *B-grade thriller*, the viewer prepares to forget it completely. On the other hand, the sooner one does it, the better. In these cases, whatneed is there to retain data or to poison oneself with laboratory intrigues? (Everyone should know that the most common form of domestic violence is television. Light television *kills more creatures than Shakespeare, but unlike this outdated figure,* it leaves nothing behind.) Intrigues that are often geopolitical proselytism. Better for the health of bulimic viewers and better for the channels that, thanks to systematic forgetfulness, can repeat the same "mystery" movies without the forgetful viewer remembering that the butler was the killer.

135, INTELLIGENCE. Intelligence is not funny, which is why it can only make us laugh when it disguises itself as an idiot; what we sometimes call humor or irony. Humor needs intelligence, but comedy is obliged to absurdity or foolishness. The most famous comedians play foolish characters, although none of them are, because one can feign stupidity but not intelligence. Socrates or Galileo could pass for fools, but none of those fools who condemned them could pass for them. That's in theory, because as Democrates said, "*he who admonishes a man who believes himself intelligent works in vain.* "

336, INTERNET. The internet is a superior instrument to television. It is a true communication channel, as it has surpassed the one-way sender-receiver relationship of previous inventions. With the internet, many things have been lost for the dictators of the moment: censorship and the manipulation of information. This does not mean that the metaphysical creature is free from other dangers, such as, for example, optimism and lack of critical thinking. Let us not forget that racism, insults, vulgarity, misinformation, and even typographical errors are an epidemic on the internet. Anyone who wants to have a bit of fun can add errors and cultural viruses to the web, anonymously or under the author's name, which is almost the same thing. For now, assuming any equivalence between the Internet and books is a sign of little intelligence. The same amount of intelligence needed to suppress a library in favor of the Supernet.

337, BEAUTY. Almost all creatures on Gaia can boast of intelligence, while no one, or almost no one, boasts of being beautiful. Hence, creatures are always willing to repeat the phrase: "what matters is inner beauty." And they are not referring to kindness, precisely. —Because the exterior is always more evident; anyone can imagine themselves as better on the inside than they appear on the outside. Therefore, intelligence is declared a universal virtue, while physical beauty remains superficial. We know that both beauty and intelligence decline with time, but only the first decline is noticeable. The other is concealed by experience or goes unnoticed due to its own absence.

338, IMAGE. The momentary (and sometimes permanent) success of any human endeavor depends on advertising: deodorants, detergents, presidents, hamburgers, poems, religions, bibles, and water heaters. The success or failure of a soap depends on the fame of the model who advertises it. Everyone knows that the praises of a famous person for a product are not sincere and that they could have said the same about the competition if the competition had paid them a bit more. But everyone also knows that without that lie, the brand would not sell as well as it does. That is to say, people easily recognize what is true and what is advertising. But they choose the advertising. —Of course, it is not always like that; sometimes people do not easily distinguish one from the other. In 1996, the magazine NOTICIAS from Buenos Aires published a survey commissioned by the consulting firm Germano & Giacobbe. Among the five most "trustworthy" people in the country was the writer Ernesto Sábato (which seems to demonstrate, once again, that people celebrate writers who do not represent them. I refer to Sábato's incorruptibility, to the "discreet charm" of Bioy Casares, to Borges's modesty...) Additionally, among those five most trustworthy people in the country was the beautiful model Valeria Mazza. That is to say, while beauty is considered a superficial attribute, everything indicates that it is valued as much as it is discredited. A year after the survey, the model found herself in Chile with General Augusto Pinochet. It seems that this gentleman gave Valeria one of his highest compliments on her beauty. When asked about this chance encounter, Valeria expressed that while she never spoke about politics (anyone can make a mistake), she thought Augusto was a charming man. I suppose she was also trustworthy.

339, HAPPINESS. The happiness of consumption is not just a business; it is also an illusion. Let us leave it as the tired argument of the frivolous. They, I will never know why, always assume they are happier than the Greek tragedians. Perhaps because depth terrifies them. Since Aeschylus, tragedy has reexamined the great Questions, has exercised the will to confront the Enigma of existence. Not to solve it (because it is unsolvable) but to admire it. On the contrary, comedy has always sought disqualification and forgetfulness. Which is also healthy because, like laughter, it relaxes.

340, DISNEYLAND. It must be acknowledged that technological magic is admirable. Virtual reality journeys to fantastical worlds are a good example of how creatures can dream while awake, all thanks to their intelligence. At Universal Studios in Hollywood, for example, a creature can experience almost the same amount of emotion as one of those mystics who roamed the skies of Asia two thousand years ago. Those Buddhas or Christians were so poor that they could not rely on a million-dollar scaffold to ascend to heaven, like today's creatures. A Buddha, a guru, or a shaman depended only on their wisdom. The case of the American Indians is even worse: they experienced more ghosts than in the movies, and they didn't even do it out of wisdom but out of ignorance.

341, SELF-DOUBT. Self-help books are the amulets of our time. In them lies all the superstition of fearful creatures. Without the aid of fear and modern superstition, these books would not be *best-sellers* and much less would they be considered profound or necessary. We can list some examples of this depth (a selection made by the newspaper *El Observador*): "Hug your wife four times a day" (John Gray); "Praise yourself as much as you can," "Criticism is a useless act," "Look at yourself in the mirror often and say: *I love you*," "Do what you like to do," "Your thoughts can help you get the perfect job" (Louise L. Hay); "Control means being the master of your own destiny," "We can all do something," "Make someone laugh today and tomorrow, every day," "No one can deceive you without your consent," "Remember that you cannot fail at the task of being yourself" (Wayne W. Dyer). —The insecure creature seeks in self-help books to be told what they already know; but they need an authority (priests of solitary success) to repeat it to them, because they no longer believe in themselves. They cannot believe in themselves because they are accustomed to believing and accepting the orders and advice of the media. Their freedom is virtual or illusory, because to be free, it is necessary, at the very least, to start by believing in oneself.

342, MŪNI. Peace is a state of consciousness and, in our world, it depends on another reality, which is physical and never entirely controllable. Or it depends on its own reality, on consciousness itself. The latter is what Buddha understood and we others have forgotten.

343, RATING. Sophocles and Aeschylus competed for the applause of the Greek people. Shakespeare wrote for the theater, not for the eternity of the printed word. Unlike the great writers of the 20th century, the Englishman was especially concerned with the judgment and acceptance of the audience that night. Like any Hollywood or television screenwriter. Because there were times when depth and intelligence had *ratings*.

344, FORGOTTEN. Granted, there are golden times and there are shitty times. It is also likely that one always tends to consider their own time as decadent or disappointing. And perhaps this is due to the fact that we know the past through its geniuses, who are the ones most remembered by libraries. We do not consider, then, that in the times of Newton and Homer there were as many fools as there are now and that almost all of them were forgotten as one day we will be forgotten. Unless, unlike libraries, electronic memories continue to store fools instead of geniuses.

XXXVII: The story will continue

345, TRANSFORMATION. For almost all of history, creatures have been conservative beings. If great changes were made from time to time, it was more due to the influence of prophets, thinkers, military leaders, and other isolated individuals than to the will of the people themselves. Peoples, in general, have always aspired to preserve and repeat an inherited order. The need to transform the world was a novel need of that brief historical period of a few centuries called the Modern Era, and its paradigmatic event occurred in France in 1789. From that point on, creatures began to kill one another with the same goal: to change everything. If thousands of compatriots had been decapitated to impose the Rights of Man, why not do the same to impose the Rights of the Proletariat? —The Marxists argued that while philosophers had been busy interpreting the world, what truly mattered was transforming it. This maxim, not so much revolutionary as modern, guided the thought and action of revolutionaries and counter-revolutionaries throughout the 20th century. Until they finally succeeded in North America. There, almost all the utopias of old and dreamy Europe were realized: a welfare society, secular, conformist, progressive, and imperialist. For this reason, there are no longer projects for great changes, but rather an excessive effort to bury history, along with all its prophets and thinkers. As in the previous millennia, the people no longer want to hear about changes or uncomfortable speculations. Something has finally been lost in this process: the abominable depth. And the people sing what Edie Brickell sings:

> *Philosophy is a walk on the slippery rocks.*
> *Choke me in the shallow water before I get too deep.*
> *What I am is what I am.*
> *Don't let me get too deep.*

346, PHILOSOPHERS. The entire education of the last creature is single-themed: from childhood, they are prepared for competition. Everything that does not aim for economic success and surpassing others is superfluous. If someone stops for a moment to question these constitutional articles, they risk falling out of the system. In the fatherland, they are called *homeless*; in almost the entire world, *incompetents*. And of course, which parent would prefer a reflective *hippy* to a successful *yuppy*? Thought and the works of the spirit do not pay unless they are best-sellers; and there are no best-sellers that include thought and spirit; and if there are, they are not best-sellers precisely because of that. —Our time imagines that philosophy is no longer necessary, perhaps because it is not competitive. But how mistaken they are! Do they not realize, perhaps, that philosophy is even more necessary in our time than in ancient Greece? Because in ancient Greece it could be a merely speculative problem, while in our time it is a matter of life or death. —It is not surprising that in this era philosophers are so poorly regarded. They represent a paleontological species on the brink of extinction, severely wounded by the fall of the Berlin Wall or by some other symbolic and virtual event. They represent the prototype of the *homo delirantes*, errant and disconnected from "reality." None of this is strange, because our time despises thought and, in the name of life and fun, embraces vulgarity. Which is not entirely bad, because we all know that truth is sad and that it is best to be happy.

347, PUNCTUALITY. Takeshi Umehara considers that "postmodernism" is more natural in Japan than in the West, since here it signifies a break with the Judeo-Christian conception of linear and progressive time, while in Japan it is a return to the circular time of *Shinto*. However, I believe it is necessary to force the "naturalistic" vision of Shintoism quite a bit to make it align with the more current "efficiency-worship" of Japan. Therefore, one might think that if postmodernism is oriental in the heavens, it still remains occidental here on Gaia.

—When I visited Japan, I was struck by the millimeter precision of the trains and the contrast between traditional neighborhoods and modern ones. When the train door aligns with the platform arrow, one need only look at the ticket to set the clock; meanwhile, in some old district of Tokyo or any other city, a man working with wicker teaches his son the craft, and on the doorstep, the elderly converse almost in silence. The traditional is peaceful, quiet, Asian; the modern, a caricature of the West, an optimistic example of Westernization with its rockers and punks, as grotesque as they are harmless. —Some time later, on May 11, 1997, as I did every day, I opened *El País* and read: "Japan: Ichiro Oshima took only half a day off in the eighteen months prior to his death. The 24-year-old publicist always arrived punctually at work at seven in the morning and often returned at one or two in the morning the next day. Until he decided to commit suicide. His death would have been considered simply another case of 'karoshi'—a Japanese word that designates something like 'death by overwork'—if it were not for the fact that his parents decided to sue his employers and demand compensation [...] There are those who instead practice 'compassionate overtime,' staying until late at night, not to work, but to offer 'moral support' to their colleagues. This is why, often, when a worker leaves their job early, they bid farewell to their coworkers by saying 'o saki ni,' which means something like 'sorry for leaving before you.'" —Walking through one of those ancient temples in Kyoto, I felt something that shouldn't have been new and that struck me as the idea of a distant Oriental: intelligence resides in large enterprises, but wisdom only in the silence of small things.

348, DOMINION. Over the last two hundred years, the creature's power to dominate nature has increased exponentially, while its power to dominate Truth, that is, the power to dominate itself, has practically stagnated. If it hasn't regressed.

349, COMMUNICATION. For millions of years, evolution has been framed as a competition among individuals while also being an association of communities. The entire biosphere is the product of an association that has resulted in a living unity, as described by the British scientist James Lovelock. But metaphysical creatures have also followed a similar path. Morality, or moralities (the consciousness of the species) has evolved toward integration, even surpassing, in many cases, the famous cultural differences. We cannot say that a global ethics exists or that something similar is near, but the tendency and the need to achieve it is stronger in our time than in antiquity, when peoples, cultures, and religions could live without coexisting, completely ignoring one another.

That is no longer possible; misunderstanding may still exist, but not total ignorance. The other exists, and we know it. —In our Post era, a new phenomenon has emerged that expresses this new associative will of the species: I refer to the super-networks of communication. About them, I conceive two images, one enthusiastic and one disappointed: I see Gaia as a body (biosphere) and as a mind or spirit (exosphere); the creatures would be the neurons, and the electronic networks the dendrites. Agreed, a geopsyche that is autistic or full of traumas, defects, and complexes. But let's not say we lack the means to understand each other.

350, AGES. Each creature repeats the history of the species. In childhood, everything is permanent, because any brief moment can be almost an entire lifetime, and any future a utopia. Maturity, on the other hand, warns that the world is no longer unchangeable but fragile and fleeting. Things and creatures pass by, and this passage, like a Chinese water torture, begins to be perceived with increasing sensitivity. New families form while the first one drifts away or is lost forever. Around the age of thirty (as with Zarathustra, Buddha, Christ, Augustine, Francis of Assisi, Kierkegaard), the creature is shaken by existential questions. The childhood of the species was the mythological age, the age without dates or order, the age of legends and the eternal cycles of prehistory. Maturity is that moment when the unconsciousness of myth or eternity is abolished by questions: by religions and by philosophy. It is the 5th century B.C. that caught Jaspers' attention. —Each creature repeats the history of the species; which also means that questioning is still our state of maturity, and that one day it will first be adolescence and then tender childhood. Will forgetfulness and nihilism be our next maturity?

351, HISTORY. In 1958, Italo Calvino wrote: "*Modern epic no longer knows gods: man is alone, and before him stand nature and history. And if at this point it is easy to say that nature and history are the gods of the modern world, renewed incarnations of ancient deities, we can immediately counter that this deification is more easily found in the pages of philosophers than in those of writers.*" Now we could say that the abolition of history is found more easily in the pages of the theorist than in the pages of writers (in the pages of newspapers it has not yet appeared). Apparently, we postmoderns no longer deify nature, nor history, nor the reason that was included in both. Nor any god, if we pay attention to the *zeitgeist* and not to individuals. It is true that architectural spaces and virtual spaces have finally abolished natural time, natural spaces, and historical spaces. The *locus* is giving way to places without identity; one is anywhere and at any time simultaneously.

There is no nature nor history in the ancient sense (two names that are metaphors, like the word "surfing" on the Internet and, perhaps, like all the words we inherited from our ancestors). But to speak of the "End of History" is like speaking of the "End of Nature." Both are possible and exaggerated. We can imagine the End of History as the abandonment of the past and the future, that is, we can see it in those virtual or identical spaces (the Internet, McDonald's, etc.). But why consider all of that as a permanent stage? Why think that if history has ended, it cannot continue? Is the "End of History" not just another chapter of History? What has ended is not History, as a process of human events; what has ended is the habit of seeing History as the enigmatic repository of all possible and foreseeable destinies of the human species. In any case, what has ended is the aspiration to project the future, and now, exhausted or satisfied, the creature lets itself be carried by that enigmatic and all-powerful entity called The-wind-of-history, without further resistance and without further romantic dreams. —If cultural diversity leads to skepticism, the erratic and contingent nature of history leads to its denial. History is no longer a coherent, logical, and predictable unity as the moderns wanted or conceived it. The past of the prophets and the future of the utopians no longer matter. Now it is the present that takes center stage in human concern. History no longer explains the future but the present, and it does so timidly, from infinite points of view. But having "deconstructed" the past does not mean, as is often claimed, having arrived at a mythological present. —We may live for some time in the End of History, but we still cannot completely end it. For two reasons: it is possible that there is still something left to build, and, above all, it is certain that there is still much left to destroy. And it is enough to create or destroy to make history.

352, RESULTS. A curious habit of creatures is to judge *all* of history by the latest results. As if the goal of all times were always our own time. In this way, one would have to assume that Pericles and Alexander the Great failed because today, ultimately, Greece is a peripheral country. It would also have been proven that the pharaohs failed with their pyramids, the futility of all the roads that led to Rome or Santiago de Compostela, the incapacity of the Catholic Church in the Middle Ages as an organizer of society, the inappropriateness of the Laws of the Indies, the final failure of the European race to conquer colonies in Africa and America, the vanity of all the peace treaties signed with Germany before 1939, and the illusion of the Nazi defeat in 1945. Thus, Marx was, successively, a utopian in 1848, an enlightened prophet in 1929, and (latest version) a terrible economist and worse philosopher in 1989. I have even heard somewhere that

Marxism has failed. But how can one say that an idea that was in fashion for a hundred years was a failed idea? When will we understand that in history, every success and every failure is always relative and partial? If there were absolute successes, there would be no reason to have stopped being pro-Alexandrian.

353, OPENINGS. If history is good for anything, it is to remind us that there are other ways of seeing the world. And if culture is good for anything, it is to return to us something of those other ways. Even the most anachronistic perspective of reality may one day prove to be so original and refreshing as to free us from the narrow limits of our time. An example is the "postmodern" thought of Nietzsche, who went back more than two thousand years to leap a century ahead of his own time. Because every era is made with the inheritance and the forgetting of a past. And above all, with the pride of that forgetting.

354, FUTURE. The future does not exist.

355, DAWN. In the 18th century, Gotthold E. Lessing thought that to suppose the creature capable of reaching absolute truth was absurd, because it implied the possibility (attributed only to God) of stepping outside of history. Undoubtedly, this observation enjoys reciprocal validity: that is, to claim an "End of History," as is done now, is an absurd claim, because it would mean that the last creature has reached absolute truth. Unless one considers absolute truth to be... *this.* —For my part, I believe that the metaphysical creature is not yet ready to think. And if it persists in the attempt, it is because its spirit is greater than its intelligence. All knowledge, even scientific knowledge, is a sign of that "preliminary babbling." (*The tools we use to understand the world*—admitted physicist Duff—*may be at fault. Perhaps the existing approaches are too primitive to describe multiple times*. For his part, James Lovelock admitted that we all know intuitively, or believe we know, what life is, but it is impossible to define it in scientific terms. The same could be said of freedom and the meaning of existence. This is because, Lovelock thinks, we have spent almost all our evolutionary time surviving rather than thinking in abstract or scientific terms.) All the culture that the creature has produced in the last ten thousand years demonstrates this: behind it lies a powerful and very particular spirit, restless, productive, and irrational; and a rather confused intelligence. —What we today call "Enlightenment" (*Enlightenment, Aufklärung*) is a historical period in the West that called itself "Enlightenment." Generally, all historical periods are considered the awakening of something, the beginning or the end. But this is always due more to the creatures' ignorance of other times than to their own wisdom or "enlightenment." And when I say "ignorance," I do not simply mean illustrative or conceptual lack of knowledge: *one is ignorant when one ceases to feel something.* In this sense, we can say that we are ignorant of much of the Middle Ages, we are ignorant of almost all the essence of classical Greece, we are ignorant of all that is sensual love when we have studied it exhaustively but have never fallen in love. —Why call "enlightenment" disbelief? Why is the consciousness of the masses considered the noon of history? In the same way that those creatures who coined the term *Aufklärung*, new generations will come who feel above us, who feel awakened, "enlightened." And not because they obtain more of the same (technology, nihilism, insignificance); it must be the opposite, because one awakens when one changes direction. Then they will consider us as dark or darker than our Middle Ages. The desirable thing will be not only that they believe they are awakening but that they actually awaken (though this last part is harder to assess). That "awakening" will perhaps be the end of the nihilism of the 20th century, already warned by Nietzsche before it spread to the "masses." —Unimaginable generations are yet to come. My utopia is a project of a creature capable of integrating the fundamental opposites: the religious spirit and the aesthetic spirit. A religious (transcendental) spirit that is neither renunciant nor fearful, that possesses the challenging impulse of the aesthetic spirit; that recovers or preserves its thirst for *knowledge* in the deepest sense, resorting to existential experimentation rather than asceticism. —Someone (I don't remember who) compared the era of industry and atomic energy to that which followed the discovery of fire. The comparison is pertinent, from many points of view, even in the information age. This suddenly gives us some hope. Because after this neo-Paleolithic (let us think) a new Promethean Era will return; like the Greek, like the Oriental. A new Promethean Era or the destruction of fire without control. Because now two extreme alternatives appear on the horizon, not a simple continuity. (At the extremes are those who only see a bright present and those who foresee catastrophes. In the middle are not the realists; in the middle are always the plausible.) For the first, we need Prometheuses; for the second...

Breaking news

The world spends 130 times more on Armed Forces (780 billion dollars) than on education (6 billion), according to the United Nations report on human development.

Furthermore, the document states that the richest 20 percent of the world's population monopolizes 86 percent of global consumption, indicating a worsening of social inequalities.

The document concludes that "a gross inequality in consumption opportunities has excluded more than a billion people who fail to meet their basic needs."

The United States is, at the same time, the country with the greatest material wealth and the greatest material deprivation in percentage terms, as it has the highest per capita income and 16.5 percent of its population lives in poverty. Similar situations occur in the United Kingdom and Ireland.

Furthermore, unemployment has reached "surprising" levels. Among young men and women, unemployment stands at 22 and 32 percent respectively in France, 30 and 39 percent in Italy, and 36 and 49 percent in Spain.

It adds that "unequal income distribution translates into social exclusion when a society's value system places excessive importance on what a person owns rather than on what a person is or can do."

As an example of the consumerist explosion at the end of the century, global consumption of goods and services in 1998 will exceed 24 trillion dollars, six times the amount spent in 1975.

"Advertising can provide incomplete information... and can be particularly misleading for those with few alternative sources of information, such as children, those with little schooling, and those who read little," the report states.

Global advertising spending has increased by 700 percent since 1950 and currently exceeds the pace of economic growth by one-third.

A child born in New York, Paris, or London today will consume, spend, and pollute more in a lifetime than 50 children from a developing country, and by a cruel twist of fate, those who consume less will bear the brunt of environmental damage," the UN report asserts.

Respiratory diseases are commonplace in Asia and Latin America. The report determines that in our continent and the Caribbean, about 15 million children under the age of two are at high risk of brain damage as a result of lead emissions.

The report cites that "the land area of Bangladesh could shrink by 17 percent due to rising sea levels, even though this country produces only 0.3 percent of global carbon dioxide emissions."

El País of Montevideo
September 9, 1998.

www.ingramcontent.com/pod-product-compliance
Lightning Source LLC
LaVergne TN
LVHW091212080426
835509LV00009B/964

* 9 7 8 1 9 5 6 7 6 0 4 2 2 *